MW00987316

How Creativity Happens in the Brain

Also by Arne Dietrich

INTRODUCTION TO CONSCIOUSNESS

How Creativity Happens in the Brain

Arne Dietrich

Professor of Psychology, American University of Beirut, Lebanon

First published 2015 by
PALGRAVE MACMILLAN

Palgrave Macmillan in the UK is an imprint of Macmillan Publishers Limited, registered in England, company number 785998, of Houndmills, Basingstoke, Hampshire RG21 6XS.

Palgrave Macmillan in the US is a division of St Martin's Press LLC, 175 Fifth Avenue, New York, NY 10010.

Palgrave Macmillan is the global academic imprint of the above companies and has companies and representatives throughout the world.

Palgrave® and Macmillan® are registered trademarks in the United States, the United Kingdom, Europe and other countries.

ISBN 978–1–137–50179–0

This book is printed on paper suitable for recycling and made from fully managed and sustained forest sources. Logging, pulping and manufacturing processes are expected to conform to the environmental regulations of the country of origin.

A catalogue record for this book is available from the British Library.

Library of Congress Cataloging-in-Publication Data
Dietrich, Arne.
   How creativity happens in the brain / Arne Dietrich, Ph.D., Professor of Psychology, American University of Beirut, Lebanon.
      pages   cm
   Includes bibliographical references and index.
   ISBN 978–1–137–50179–0
   1. Creative ability.   2. Brain.   3. Cognition.   I. Title.
   BF408.D534 2015
   153.3'5—dc23   2015013978

Contents

Figures and Tables

Figures

Tables

About the Author

Born, for obscure reasons, in Northern Europe, Arne Dietrich gave early promise of being nothing special whatsoever. As a child, he was annoyingly hyperactive and exceptionally stubborn, so some people predicted a career as a clown while others foresaw an early death. To everyone's intense disbelief, he finished school and left his ancestral home just in time to avoid yet another rainy and overcast summer.

After an entirely uneventful time in college, he spent several years globetrotting, climbing little known mountains, and bushwhacking through the jungle; a lifestyle interrupted only by the occasional date and a few phone calls to his mother. During this time, he also embarked on extended do-it-yourself introspective voyages into the hinterland of the mind. On these trips through inner space, he realized that soul searching is too treacherous without a detailed map of neuroland.

For equally obscure reasons, he spent his graduate years at the University of Georgia, where he, over a hectic period of a few years, learned the nuts and bolts of neuroscience, including the 'how to' of publishing entirely useless stuff about the brain. He surprised his dissertation committee with a thesis that concerned such an opaque topic of neuroscience that no one even bothered to read it. But the committee refused to flunk him in utter fear he wouldn't leave as promised.

Arne Dietrich is now a tour guide into the bizarre world of brain cells and human behavior at, of all places, the American University of Beirut in Lebanon. He is still surfing the stream of consciousness every chance he gets. He prefers to work on, and spend his time in, various altered states of consciousness. His favorite one is daydreaming but he also enjoys the exercise-induced state of transient hypofrontality that comes from swimming, biking, running, or hiking for miles on end. His other interests are just as opaque as his work but somewhat more suitable to his restless and obstinate nature.

1
A Sneak Preview of the Journey Ahead

This is a book about creativity. Specifically, it's about the brain mechanisms of creativity, how a grapefruit-sized heap of meat crackling with electricity conceives of mathematical theorems, creates beautiful art, discovers the laws of nature, thinks of space rockets, invents kitesurfing, and designs buildings that look like sea shells. To get a grip on this thorny issue, I will take you on a little trip into the hinterland of the mind to see how, exactly, it manages to be so outrageously creative.

Creativity is a topic where respectable people, even those of the highest scholarly standing, regularly rise to levels of speculation that can safely be called imprudent. Everyone, it seems, is an expert on creativity, what counts as creative (and what doesn't), what makes a person creative, and how best to bring it out. Whole shelves of books exist that venerate the creative genius, tell you the seven traits of highly creative people, or list ten easy steps to tap into your unused creative potential. If you are looking for such a read, this isn't it. I will neither attempt an exercise in advanced hindsight nor go for a proof by verbosity. The book you have started to read is a concise affair with a sharp focus: to convey what we can, and cannot, say about how brains give rise to creative ideas. The plan is to stick exclusively to sound, mechanistic explanations of how ideational combinations of information happen in the mind.

In the general spirit of truth in advertising, allow me to follow this up with one caveat and one reassurance. What you are about to read will almost certainly challenge some of your deepest intuitions about how the mind works. But the reward will be a better understanding of creativity, grounded in solid neuroscience thinking. One thing you shouldn't fret over, though, is the neurolingo. I will make a concerted effort to decrypt the often impenetrable thickness of brainspeak that makes modern neuroscience seem so inaccessible to people.

The fountainhead of civilization

Suppose an advanced alien lifeform visits Earth to investigate if *Homo sapiens* is worth saving. Suppose further that they don't have a portable consciousness-detector, a small antenna-held gizmo they can conveniently hold to our heads to check for signs of inner musings. What would they identify as the defining characteristic of being human? Taking a quick look around and seeing what we have done with the place, they'd be hard-pressed to put any other item on top of their list than our creativity and inventiveness. We are an intensely creative species and there isn't an element of the periodic table we haven't tinkered with to utterly transform the world we live in, modifying our own minds and bodies, too. Human culture, indeed all progress in the arts, sciences, and engineering, originates from the capacity to change existing thinking patterns, break with the present, and create something new. Creative thinking and its derivative products – the knowledge and artifacts that make up human culture – are the quintessence of our humanity.

At an ever-accelerating pace, new empirical evidence on the neural basis of the mind pours out of neurolabs at a dizzying pace. Trying to take in the contemporary writing on the topic, professional or popular, is a bit like drinking from a fire hose. No wonder many people feel that the meteoric rise of the intersection between neuroscience, psychology, and cognitive science is nothing short of a revolution. Clearly, the brain no longer is the inscrutable clump of goo it once was. Arguably the single most notable gap in this triumphant parade is creative thinking. For all its prominence at the apex of human mental faculties, we know next to nothing about how brains generate creative ideas, let alone facilitate their occurrence. From a perspective of a few steps back, this is stunning. Given that creative achievements represent, perhaps, the clearest expression of our humanity, one would have thought that psychologists and neuroscientists would attack this problem with much greater resolve.

But the bare fact is that creativity has a dubious distinction in the behavioral and brain sciences. I cannot think of a mental faculty so central to the human condition for which we have so little understanding as to how brains do it. One might be tempted to argue that this lamentable position is held by the problem of consciousness, but at least there we have some load-bearing proposals – global working space, social brain hypothesis, competing neuronal coalitions, higher-order thought, among rather many else – that have so far escaped the dustbin of wishful thinking. Not so for the underlying neural mechanisms of creativity, as we will see in Chapter 2. We may find, in due course, that this is an even harder problem.

The central, motivating intent of this book is to show that there is a way out of the disciplinary insolvency where the neuroscience of creativity finds itself. We know less about creativity than the gurus of the innovation industry and some of my phrenology-tinged neuroscientist colleagues pretend, but more than you might think. And a genuine neuroscience of creativity is stranger and more fascinating than the recycled clichés about right brains, divergent thinking, autistic savants, bipolar disorder, the mad genius, or grand proclamations that original thinking is located in some unpronounceable part of the neocortex. To pursue in earnest the question of how brains compute creative insights, I will bring to the fore, and then interconnect, a number of concepts that, despite being securely anchored in the bedrock of mainstream cognitive neuroscience, have so far been ignored in the quest to find the *how* and *where* of creativity in the brain and, by extension, the wellspring of human culture.

Separating the Schaden from the Freude

Given the time-tested ability of pop-psychologists and self-help gurus to expand in a vacuum, creativity has become a hotbed for useless piffle, nebulous fluff, and – to adopt an expression of art from the philosopher Harry Frankfurt – bullshit. A battle-hardened legion of creativity couches and leadership consultants circle the globe in a tireless effort to emit such vacuous banalities about the creative process as this: "Don't be afraid to fail; your ego is the biggest obstacle to creativity." Or consider this hidden gem: "Always look at things from a new perspective; if you are passionate about what you do, your true creativity, your true self comes out." And, don't forget: "Always think positive; the worst enemy of creativity is self-doubt!" This is probing stuff.

To forestall the risk that the content of this book ends up as fodder for a Gabfest where meme-laundering motivational speakers go to seek audiences suffering from uncritical idolatry, I'd like to make an opening announcement: Here are the ideas you will not find in this book:

You will not read anything about lateral thinking, collective creativity, out-of-the-box thinking, or brainstorming. I will not give you neuroscience-informed tips on how to break the ice, rediscover your inner child, or go with the flow. I will also not tell you to listen to your intuition, wait until it comes to you, or go for a run. And I definitely will not analyze the creativity crisis in America. I promise not to refer to anyone's creative juices, creative personality, or creative state of mind. And we will not unleash our creativity by sitting in a circle, throwing a bean bag around, and reporting the first thing that comes to mind. If you want to know what a stunted idea that is, all you have to do is realize that this is all what cavemen did after sundown 30,000 years ago. I will also not be claiming that education kills creativity, that kids need to reach beyond the traditional four-wall classroom environment, and that we all need to keep an open mind. Open minds are good, but you should never open your mind so far that your brain falls out.

There will also be no social media jargon on offer in this book. No re-tweet to announce a #hashtagcreativity podcast. There will be no hands-on state-of-the-art networking, no problem solving using big data, no crowdsourcing for innovative partnerships, and no user-generated content. This book will not go viral in the blogosphere and you will not like it on Facebook. We will not push past creative barriers, interface in the cloud, or rewire our brains for the digital age. And we will definitely not let the unconscious mind take over.

There will also be no academese used here. No long passages in the passive voice that seemingly emanate from no-person or a series of life-less paragraphs that have the appearance of being committee-written. For instance, I will not argue for or against some obscure position only to conclude with the need for more research. You will not find a long-winded analysis of the pros and cons of creativity-with-a-big-C, get treated to the nuances of various definitions of creativity, or see foot-notes that provide a painstaking elaboration of the references cited in the text. And you will not be asked to ponder the psychological conse-quences of Andy Warhol's childhood experiences or digest the deeper meaning of cute creativity quotes like "imagination is more important than knowledge" or "creativity is 98 percent perspiration." If that is what you are after, you certainly grabbed the wrong book off the shelf.

You will also search in vain for an in-depth discussion on the thin line between genius and madness. Take, for instance, troubled Vincent van Gogh, famed nineteenth-century painter who suffered from bipolar disorder, cut off part of his left ear, and eventually committed suicide. Or Isaac Newton, eccentric seventeenth-century physicist, general head-case and, judging from his leviathan superego, a candidate for making the diagnostic criteria of at least half a dozen psychological disorders. No sooner do we contemplate this aberrant pair, a whole army of mad geniuses springs to mind led by such illustrious figures as autistic Wolfgang Amadeus, depressed Ludwig van, or tortured Edgar Allan. Like Franz Kafka, Robert Schumann, Michelangelo, Virginia Wolf, Richard

Strauss, John Nash, or Ernest Hemingway, they were all, at some point in their lives, anguished, tormented, alcoholic, angst-ridden, manic, outright psychotic, or just plain weird. Add the mind-boggling savant syndrome, throw in a quote from a venerable ancient Greek for good measure – say, Aristotle: "No great mind has ever existed without a touch of madness" – and we have the making of mythconception.

Tales from the insanity zone are nuggets of pure gold for the true believer. What if we could just open "the doors of perception"? What would we have lost had Prozac turned Nietzsche into a regular bloke? It isn't uncommon, even in the rarefied air of peer-reviewed psychology journals, to read articles galloping through so many esoteric life episodes, irrelevant factoids, and delicious gossip (did you know that the reclusive William Cavendish insisted on having a chicken roasting at all hours of the day?), that the veracity of the mad genius link is all but a foregone conclusion. But it is one thing to be enchanted by folklore, it is quite another to forego the purifying powers of statistical reasoning for anecdotal storytelling. For the entire thesis of the highly gifted mentally ill is simply the result of a lethal dose of selective data reporting.

Finally, I promise that this book is guaranteed, 100 percent phrenology free. Unlike physics, neuroscience is data rich and theory poor. But this is no reason to pull conceptual rabbits out of metaphysical thin air. One would think that serious researchers need not set foot in pop-neuroscience land, but, alas, some of my colleagues' writings brim with just as many thoughts that are either so simplistic that nothing good can possibly come out of them or, given what we know about the brain, factually mistaken. I pledge, for instance, not to sell you a colorful brain image from a neuroscanner as a substitute for an explanation. And I will not present you with a location in the brain when I mean to provide you with a neural mechanism. You will not read here that creativity is in the superior temporal gyrus, associated with white matter density, dependent on alpha enhancement, or boosted by neurogenesis in the hippocampus. To not put too fine a point on it, this is neurobunk, fragments from an imaginary science.

I could go on and on. In fact, I think I will. Creative people are said to use more of their brain – somehow, for no one can tell you exactly how, let alone link this to creativity – use less brain more efficiently (which is, come to think of it, the opposite claim), have more dopamine receptors (or was it serotonin?), have more densely packed neurons, or more synaptic connections, or a thicker corpus callosum. Einstein's brain, for instance, was unremarkable in all these aspects.

And what would we do if we find out that Stephen Hawkins or Quentin Tarantino had a bigger visual cortex or more acetylcholine synapses in the basal forebrain, eh? Surely, they must have, like all of us, some quirk upstairs.

What we should expect to see, based on what we know

For the challenging task that lies ahead it is a good idea to get a brief overview of the book. The upcoming attractions are organized into eight chapters, each designed to take a small step toward the goal of understanding how creative ideas might come into existence in the vast inner space of the human brain. Paradoxically, we are forced to begin the project by first getting back to square one. This is because the neuroscientific study of creativity has been moving in the wrong direction for some time and gotten itself thoroughly stuck in a rut. But as Artemus Ward put it: "It ain't so much the things we don't know that get us in trouble. It's the things we know that just ain't so." So, before we can pursue our quest, and prevent it from derailing prematurely – or anywhere along the way, really – it is necessary to give the myopic theorizing causing all the trouble its proper neuroscientific funeral.

As a consequence, Chapter 2 should be understood as a sustained and disciplined demolition project aimed at sanitizing our bad habits of thinking about creativity. It first logically, and then empirically, demonstrates that the ideas currently floating about – right brains, divergent thinking, defocused attention, low arousal, alpha enhancement, dreams states, or unconscious processes, to name a few popular ones – are irreparably incoherent and cannot do the explanatory work we need. Being false category formations (with their opposites also leading to creativity) as well as compound constructs involving many different cognitive processes (with no one knowing what, exactly, is creative about them), they beg the question. And if you fail to isolate the subject matter under study in your experimental paradigm, you cannot use neuroimaging tools to hunt for brain mechanisms. You just don't know what the brain image shows! It shouldn't come as a surprise to learn, therefore, that review studies have exposed the data set of the field to be a total mess. To be clear, the primary target for demolition here are not the ideas themselves but the basic error in thinking that underlies them. They all emanate from the monolithic entity fallacy, the failure to understand how thoroughly distributed in the brain and multifaceted in its processes creativity must be, given all the diverse forms it manifests itself in the human population. The chapter concludes by arguing that the current experimental work on the neural basis of creativity satisfies the criteria for phrenology. Ouch.

So where do we go from here? Once we are clear that the conceptual foundation of the current paradigm is leading us nowhere good, we can leave it behind and consider more capable candidates. If Chapter 2 is the reset button, Chapter 3 is the starter pistol for a fresh attack. From here on, we marinate our minds in the latest the brain sciences and related disciplines have to offer. Most of the ideas I bring to the fore are part and parcel of the standard conceptual toolbox of cognitive neuroscience, only their combination and application to creative thinking are original.

Without getting too technical about it, Chapter 3 lays down some groundwork by highlighting how the brain, in general, operates. It describes the brain's connectionist or network architecture and its dual information-processing system (explicit vs. implicit) as well as basic concepts from cognitive psychology, such as task set, task-set inertia, and speed of processing that will become important later on. By definition, creative insights occur in consciousness, so a big part of the chapter tackles the intriguing topic of how information in the brain goes from unconscious to conscious, or at least what we know about these far reaches of conscious awareness. This, in turn, raises the specter of the Cartesian theater, perhaps the most powerful cognitive illusion we have about how the mind works. In fact, it is so intuitive, and so misleading, that breaking its back is a recurrent theme of the book and goes by the mantra of taking the Designer out of the design process.

With the ground cleared, and a few corrective thinking devices in hand, we are now in a better position to take the next step. Chapters 4 and 5 form a unit that rests squarely on Darwinian, not Aristotelian logic. The curious fact is that we already know of a functioning mechanism for creativity, namely the variation-selection process that does all the creating and designing in the biosphere. Extending Darwinian thinking upwards into culture remains ideologically controversial because of its implications, but all sides in the debate on cultural evolution concur that the basic generate-and-test algorithm holds for culture. What's more, all parties also agree that in contrast to the algorithm driving Mother Nature, the cultural evolutionary algorithm is partially sighted, not blind. In other words, a common denominator exists that is, on the whole, unobjectionable. Culture is a variational evolutionary system involving some degree of coupling between variation and selection and the copying and transmitting of cultural information happens in brains! Despite this universal consensus, almost no neuroscience study has used the rationale of the evolutionary two-step to set up empirical protocols. A remarkable case of interdisciplinary disconnect.

Since this common denominator isn't exactly news to those working on cultural evolution, the questions arise: Why hasn't it percolated through to those working on the neural mechanisms of creativity? Why hasn't it already trumped the current neuroimaging phrenology it must replace? The search for the brain mechanism of creative thinking is at the heart of anxiety about our creative agency and often gets distorted by a biophobia that is quite distinct from thoughtful skepticism. Some who have sensed the threat posed by taking the Designer out of the design process have seriously misrepresented the generative mechanisms of how brains compute new ideas. To close all the exits on this part of the journey, Chapter 4 x-rays the core issues of the cultural evolution debate for the sole purpose of securing this common ground. There is much to enjoy in this book but there are also no free passes here. A mechanistic explanation of creativity comes with hardcore materialism, a position that tends to give people existential vertigo in short order.

The fact that neuroscience has failed to ground its empirical studies in the most obvious of paradigms, the variation-selection algorithm of evolution, is surely the main reason for the lack of progress in the field, for variation and selection processes are likely to be very different beasts in the brain. As will be argued on several occasions in the book, both are distributed, occur at conscious and unconscious levels, and engage, at each of these levels, different cognitive processes and different brain regions. It is hard to imagine useful neuroimaging data from studies on creativity that blend them!

But once we have accepted the evolutionary paradigm, we have a clear way forward. So long as it is agreed that the common denominator of cultural evolution – a variational system with a coupling upgrade – is the bedrock on which to anchor our search for the mechanisms of creativity (and this much is unobjectionable at this point), we can ask more constructive and competent questions about the creative process in brains and start making theoretical hay. The main theme in subsequent chapters is to answer the question thrown up by this conclusion. How do brains manage to accomplish this partial sightedness in their explorations of terra incognita? Obviously, creative people are not a special class of prophets.

At the conceptual level, this question has a deceptively simple answer: Brains produce representations of the world that can inform – give direction to – the search process. That is to say, brains produce mental models that simulate the consequences of generate-and-test trials that are then fed into the variation process. But this doesn't even begin to tell the story of what happens in neural networks during creative thinking. How does this work exactly? Which parameters of the evolutionary algorithm are changed? And why does this give us the feeling of foresight and purpose when we think creatively?

The main goal of Chapter 5 is to describe the brain's upgrades to the evolutionary algorithm. It hones in on four features that distinguish evolutionary algorithms occurring in brains from their biological cousins, as it is these features that are most in need of a neural explanation. They are (1) heuristics, which provide a causal arrow from selection back to variation conferring degrees of sightedness, (2) the establishment of fitness criteria for selection processes that are necessarily hypothetical, (3) cognitive scaffolding that enables multistep thought trials, and (4) the experiences of foresight and intention that accompany human creativity.

Chapters 6 and 7 together represent the crux of the book. Chapter 6 brings us in contact with one of the most exciting developments in all of neuroscience, the newly emerging prediction paradigm. Theorists have been converging from quite different quarters on the idea of prospective processing as a central purpose of brain function. Readers who accept the primacy of the brain's prediction imperative in organizing neural computation should have little trouble seeing the profound implications of this new framework for the creative process. For, one of the most fascinating yet completely unmapped implications of the prediction framework is the prospect of a brain mechanism that drives the four upgrades to the mind's evolutionary algorithms and, hence, our understanding of the neural basis of human creativity. Indeed, our ability to run offline simulations of expected future environments and action outcomes informs the way brains carry out variation-selection thought trials, both at the level of variation and at the level of selection. After introducing the key ideas of the proactive brain, I develop in some detail the notion that internal representations of the emulated future provide the neural mechanism that enables brains to partially couple variation to selection and, in so doing, impart degrees of sightedness for the evolutionary search algorithms that run in our minds. This gives us a way to account for the seeming paradox of how a process like biological evolution that is blind, clueless, and reactive can evolve a machine – the human brain – with processes that are (a tad bit) foresightful, purposeful, and proactive. This must necessarily be driven via predictive processes.

Having equipped ourselves with a bag of thinking tools that can extend our epistemic horizons, my task in Chapter 7 is to apply this newfound knowledge. I start by considering neuroanatomy. The focus up to that point will have been on "how" questions that outline cognitive or computational processes for variation and selection in the brain. But what about "where" questions? What can we say about the location of variation and selection in the brain? To keep the bugbear of phrenology at bay, I will develop what I call the vaudeville conception of creativity in the brain. The position follows, as a matter of consequence, from two basic concepts in neuroscience – modularity and nonlinearity – and presupposes that creativity is completely distributed and fully embedded into neural networks. Like other complex, higher-order psychological phenomena – political orientation or religious conviction, for instance – creativity, or its purported subcomponents such as divergent thinking, just doesn't exist as a cohesive entity at the neural level. Creativity, therefore, doesn't merit elevation to the status of a phenomenon with a distinctive neural signature. Too different is what scientists, entrepreneurs, fashion designers, or choreographers must do to be creative in their respective spheres. Although this seems like common sense, it runs counter to the prevailing rationale of current neuroimaging studies of creativity and their interpretations.

The centerpiece of Chapter 7 is the proposal that there are two distinct modes, or types, of creativity that differ from each other in several important ways. There is a top-down or deliberate creativity mode that is strongly biased by top-down projections from the prefrontal cortex. These top-down influences tend to restrict the heuristic search function to more commonsense solutions so that the deliberate mode is liable to yield creative insights that are more paradigmatic in type and rely on more close associations. This can be contrasted with novel ideas that emerge from a bottom-up or spontaneous creativity mode in which top-down influences are weakened and the heuristic algorithm is less directional. Although this comes with a speed and efficiency tradeoff, the spontaneous mode has the potential to chance upon more paradigm-shifting ideas or remote associations. To flesh out the details of how exactly these two creativity modes are implemented in the brain, I bring back into the picture the relevant concepts covered in earlier chapters, including connectionism, competitive processing, task sets, task-set inertia, speed of processing and, of course, the prediction mechanism. The decomposition of creativity into variation and selection aside, this deliberate-spontaneous partition of creativity is the only one that I think has currently sufficient empirical and theoretical support, and it can account for the boosting of *some kinds* of creative thoughts in *certain kinds* of states of consciousness, such as daydreaming, dreaming, or meditation.

Chapter 8 is devoted to the flow experience that I have kept clamped up to this point. Creative behavior emerging from flow demands its very own chapter because it is powered by an utterly different neural drivetrain than either the deliberate or the spontaneous mode. The theoretical considerations of the preceding chapters will make plain that the rapid-fire, smooth sensorimotor interplay so characteristic of the flow state cannot arise, as is the case for both the deliberate and spontaneous modes, from the complex explicit system with its fancy offline prediction machinery. Instead, flow is based on processing in the implicit system, which changes a great number of parameters of the evolutionary algorithm, from predictive computations to just about all other higher-order cognitive processes. As such, flow represents a third mode of creativity, alongside the deliberate and spontaneous modes of creative thinking. Once this final piece of the puzzle is in the bag, we are ready to appreciate a bird's-eye perspective of all the creativity mechanisms in the brain. Chapter 8 ends by directly comparing the neural processes underlying the brain's trinity of creativity modes.

This leaves open only one more thing in a book that is uncompromisingly and unapologetically mechanistic: Artificial intelligence – AI. If the creative mind is nothing but a complex network of neurons computing generate-and-test algorithms – no ineffable extra soulstuff anywhere in sight, no muse to ignite sparks in the occipital cortex – why couldn't there be one made from silicon? The matter of machine creativity has never been a topic that lends itself naturally to sober, intellectual discourse. The stakes are just too high, nothing less than the nature of our souls, if you think about it. People seem to be sure that computers are not, by themselves, creative and that this isn't going to change – not tomorrow, not next year, not ever! But what makes them so sure? In their zeal to protect the human mind from the steady march of science, opponents often erect barriers too early, thinking it is better to defend too much than risk losing the precious mind to materialism. Following a brief history of AI, just so we understand what is involved at the computer end of things, the main section of Chapter 9 is a roundup of the top naysaying claims against robotic creativity to see if any of them can be made to stick. Turns out, the perennially attractive conclusion everybody is aching to make – machines just don't have it – cannot be achieved. We simply cannot find a secure hiding place from the relent-less advance of AI. It isn't my goal to convince you of the opposite claim, the inevitable coming of the creative machine. I am rather out to plant the seed of doubt that the absolutist dichotomy of us and them, of soul-less machines with no creative potential whatsoever and inspired brains that have it all, is much harder to defend than you might think.

For the purpose of edification and entertainment, I also want to turn the tables and give robots a chance to make their case, to show us how far they have already come and what they might be capable of in the future. We consider two remarkable projects from AI. You might think that they fall comically short of true and genuine creativity but keep in mind that all we are after at this stage is a proof of concept.

And now for the journey...

2
A Disciplined Demolition Project

In response to "Hey Yogi, I think we are lost," Yogi Berra, former player and general manager of the New York Yankees once said: "Yeah, but we are making great time." It's hard to think of a more fitting depiction, in my view, for the present-day, ill-conceived efforts to identify the mechanisms of creativity in the brain. Let me come right out and say it: It's phrenology. Neuroanatomically upgraded phrenology perhaps, but still phrenology. To be fair, studying creative thinking in the lab, under tightly controlled conditions, isn't the easiest way to make a living as a neuroscientist. Even for the wilderness of human thinking, creative ideas seem to be deliberately designed to defy empirical inquiry. There is something elusive, perhaps even sacred, about them. They come as they please – often with a resounding Homer Simpson DOH quality – and there is little you can do to force their appearance. Lucky those who have them.

No wonder we have always mystified creative ideas – visits from the muse and light bulbs come to mind. So what are neuroscientists to do if they want to catch creative thoughts *in flagrante*? Obviously, they cannot simply take volunteers, shove them into the nearest brain scanner and tell them: now, please be creative! This is perhaps why most paying members of the Society for Neuroscience consider the prospect of studying creativity akin to trying to nail jelly to the wall. It is likely to leads to unemployment and ostracism.

Yet, finding the cognitive and neural mechanisms of creativity, the wellspring of all our cultural achievements, scientific triumphs, and technological innovations, is an enterprise that couldn't be more important. For starters, there is the perennial desire to figure out who we are, which in the case of creativity is a quest that is likely, without hyperbole, to identify a defining characteristic of what makes us human.

Clearly, when it comes to creative behavior, we aren't just slightly better chimps. But in addition to this loftier, humanist goal is an equally important, if more practical, reason to push this objective. By uncovering the basic principles, the nuts and bolts if you like, of how exactly the brain manages to be so inventive and original, we might be able to enhance this process with potentially enormous benefits for society. Indeed, it would be an instant game-changer for any nation that gets an initial handle on this.

But for reasons we will lift from the muddied water in this chapter, the search for the underlying neural basis of creative cognition didn't develop over the past 60 years like other areas of the brain sciences – relentlessly forward and upward, in case you weren't paying attention. As cognitive psychology, joined by neuroscience a little later, delved into the meat-and-potatoes business of our higher mental functions discovering new facts and devising fresh theories at an ever accelerating pace, the experimental study of creativity, even if we allow for some breathers, held on like grim death to the few ideas and methods developed in the early days of the cognitive revolution. A cursory look at the contemporary literature readily corroborates this. Pick up any neuroimaging article and you likely find it beginning, in 2015 no less, by describing concepts and methods from the 1950s and 1960s – divergent thinking or the Alternative Uses test, for instance – not as a historical background for the benefit of the reader mind you, but as part of the rationale that sets up the upcoming experiments. I don't know of another research area like this. Doesn't it strike you as mildly ironic that perhaps the least creative domain of the cognitive neurosciences is the field of creativity?

After a half-century of working with this narrow paradigm, which increasingly looks like a cul-de-sac, the neuroscientific study of creativity finds itself in a theoretical arid zone that has perhaps no equal in the cognitive neurosciences. It isn't too much to say, I think, that we don't have a single brain mechanism we can lean on in earnest to explain the extraordinary creative capacities of an Einstein or a Shakespeare. The aim of this book is to help close the gap in the fabric of organized neuroscience knowledge where creativity should be. Before we can make the first steps in that direction, we must, from the outset, clear the ground of these pernicious fossil traces from a bygone era. They must be highlighted and consciously abandoned because they are not viable candidates but misdirectors of attention that, as long as we keep them, seduce us into taking paths that lead nowhere good. This chapter is intended to do just that. You can think of it as a sustained and disciplined demolition project aimed at sanitizing our bad habits of thinking about creativity.

Trying to nail jelly to the wall

Phrenology is to neuroscience as astrology is to psychology, the quintessential pseudoscience of the field. Mention the P word to a group of neuroscientists and you won't be able to finish your sentence so eager would they be to interrupt you and put ideological distance between themselves and phrenology. The trouble is, however, that the basic fallacy that fueled phrenology some 200 years ago is very difficult to shake and it keeps on making appearances, even if cryptic and implicit, in the most erudite of places (Uttall, 2001), especially in modern neuroimaging research on creativity.

Take a deep breath – this is a slightly longer tale. Phrenology started around 1800 with Franz Joseph Gall who reasoned that (1) the mind is in the brain (which got him into trouble with the Holy Roman Emperor Franz II for reasons that can safely be left to the imagination), (2) the brain is compartmentalized such that different mental faculties reside in different brain regions, and (3) a person's strengths and weaknesses would be reflected in the anatomy of these different brain region. So far so good. In fact, this was all revolutionary stuff back then and helped established the idea of localization of function. But from there, Gall got everything else wrong. He reasoned further that if the brain is formed according to your talents and faults so should the skull. Bumps on the skull would indicate increased capacity and pits decreased capacity. By examining the skull, a phrenologist could then determine a man's personality. The idea as such wasn't entirely new. Phrenology is only a more convoluted system for the common prejudice of judging the content by its package. The ancient Greeks, for instance, widely practiced physiognomy, the belief that one can tell character from the way a person looks. Actually, it's something we all do, every day. We betray an adherence to the same belief when we are surprised that a big, muscular guy with a mean-looking face is sweet and nice, or, to use another stereotype, a tall, gorgeous blond is introverted and intelligent.

Gall's effort to localize function went bunk because neither his mapping of mental faculty to brain region nor the conjecture that this affects skull shape had any empirical basis. He thought, for instance, that the brain's memory center is located behind the eyes and a good memory would cause the eyes to protrude. With the help of his disciple and later rival Johann Spurzheim, Gall associated regions on the skull with particular mental faculties, a total of 27, all without so much as a shred of evidence. The final chart contained such doozies as a center for mirthfulness, combativeness, marvelousness, secretiveness, and, my personal favorite, the organ of philoprogenitiveness (tending to produce many offspring and loving one's offspring), which he located, if you must know, just above the middle of the cerebellum. It's easy to laugh at this bumps-on-the-skull idea today, but few people appreciate the enormous popularity phrenology enjoyed at the time. In Victorian Britain, it ranked with Darwin's theory of evolution and a phrenological exam was a normal practice for job interviews. If you had the right bumps in the right places you'd get the job! I am not kidding. Ambrose Bierce spoke for many when he quipped that "phrenology is the science of picking a man's pocket through the scalp." The unlikely enthusiasm and longevity of phrenology had probably as much to do with gullibility as with the fact that it filled a vacuum, the enduring wish to find a marker that could foretell a person's behavior, for marriage, job performance, or some other purpose.

The task of debunking phrenology fell to Pierre Flourens, who, in a twist that isn't without irony, was a Cartesian and thus motivated by the desire to show that the mind wasn't in the brain at all, let alone compartmentalized leaving impressions on the skull. He pioneered a method technically called experimental ablation that studies brain function by removing precise brain areas and observing what an animal can no longer do. The control of the missing behavior is then attributed to the ablated region. To take an example, Gall ascribed amativeness to the cerebellum but when Flourens removed it he found nothing of the sort absent. Following this logic, Flourens' technique quickly disposed of phrenology in the scientific community.

The pendulum soon swung back to the localizationist's camp, but this time for good reason. Flourens' own work already showed him that subcortical regions, such as the cerebellum, do have specific roles. It was only in the cortex he couldn't find functional differences. No matter where he placed a lesion, he failed to find a neat correspondence. He eventually concluded that mental faculties are distributed in the cortex. But that conclusion soon turned out to be premature. In 1861, neurosurgeon Paul Broca was in a unique position to use the rationale of experimental ablation on a stroke patient and infer a specific higher cognitive function – language production – to a specific cortical region in the frontal lobe, known since as Broca's area. Shortly thereafter a similar event happened to the neurologist Karl Wernicke, only this time the deficit involved language comprehension and the focal lesion occurred in the left temporal cortex, a region known today as Wernicke's area. Both cases provided indisputable evidence that language had a precise locale in the brain. At around the same time, physiologists Gustav Fritsch and Eduard Hitzig discovered the primary motor cortex, the brain region responsible for controlling voluntary movement. This provided even more momentum for the localizationist project. And this was just the beginning. Almost a century of work followed yielding one triumph of localization after another.

In the 1940s, the psychologist Karl Lashley entered the debate and swung the pendulum back toward a more holistic view of cortical function. He systematically removed sections of cortex in rats and observed their ability to learn various mazes. What he found was contrary to expectation. No matter where the lesion was, it didn't correlate with a specific deficit. All he found was that the amount of damage was associated with the severity of the deficit. From this he formulated two principles: mass action, the larger the lesion, irrespective of location, the poorer the performance, and equipotentiality, the idea that all regions of the cerebral cortex are equally likely to take on any function.

Eventually, localizationists prevailed. Progress on two fronts proved decisive. First, single-cell recordings in the 1950s started to reveal detailed functional maps that correlated the behavior of individual neurons with specific mental processes – the large-scale mapping expedition of the primary visual cortex by the physiologists David Hubel and Torsten Wiesel springs to mind. Second, the appearance of neuroimaging techniques in the late 1980s provided the ability to study healthy, living brains and diminished the reliance on experimental ablation. However, while both tools supplied overpowering evidence for the view that higher cognitive functions are localized, they also substantially changed the traditional notion of what, exactly, is localized. Consider memory. We know today that memory is a widely distributed representation. Many, and quite different, individual cognitive processes are coordinated to form the memory of, say, your grandmother. Some areas contribute specific visual features; others provide different visual features; while still others add auditory elements or contain information about your past interactions with her. Like the internet, your grandmother isn't implemented in a single location or network; but, *single cognitive processes* that combine to make your grandmother – like the actual computer terminals that make up the Internet – *are* localized.

While single cognitive processes are localized, there is no particular brain center for a complex behavior or mental ability, a particular bit of gray matter in charge of God, imagination, consciousness or, for that matter, creativity. These are multipart representations in the brain that are composed of many different and separate mental processes, each of which is computed in its own specific place or network. When they all come online together to form a complex mental representation, like the belief in Santa Claus or the tendency to vote Republican, that representation is, to a first approximation, global.

For creativity, the matter comes to a head with modern neuroimaging techniques like functional magnetic resonance imaging (fMRI). The first question we have to ask, and answer, is what exactly these colorfully pixelated images from modern brain scanners can and cannot show. To be clear upfront, there should be no doubt that these tools have brought an enormous amount of information to light, especially in localizing specific mental processes, such as working memory processes, focused attention, memory retrieval, different perceptual processes, among rather much else. They have even worked well for some multifaceted functions, such as moral reasoning, decision-making, or the sense of agency. Why, then, don't they work for creativity? In exploring this question in the coming pages, we will see the same loopy logic resurface – wrapped in modern neuroscience speak, of course – that made Gall's phrenology such a house of cards. With this in mind, we are ready for the first target scheduled for demolition.

The brief and frightening reign of the right hemisphere

Must we talk about the right brain? Apparently, we do. Save for a curious lapse (Kounios & Beeman, 2014), everyone in the field of creativity (Dietrich & Kanso, 2010; Fink & Benedek, 2014; Sawyer, 2011; Sureyya & Runco, 2014; Weisberg, 2013) recognizes the right brain theory as a fallacy, a particularly striking instance of modern-day phrenology, and it wouldn't be worth mentioning in a list of demolition targets if it weren't for the fact that neither the basic underlying error in thinking that led to this real blooper of a proposal has been properly exposed and discarded nor have its grisly side effects in the popular imagination been properly counteracted. So, while holding my gag reflex, here it goes.

The unlikely story of the right brain theory begins with Roger Sperry and Michael Gazzaniga (Gazzaniga, 2000), two bold cartographers of inner space, who built a career around studying split-brain patients, a small group of people who have been called the most fascinating people on Earth. By the 1940s, it was known that epileptic seizures tend to spread by way of the corpus callosum, a large bundle of 200 million fibers connecting homologous regions of the cortex. The corpus callosum puzzled early functional neuroanatomists. From its large size and strategic location, smack in the center of the brain, they expected it to control important functions. Yet when they ablated it in animals, they were dumbfounded to find only minor detrimental effects on behavior. Some even quipped that it is nothing but a set of cables holding the two cerebral hemispheres together. This curiosity, coupled with reports implicating the corpus callosum in the propagation of seizures, fermented the idea that epileptic patients might benefit from callosotomy, the dissection of the corpus callosum. It seemed a drastic treatment option but for patients who do not respond to drugs, the consequence of not doing it – death, for most of them – is infinitely more drastic. The first successful split-brain operations were done in the 1960s. By severing this inter-hemispheric superhighway, seizure activity was indeed prevented from reaching the other side of the brain. That was the good news! The bad news was that, because callosotomy disconnects the right brain from the left one, it also prevents other things from reaching across, things like information. In short, the surgery created people with two independent, non-communicating symmetrical brain halves, a left hemisphere (LH) and a right hemisphere (RH).

If you were to meet a split-brain patient you'd not suspect – save for some momentary quirky behavior confined mostly to the post-surgical period – that something is special about them. But there is. When tested in skillfully contrived psychological experiments, they reveal a mental world so bizarre, it defies belief. The trick in a typical split-brain study is to present a stimulus so as to deliver the information to one hemisphere only. This is possible because the wiring diagram of the nervous system is such that each hemisphere receives information primarily from only one – the opposite – side of the body. So, for instance, a tone entering into the left ear would only reach RH. Motor fibers also show the contralateral arrangement with LH controlling muscles on the right side of the body and RH controlling those on the left. With this in mind, consider the basic split-brain experimental design. A patient is blindfolded and asked to identify an object, say, an apple, with her right hand. Using this setup, only LH learns about the apple. When asked to name the object in her hand, she'd report without trouble, "it's an apple," for the simple reason that LH – in most people – also controls language production. It gets more interesting when the patient is asked to repeat the test with the left hand. This time the tactile information goes exclusively to RH. But since the corpus callosum is cut, information in RH cannot reach the speech areas of LH and she is unable to say what is in her left hand. If the patient is subsequently allowed to open her eyes, LH would be informed as well about the apple and she'd say right away: "Oh, it's an apple." It is for this reason that a casual encounter with a split-brain patient does not reveal a split person; in the real world, sensory information is never delivered exclusively to RH.

In reality, the most common testing arrangement uses vision. Here the patient is instructed to fixate on a dot in the middle of a screen while a stimulus is briefly flashed to one side of the visual field. In one study, investigators flashed the words "key" to the left and "ring" to the right of the fixation point. When asked what he saw, the patient said "ring," as this was the only word the speech dominant LH knew about. But RH also saw something – namely the word "key." RH, however, cannot report its knowledge using language. So to give it an opportunity to demonstrate what it saw, the investigators showed the patient a box of objects. Naturally, he picked out the key with his RH-controlled left hand. On the other hand, as it were, his right hand is controlled by LH and therefore picked from the box what it knew, the ring. Roger Sperry, who shared the 1981 Nobel Prize for this work, and Michael Gazzaniga studied these patients extensively. The basic conclusions they have drawn from testing split-brain patients using this paradigm boil down to this. First, neither LH nor RH saw the combination "key ring." It follows that each hemisphere is evidently blind to what the other is seeing. Second, it seems that we become fully conscious of something, at least to the extent that we can verbalize it, only if information reaches the language-dominant LH. Full, explicit representation doesn't occur when knowledge exists only in RH. This is a stunning find. Not only is LH the site where full-fledged consciousness happens, the capacity for symbolic language seems a necessary condition for it.

Given this, it is natural to wonder why split-brain patients behave coherently at all. In the end, they have, in a way, two independent minds, each one controlling the opposite side of the body. Why, then, don't they behave as if composed of two selves, each with its own will? Well, instances where the two hemispheres are at odds with one another do occur and they make for truly grotesque examples of our fascinating ability to disagree with ourselves. Upon waking up from the surgery, one of the first complaints many patients have – aside from, as one patient put it, the "splitting headache" – is that the left hand has a "mind of its own." This commonly dissipates with time but in some cases the fact that information between the hemispheres is not shared intrudes in everyday behavior. For example, in a little vignette retold in countless popular outlets, one man found himself beating his wife with the left hand while trying to prevent it with his right (Gazzaniga, 1992). And you thought you had problems! In another case, a woman reportedly unbuttoned her blouse with one hand while buttoning it with the other. How is that for a mixed signal?

Overall, though, those stories are greatly exaggerated. The effects of the disconnection are negligible in most patients and rarely persist beyond a few months. One has to wonder though why that is the case. It cannot be simply explained by the fact that sensory information in the real world never enters exclusively through just one side. Just because both sides know about some event does not mean that RH might not want to do something different with it. Yet, one cannot help but wonder what this tells us about the extent to which we do react automatically to our environments. Why else would RH play ball so much with the consciousness harboring LH? One reason for this surprisingly high degree of coordination is certainly the fact that most motor behaviors – walking, chewing, clapping – are controlled by lower brain regions that are still connected across the midline. Strictly speaking, a callosotomy disconnects the right from the left cortex; there are several other commissures, fiber bundles that link the two hemispheres, left intact after the surgery.

This initial split-brain research sparked a flurry of studies exploring which hemisphere does what, or more accurately, which hemisphere does what better. For instance, most people process language in LH, but RH also handles some aspects of language, such as the rhythm and the emotional content of language. Evidently, for language to be full-flavored, we need both hemispheres. One surprising finding was that the non-language hemisphere has very poor inference skills. If a causal situation is presented to a split-brain patient so that the cause is presented exclusively to LH and the effect to RH, the association is totally lost on the person. The same is true if both, cause and effect, are presented solely to RH. Only when LH learns about both, cause and effect, does the person extract the causal relationship. This lends further support to the notion that full-blown consciousness is dependent on LH.

The acceptable generalization commonly extracted from research on hemispheric specialization is that LH is more skilled at analytical tasks, such as sequential reasoning or language. This raises the obvious question: if such higher-cognitive functions are predominantly controlled by LH, what does RH do? Is it stupid? It very well might be, as it happens. Michael Gazzaniga (1992), who studied RH for decades, considers it "vastly inferior to a chimp." But that doesn't tell us what it does. In contrast to LH, RH seems to be more skilled at tasks that require synthesis, such as taking the parts of a picture and seeing the whole.

Anyone with two neurons to rub against one another can readily imagine what happened next. For, no matter how careful such a trend is formulated, or how many caveats and qualifying remarks are attached to it, generalizations that feed into our phrenological thinking habits inevitably set the stage for an unrestrained broadside of flag-waving oversimplifications. And creativity was such an easy target because this new understanding seemed to fit so beautifully with our self-affirming, romantic view of creativity. Isn't regular old thinking conscious, analytical, and systematic, perfectly suited, in other words, to the logicality of LH? And isn't creative thinking intuitive, primal, holistic, and delightfully irrational, custom-made, as it were, to the mysterious ways of RH? All that remained was to cement the processing predispositions of LH and RH into a rigid, categorical division, et voilà, the gobbledygook was complete. Sadly, LH has since been the go-to brain half of methodical and unimaginative engineers, while RH has become the imaginative playground of creative artists. There is even a modern version of the right brain creativity idea by the neuroscientists John Kounios and Mark Beeman (2014) who propose that RH is responsible for coarse semantic coding related to insight. This proposal has been given a thorough shakedown (Dietrich & Kanso, 2010; Sawyer, 2011; Weisberg, 2013). Indeed, just about everyone else in the field thinks – rightly, in my opinion – that the whole idea of the creative right brain needs to be treated like nuclear waste and buried for a million years.

The left-brain right-brain craze that has taken hold in popular culture underscores the need, in clear and vivid form, of how important it is to systematically demolish ideas gone bad. As is so often the case when science moves on, the outdated ideas take on a life of their own, fueled, as they must be, by forces entirely outside logical reasoning. But when a meme has so much sex appeal, as phrenology natural does, more care must be taken before it is let out of the bag. Michael Gazzaniga once put it in an interview this way: "Some scientists oversimplified the idea, and clever journalists further enhanced them. Cartoonists had a field day with it all." But at the same time as the media went all fuzzy about it, more data on the lateralization of function poured in and it became quickly clear the idea is wrong outright. That's, of course, not a problem, as science is inherently self-corrective, but while this drama of self-correction played itself out in the scientific community, we let loose a runaway train that has become next to impossible to stop. There is the business seminar on how to think with both sides of your brain and a seemingly endless supply of books and magazines promising an easy step-by-step program on how to tap into your creative right-brain potential. You might as well ask someone to make better use of the hypothalamus.

The primary target for demolition here are not myths circulating in the public at large but the phrenological thinking that underlies this kind of myopic theorizing in general. The error comes into clear view when we examine the many close cousins of the right-brained-creativity theory that are currently making their rounds. These mutants of the original are so infectious that they have metastasized to many domains of psychology and neuroscience (Dietrich, 2007b). To compound the trouble, they come in so many cute and convincing disguises, newly neuroanatomically upgraded as they are, that they are rarely recognized for the threat they pose. You can spot them when you read in the latest study that sudden insights activate the superior temporal gyrus or creativity is associated with white matter density. What, we have to ask ourselves, does information of this kind tell us about the nature of creativity? For starters, we mustn't forget that a location is not an explanation. A true explanation contains mechanisms! So, at a minimum, proclamations like these fail to explain what needs to be explained, certainly as far as fundamental processes go. But the greater harm still comes from seducing us into believing that we are hot on the trail of an explanation when in fact we are looking at phrenology window-dressed as neuroscience.

Often these days a mental function is already considered "explained" when neuroscientists can show in their oversized neuroimaging pizza ovens which brain area turns active. The prefrontal cortex has become the latest frontrunner in this mad dash to localize creativity in the brain, but, alas, one can find claims in the contemporary literature for the whole funhouse of brain structures in the forebrain – hippocampus, amygdala, visual cortex, temporal lobe, and, why not, the basal ganglia. The next thing in tow, given the drift of things, is surely the cerebellum or some unpronounceable set of nuclei in the limbic system.

What makes all this a cargo-cult science isn't, as said, the neuroimaging technology *per se* or the principles of localization. The trouble is at the other end of things, our theoretical knowledge of what is involved in creativity and the no-good psychometric tests used to inspect the brain for signs of its occurrence. The best neuroscans tell us nothing if we don't know what to look for.

The rise of divergent thinking and the fall of everything else

A few clever studies in the early 1900s by Gestalt psychologists aside, creativity research is commonly said to have begun with Joy Paul Guilford's farewell address as president of the American Psychological Association in 1950. In this paper, Guilford (1950) called for the study of creativity and backed his call to arms with a proposal on how to go about doing so, the concept of divergent thinking. The idea of divergent thinking, defined as the ability to generate multiple solutions to open-ended questions, was quickly taken up by others because it represented the hope of bringing a hitherto intractable problem into the folds of empirical science. Several standardized testing methods for creativity were subsequently developed. The most popular of these psychometric tools – to this very day – are Paul Torrance's (1974) Torrance Test of Creative Thinking, which is entirely based on divergent thinking and Sarnoff Mednick's (1962) Remote Associates Test, which is based on the related construct of associative hierarchies. The single most frequently employed divergent thinking task is the Alternative Uses Test, or AUT as it is known in the field. It asks participants to generate alternative uses for common objects such as a brick, safety pin, or automobile tire.

To see what the limitation of these alleged creativity tests is, take a minute and write down all the alternative uses of what to do with a brick. Then score the test on three factors. First is ideational fluency, which is simply the total number of ideas you had. If you came up with 8 items your score would be 8. Second is flexibility, which is the number of different types or categories of ideas. If all you could think of were uses as a weapon (hit an enemy, throw at a blocked door, etc.) your score would be a meager 1. Third is originality. While the first two factors, ideational fluency and flexibility, are variables that can simply be counted, the originality variable is usually assessed with the so-called consensual method, in which naïve judges rate the originality of the answers. Alternatively, this factor can also be assessed quantitatively if the test is administered to a large group – a school setting, for instance. In this case, you take each response and compare it to all responses of the group. An item occurring in fewer than 5 percent of responses is considered unusual and gets 1 point. An item occurring in fewer than 1 percent is considered unique and gets 2 points. Suppose you had one unusual and one unique item, your originality score would amount to 3. Sum up all points $(8 + 1 + 3)$ and your overall creativity score would stand at 12. And now for the real issue: Do you think this captures your creativity? Do you think that a score of 12 as compared to, say, a score of 8 would tell you about your creative thinking ability. How do you think creative giants like Ludwig van Beethoven or Marie Curie would have scored on the AUT?

Whenever I give the AUT to my students in class and ask them the same question, they laugh. No way, they say. It has to be said, though, that proponents of divergent thinking tests admit that these tests measure creative potential, not creativity. And that claim they can support with solid data, as such tests do have decent predictive properties (Runco et al., 2011), probably because they capture some aspects of intelligence and some relevant personality characteristic, such as openness to experience. But for reasons we are about to see, they don't work for neuroscience, and here we have to have the guts to shout that the emperor has no clothes. In all honesty, can we really expect a test that asks you to imagine alternative uses of a safety pin to differentiate the brain of Einstein from one that belongs to a certified public accountant?

Granted, all standardized psychometric tests have limitations, and I want to restrict my critique of these purported creativity tests to their use in the hunt for creativity mechanisms in the brain. By tentatively distinguishing creative from non-creative – convergent, in this case – information processing, divergent thinking was an attempt to get an initial grip on creativity. It was the kick start creativity research needed to get underway. But from this rather promising beginning, in a development that even Guilford didn't intend, the humble notion of divergent thinking has morphed from a first crack at this hard-to-pin down phenomenon into *the* standard conception of creativity. In no time, tests of divergent thinking became, for convenience sake, tests of creativity and, on the basis of this sleight of hand, people drew conclusions about creativity *per se*. In fact, divergent thinking and its derivative testing products have come to so completely dominate theoretical and empirical work in the field that everything else has fallen by the wayside. I'd bet that most of what you have ever read about creativity in reputable outlets is drawn from these divergent thinking tests. It isn't that this early work from the 1950s and 1960s is all wrong; oh no, after all, you have to start somewhere. The trouble is that this very respectable first piece of theoretical Lego hasn't been developed to the same extent, broadly along the same lines as other areas of cognitive psychology and neuroscience in the past 50 years.

It's embarrassingly easy to show that the proposal of taking divergent thinking as proxy of creative thinking is an incoherent foundation for neuroscientific studies. There are, in fact, two separate but nested problems with it, and either of them alone is lethal for neuroscience research. I have labeled them the monolithic entity fallacy and the false category formation. Together, they propel divergent thinking to the number two spot in our list of demolition targets.

To start with the latter, one cannot help but wonder how divergent thinking ever became effectively equated with creativity? Perhaps this is just the way things go but it couldn't have well escaped generations of psychologists – it certainly didn't elude Guilford – that a creative product can just as well be the result of a convergent process – think Bach, Edison, or creative achievements in mathematics. This raises the following, rather obvious question. What, exactly, is it about divergent thinking that is creative? What use is the concept for the experimental study of creativity if divergent thinking can also result in ordinary outcomes and its exact opposite, convergent thinking, in creative ones? The fact that divergent and convergent thinking can generate both, ordinary and creative solutions, renders the concept of divergent thinking incapable of identifying the fundamental processes, cognitive or neural, that turn normal thinking (whatever that is) into creative thinking. Divergent thinking, in other words, is a false category formation (Dietrich, 2007b).

Once we understand that creative acts arise from both, divergent and convergent processes, the distinction becomes meaningless as the theoretical basis for the study of creativity. To hammer this piton in tight, what good is the distinction – for uncovering the fundamental nature of creativity – if it doesn't discriminate between creative and normal thinking? It isn't strictly true, I must quickly interject, that this matter has escaped the notice of psychologists and many who work on creativity have questioned the usefulness of divergent thinking as a construct. But this – and here is the rub – you could hardly tell from the perusal of the psychological literature. Even when investigators acknowledge the problem in their paper's introductory remarks, mostly because some referee in the peer-review process forced them to, they, undaunted, proceed to use the flawed construct anyway. This has had the curious effect that we have an experimental study of divergent thinking. This is not what we want. We want an experimental study of creativity!

The issue seems simply to be a case of logic 101. If you wish to better circumscribe a phenomenon's existence, you must delineate your proposal from something, a control condition of some kind that either contains its opposite or at least is marked by its absence. How else would you know if you carved nature at its true joints? Actually, divergent thinking is only the most influential of a whole stack of such false partitions. Psychologists and neuroscientists, often with more enthusiasm than sense, have put forth a number of such forlorn proposals. Open any source on creativity, academic or otherwise, and you will find an extended list of false category formations that aligns creativity with, say, low arousal, defocused attention, flow states, lateral thinking, latent inhibition, remote associations, unconscious thinking, altered states of consciousness, madness, alpha power enhancement and, not forgetting, right brains, to name the popular themes. We can add each and every one of them to the list of demolition targets because commonsense alone tells you that their exact opposites are also wellsprings of creative thinking and, to complete the factorial crossover, each and every one of them is associated with non-creative thinking. Such category formations flout basic logic.

Although widely recognized as not selective for creativity, it didn't follow, as it should have, that these false categories were either rejected and replaced by new ones or deepened to see what, exactly, is creative about them. Instead, like a bad meme out of hell, they have happily self-replicated and contaminated large areas of the intellectual landscape. Insult was added to injury when this premature this-but-not-that thinking became the launch pad for tests of creativity.

Given the time-tested ability of academics to expand in a vacuum, some researchers have responded to this critique by back peddling and admitting that there is such a thing as convergent creativity. The Torrance Test of Creative Thinking, for instance, now contains convergent thinking items that have only one right solution. But this is a bizarre theoretical backflip. Look what this does. It turns the paradigm of divergent thinking, on which the Torrance test is based you will remember, from a category error into a circular argument. One more time and with apologies, if both divergent and convergent thinking lead to both creative and non-creative thinking what is there about either divergent or convergent thinking that is creative or non-creative? In consequence, the inclusion of convergent creativity is question-begging. The refusal to come to grips with this is truly remarkable.

And this isn't the only offense. The other lethal problem is the monolithic entity fallacy, the bad habit of thinking about creativity as a single, unitary thing. Perhaps because we tend to think of creativity as a discrete phenomenon or personality trait – as in, Steve Jobs had it (notice the singular) and my grandfather didn't – we also tend to think that creativity must be due to one, distinct factor, an extra something – the creative bit, if you like – that's specifically added to the plain mix to make the sparkling difference. Many have found this an attractive idea and, if you step back and think about it for second, it's actually a necessary assumption to justify pointing neuroimaging cameras at the brain. In fact, it's the monolithic entity fallacy that fuels the phrenological theorizing about the neural basis of creativity, because a single unit, the thinking goes, must be located someplace specific or have a distinct brain wave pattern, mustn't it?

This book will bring into sharp focus that creativity is highly distributed and embedded, a complex phenomenon that emerges, like all multipart psychological traits, from goodness knows how many processes and places in the brain. Asking cognitive neuroscientists for the neural location of creative thinking is like asking them for the neural location of thinking. It's the brain, stupid!

So here is the perplexing part. Creativity researchers seem to know this and waste no time at all in openly distancing themselves from any commitment to a monolithic entity conception of creativity. They will climb over one another to tell you that there is no special brain structure, no single process, and no magic switch that turns on the muse. Implicitly though, likely due to a lack of theoretical alternatives, they hang on to this way of thinking, albeit in a more refined form. How else, I ask you, can we understand the rationale for using neuroimaging tools in the study of creativity. They all rest on the assumption that the creative bit exists as such and does so as a definite and localizable entity. The writing in the professional literature clearly demonstrates that it hasn't yet sunk in how thoroughly scattered in the brain and multifaceted in its processes the superduper complex behavior of creativity, in all the different forms it manifests itself in the human population, must be.

So what about divergent thinking then? Sure, the concept does represent an attempt to start parsing the compound construct of creativity into constituent elements to make the search for mechanisms more tractable. But even if we bracket the false category mess for a moment, is divergent thinking really a step forward in the search of a brain mechanism? Of course not. Divergent thinking is still a complex, multipart concept, consisting of various different and quite separate mental processes that are highly distributed and embedded. What's more, no one has the slightest clue what divergent or convergent thinking involves in terms of actual – meaning localizable – cognitive processes, such as working memory, top-down attention, face recognition, or visual perception. Just as there is no creative bit, there is no divergent thinking bit that exists as a definite and localizable entity. In consequence, the monolithic entity fallacy holds for divergent thinking, without modification.

It follows that creativity tests based on divergent thinking are method-
ological sledge hammers that cannot produce useful neuroimaging data.
The main take-home message is this: the subject of interest simply
cannot be isolated. The irony is, again, that everyone seems to agree
on this; yet, believers in this paradigm fall prey to the same error in
thinking and treat composites like divergent thinking as monolithic
entities. They are so hooked on phrenology that they don't see the
clear contradiction. For neuroscience, the concept of divergent thinking is an artifact of misguided theorizing, an amorphous monster that
will remain forever intractable by the methods of neuroscience, no
matter how high the spatial or temporal resolution of future imaging gizmos. Remember the organ of philoprogenitiveness? Exact same
problem.

If you think that does it, that's the end of divergent thinking in
neuroscience, you'd be sadly mistaken. People defending a paradigm in
its dying stages are nothing but tenacious. They will persist with an idea
even if its wobbly underpinnings are laid bare. Too much invested; too
much cognitive dissonance! Proponents of divergent thinking have por-
trayed the monolithic entity fallacy as a straw man argument because
everyone, they say, recognizes that it draws on many component processes. But this invites the obvious retort of the false category formation
and the follow-up question of what, exactly, is creative about sub-
processes of divergent thinking given that their counterparts also do
creative work. That's the question I want answered. To stop the circularly
defined elaborations, one would have to break such complex constructs
down further into *valid divisions* that allow researchers to detect creativity on one side of the category boundary because of its absence on the
other.

Some have even argued that divergent thinking can be parsed appropriately by breaking it down into fluency, flexibility, and originality –
remember the AUT? The trouble with that defense is, of course, that
these parts aren't selective for creativity either. Again, one would have
to demonstrate what, exactly, is it about fluency that is creative. To see
this point more clearly, consider the complement of fluency by way of
a story told about Albert Einstein. When he was asked if he kept a note-
book to record his ideas, Einstein responded with genuine surprise: "Oh,
that's not necessary. It's so seldom I have one." We can safely conclude
from this episode that Einstein wouldn't have scored high on fluency,
which, incidentally, is the part of the AUT people get the most number
of points on.

If we want to leave this definitional trap and develop a science of creativity that puts us out of our misery, we must heed the lessons of the

past and prevent ourselves – no matter how difficult – from backsliding into thinking that, at the current theoretical resolution with which we see the issue, creativity can be localized in a specific place or defined by a specific mental process or brain wave signature. Just as there is no place where you can find creativity in the brain, there is no one process that makes it. The exact same thing holds – and this is the important message for the research community – for divergent thinking or any of the currently circulating false category formations – defocused attention, remote associations, unconscious thinking, alpha power increases, and so on. They are all ontological danglers that don't do any explanatory work for the study of creativity. The concept of divergent thinking is a case of a once good idea that became over time a straitjacket out of which the field has yet to escape. I have been urging people to abandon it, at least for the purpose of doing neuroscience research, and, thanks to neuroimaging technology, its days in neuroscience are perhaps finally numbered.

Weird mental test X gives pretty brain image Y

Suppose now that we recruit a dozen college students, administer a divergent thinking test to them – the AUT would do – and scrutinize their buzzing brain activity with the probing beam of a neuroimaging lens. What, after all we've learned, can we reasonably expect to see? Sure, something is going to light up; it's a mental test after all. But the all-important question is this. What can the activity tell us about the neural mechanisms of creative thinking?

Modern brain science is on a roll. The new neuroimaging tools seem able to take a snapshot of your mind in 256 million colors while you ponder Buddhist koans, solve moral conundrums, or perform some other test of mental ability. And everyone wants a piece of the action. Hunting for the neural basis of our higher cognitive functions has always held great appeal for the simple reason that it seems to get us a step closer to understanding something fundamental about the human condition. However, progress on the matter, for most of the last century at least, seemed to fall laughably short of this noble goal. There just wasn't a way, some clever eavesdropping device perhaps, that could deliver the goodies. Neuroscientists and psychologists had to contend with studying the human mind by proxy – rat brains, monkey brains, brain-damaged humans, etc. – and by approximation – rather basic learning paradigms of one sort or another. As invaluable and productive as this research program was, this just wasn't ever going to mesmerize the general public. What was needed, clearly, was some glitzy new contraption that could collect shiny, real-time data from the innards of the machine while it was doing the sort of thing that seems to define us as humans – language, mental time travel, emotions, cultural differences, creativity, or consciousness.

When this new technology came, in the shape of brain scanners, neuroscience quickly turned, within the short span of two decades, into a massive tidal wave that has been sweeping, though some might prefer bulldozing, through all but the most remote outposts of the social and behavioral sciences. Even anthropologists, philosophers, and economists want to play with the new neuroimaging toys. The general public, too, has fallen in love with the hypnotizing images of the color-coded human brain. It's a bonanza, a feeding frenzy not seen since molecular biology came of age.

It's not my intention here to mount a general critique of neuroimaging technology. Far from it. The great neuro show of recent decades has revealed a great deal about the human brain and how it functions. At the same time, such a frenzied and hyped atmosphere invites excesses. Consider just one. The insula, a little-known region in the forebrain, has enjoyed a rather quiet existence so far, happily doing its thing under the radar screen of neuroscientists' attention. But the arrival of fMRI changed all that. Turns out, the insula is an artistic multitasker, a polyglot extraordinaire. Depending on which study you read, it's variously responsible for sex, pain, disgust, and lust as well as attention and the sense of time. In the hope of striking neuroscience gold, many people took the road to phrenology and met a dead end.

In creativity research, this road had the following mileposts. Take a divergent thinking test, secure scanning time in the department's new brain imaging center, recruit some student volunteers from the current Psychology 101 class, and stir well. Add a randomization scheme and a double-blind procedure for scientific rigor, analyze the data stream with a good statistical software package, and write up a glowing discussion section about your breakthrough discovery on the mysterious neural underpinnings of creativity. How can you fail? For – surprise, surprise – some brain region was indeed firing away with extra oomph and the topic itself, gee, does it get any sexier than that? And who is ever going to ask about the petty little distinction between divergent thinking and creativity, or the conceptual basis of the so-called creativity test, eh?

In time, the findings from this cortex-sapping paradigm will eventually recede into the statistical fog of false positives. Bearing in mind their theoretical incoherence, it's hard to see how they don't. For now, though, we are forced to grapple with this powerful illusion maker. This is no easy task because the recipe followed doesn't much distinguish it from a lot of the rest of the neuroscience literature. The boilerplate is the same and the imaging methodology is clean.

The difference lies, of course, in the conceptualization of creativity. In other domains of cognitive neuroscience, the devised mental task is, first, at an appropriate level of granularity so that neuroimaging is applicable and, second, ecologically valid so that the whole experiment makes sense. The first aspect avoids the monolithic entity fallacy by matching the theoretical resolution with which we understand the psychological construct to the spatial resolution with which brain scanners operate. This is the case for individual mental processes such as working memory components, fear conditioning, or visual feature detection. Because they are implemented in specific regions or networks, neuroimaging studies can also deliver meaningful information on their localization. The second aspect avoids the false category formation by contrasting the mental task with a control task that doesn't tap into the same mental faculty. It isn't too hard to come up with a control task for fear conditioning. You can probably construct one without much difficulty – by simply presenting neutral stimuli, for instance. As long as the mental faculty in question can by isolated in this manner, neuroscientists can even make progress on complex psychological constructs that would otherwise be intractable due to the monolithic entity fallacy. Take moral reasoning as an example. One can hardly quarrel with the statement that morality is a faculty that is complex and distributed. It's a composite involving many different individual mental processes that are realized in as many different pieces of neural real estate. Yet, there are excellent brain imaging studies on moral reasoning. Why? The answer, I hope, is obvious at this stage. For morality, neuroscientists have managed to construct psychometric tests that clearly divorce moral decision-making from its opposite. The resulting differential brain activation for these two conditions can then tell you something about the neural basis of this mental faculty.

The use of brain scanners to hunt for the neural basis of creativity is different. Here the monolithic entity fallacy and the false category formation combine for an unholy marriage that makes defeat certain. The simple truth of the matter is, we have no clue in these creativity studies what, exactly, is being imagined, what these fMRI pictures show. It is tempting to suppose that as it becomes harder and harder to make a name for oneself in brain research, as the pressure for high-impact factor journals and tenure mounts, some cognitive neuroscientists have sought greener pastures and filled academic journals by simply taking the same template that worked so well for other cognitive functions and apply it to the problem of creativity. And why not? There are ready-to-go so-called creativity tests in existence and the university's brand new neuroimaging center is just next door. Alas, a bit of level-headed thinking would have saved a lot of grant money and us from this pixelated Potemkin village.

I first laid this all out in a paper in 2007 (Dietrich, 2007b), but theory alone rarely convinces people. Those not caught up in the paradigm suspected this anyway and nodded quietly, while those invested in it enthusiastically ignored the paper and soldiered on. It goes to show how hard it is to overcome a conviction once it fundamentally colors your view of the world. In my other work on altered states of consciousness, I had already learned that in order to break the back of an intuition as powerful as phrenology it is necessary to block all the exits. A review article of all the existing data, I thought, might do the trick. So, in 2010 an undergraduate student and I (Dietrich & Kanso, 2010) sifted through mountains of data in professional journals with such fun titles as *International Journal of Psychophysiology, Neuroscience and Biobehavioral Reviews, Neuropsychopharmacology* and, why not, *Human Brain Mapping,* and collated a comprehensive list of studies that had looked at creativity through the lens of a brain imaging camera. There were a total of 63 papers, reporting 72 experiments, with more than half using the AUT or a similar divergent thinking test.

To avoid sugar-coating it, the results were a total mess. Skeptical me wasn't exactly expecting to find much in the way of coherent results, but even I didn't think it would be this bad. To make a long story short, when all was compared, analyzed, contrasted, summarized, and checked, there wasn't a single idea on the neural underpinning of creativity that survived close scrutiny. The data were so all over the place, in fact, that even weak trends were difficult to make out. In the end, no single anatomical locus and no single theoretical concept was supported by even as much as half of the reviewed studies. So let the record show, creativity isn't linked to RH, white matter density, divergent thinking, defocused attention, low arousal, alpha waves, or any other conjecture. Whatever notion of creative thinking you care to press, there is always more evidence against you than supports you. On the flipside, there is also always enough evidence to maintain any theoretical position. This fact, helped by the practice of selectively citing studies that suit one's theoretical taste, has led to the bizarre situation that not one of these proposals on the neural basis of creativity has been demolished and offloaded into the dustbin of neuroscience. But given the weight of the evidence, the dustbin is where all of them belong.

Divergent thinking took the biggest beating. The neuroimaging data inadvertently exposed just how inadequate the concept was for our quest to understand the nature of the creative process in brains. If the doubt over the validity of divergent thinking was once a family argument, neuroimaging was the method that aired the dirty laundry. Shortly thereafter, several more review papers came out telling the same basic story (Arden et al., 2010; Sawyer, 2011; Yoruk & Runco, 2014; Weisberg, 2013). Together, they showed that all that data from this neuroimaging paradigm can show is that – if one squints hard enough – weird mental test X produces colorful neuroimaging picture Y. Garbage in, garbage out, one might say.

Great, I thought. With this out of the way, we can now turn our attention to more promising candidates. But the movement still didn't flag. Apparently, I had completely underestimated people's resistance to change. Leo Tolstoy was on to something when he wrote:

> I know that most men, including those at ease with problems of the greatest complexity, can seldom accept even the simplest and most obvious truth if it be such as would oblige them to admit the falsity of conclusions which they have delighted in explaining to colleagues, which they have proudly taught to others, and which they have woven, thread by thread, into the fabric of their lives.

Plus, the media now got into the act. The narrative of finding the location of creativity in the brain just struck all the right chords for coverage in the tweet-sized attention span of modern news reporting. Even the BBC couldn't resist, producing a documentary on the neuroscience of creativity based almost entirely on carefully picked studies from this divergent thinking paradigm.

By the time of this writing, an additional 20 studies or so had appeared employing the same cookie-cutter template. Needless to say, they didn't bring new insights for the pile. At least now there does seem to be some indication that even proponents of the paradigm are beginning to realize that their approach needs fixing. Unfortunately, all they do is tweak the old divergent thinking paradigm – by, for instance, including convergent thinking or coming up with fresh false category formations such as fluency. So far I have heard no good solutions, and plenty of bad ones. Let me comment on this by quoting another piece of Yogi Berra wisdom:

"You got to be careful if you don't know where you are going because you might not get there."

The rocky horror pixel show

Advances in science depend on falsification, a process that eventually forces us to abandon our conceptions of the world should they not pan out. As Bertolt Brecht wrote in his play Galileo: "The goal of science is not to open the door to everlasting wisdom, but to set a limit on everlasting error." There is little indication that this process has taken place for the neuroscience of creativity. When a paradigm fails – on theoretical grounds, evidentiary basis or, in this case, both – two options present themselves. The principles of falsification demand, of course, to leave it behind and look for alternatives. This is the road we take in this book. But in the same way phrenology kept going even after Flourens had cluster-bombed the central idea, the current neuroimaging paradigm of creativity can also just march on, in its own self-sustaining echo chamber and undisturbed by theory or data. Take for instance the coarse-coding right-hemisphere theory of Kounios and Beeman (2014). The bare fact is that the evidence against it is deep, wide, and thick (Dietrich & Kanso, 2010; Sawyer, 2011; Yoruk & Runco, 2014; Weisberg, 2013, among rather many others). Yet, it lives on. The same goes for the unbroken support for divergent thinking (Fink & Benedek, 2014; Jung et al., 2013). We have to be clear however, that at this point continuing on this road leads to pseudoscience. Now that this research program has been found out, those who wish to persevere with it must, at the same time, put up with the charge of phrenology.

Now, as then, phrenology careens through three stages. Stage 1 consists of the formation of a psychological concept that doesn't exist as a unified entity at the neural level, irrespective of its seeming so at the psychological level. You will remember philoprogenitiveness. Unless better circumscribed or dissected into its constituent parts, a nebulous concept is intractable with the current neuroimaging technology we have. Creativity is such a concept. So is religious belief or political conviction. Some defenders of the paradigm have labeled this a straw man argument and countered with the proposal of new concepts that purportedly address this problem. Trouble is, the new proposals fail on exactly the same grounds – monolithic entity fallacy and false category formation. Divergent thinking, originality, fluency, low arousal, or remote associations all satisfy the conditions of Stage 1 on the road to phrenology.

Stage 2 involves a false mapping process. On that, Franz Joseph Gall is hard to beat, as his effort to map mental faculty to brain region was, willy-nilly, based on no data whatsoever. But the mapping process need not be totally bogus to be a comprehensive fail. A psychometric test that doesn't isolate the processes in question joined in an intimate embrace with a brain camera that has insufficient zooming power wreaks the same havoc. Neuroimaging experiments of creativity certainly look impressive but the generated data is a figment of misinformation if the tools don't measure what they are supposed to measure. It's not unlike using an x-ray machine to detect a quantum field. Modern brain scanners are simply the wrong tool for the job. To leave no room for confusion, the job they are wrong for is to image a complex psychological phenomenon that is defined by way of a false category formation; I am not talking about the detection of individual mental processes that are defined well. A false mapping process is a double whammy on the road to phrenology. Not only does it give wrong information on location or brain-wave pattern, it also gives the deceptive impression that we are getting closer to an explanation when all we are looking at is a colored Rorschach image.

This brings us to stage 3, the overselling of the findings. It is one thing to give in to a certain amount of naïve excitement in the early period of a new paradigm. The matter becomes considerably less agreeable, though, when the overreaching persists after the defects have been rendered explicit. Suppose they are right. Suppose that coming up with weird uses for a brick does somehow measure aspects of creative mentation. Even then, we hardly need reminding that neuroimaging data of this kind wouldn't apply to brain activation for creative behavior in other domains, such as, for instance, poetry improv, play-writing, or theoretical physics. But empirical reports don't read accordingly. Pick one up and you will see. More often than not, one finds grand pronouncements in the literature about creativity *per se*, without any of the badly needed qualifying remarks. The fact that investigators freely talk about their data as if they apply to all the diverse ways in which we can be creative shows just how difficult it is to go all the way with the idea that creativity is composed of a plethora of very different and distributed processes. And once the media gets hold of such overgeneralizations, we have the additional embarrassment of being treated to one-sided mumbo-jumbo such as this one from the *New Yorker* (Lehrer, 2008) " ... once the brain is sufficiently focused, the cortex needs to relax in order to seek out the more remote association in the right hemisphere, which will provide the insight."

Each time we read a lofty statement of this kind, we should immediately ask a series of probing questions. First, is it based on a valid measure of creativity or insight? If the answer is thumbs down we can stop considering it right there. We are evidently dealing with phrenology and should pounce on this like a pitbull. If thumbs point up, we must precede to the next question: What type of creative insights are we talking about? Followed immediately by a third question: To what forms of creative insights does this not apply? And a fourth question: Why are we talking about creative insights as if the findings are generalizable to all manifestations of it.

Will the phrenological habits of thinking about creativity go extinct? I expect not. It will not survive in its current, toxic form because it will probably run itself out naturally, at the very latest when another two dozen studies will have failed to converge on anything meaningful. But this will only prompt followers to morph it into a less virulent mutation, so powerful is the pull of phrenology. It just appeals to people. So, I won't make the tactical error of spending more time trying to dislodge with theory or data a position that is at this point beyond reason. I prefer to light a candle rather than curse in the dark, and spend the rest of the book proposing a way out of this gigantic sinkhole.

From all we know about brain organization, it is difficult to conceive of creativity, in all its shapes and forms, as emerging from a small, common set of brain networks or as depending on a limited number of mental processes that have a distinct neural signature. Too different is what scientists, entrepreneurs, fashion designers, or ballet choreographers must do to be creative in their respective spheres. Because of its complex and temporarily extended nature, the neural mechanisms that underlie creative thought surely depend on the content and purpose of particular instances. A convergence in terms of brain regions or processes would be nothing short of calling into question the modular conception of brain function that all neuroscientists accept. If painting, mathematics, and parking your car engages totally different brain areas and processes so should creative painting, creative mathematics, and creative car-parking.

Naturally, this leaves open the burning question of how else we should think about creativity in the brain. Well, at this juncture we have to seriously entertain the possibility that the opposite holds true, that creativity is completely distributed and fully embedded. I call this the vaudeville conception of creativity and it presupposes that creativity as such doesn't merit elevation to the status of an entity with a distinctive neural signature. If you have problems reconciling this with your thinking that creativity, as such, must be somewhere specific or identifiable by a single neural pattern, you are not alone. Luckily, in this book I suggest therapeutic countermeasures that will help you with conceiving of that possibility. Of course, those creativity researchers who are in love with their neuroimaging toys will think that it is I who need therapy. This I might. But not for the rational argument I outlined in the preceding pages.

I will make the case for the vaudeville conception of creativity in more detail in Chapter 7, once other complications have been suitably disentangled. For now, I just mention that it assumes that the creative bit, for any mental faculty, is in the same place and uses the same processes than the normal processing of information for that mental faculty (Dietrich, 2004b). What we are going to find with our brain scanners, then, depends entirely on how we decide to look. Use a different creativity test and you'd get correspondingly different neuroimaging results. This is an awkward moment. For, if I am right about this, the vaudeville conception, properly disciplined, fully defeats the efforts to localize creativity with our currently available knowledge and methodology. And this is exactly what the various review articles of neuroimaging studies seem to show. A single change in the testing procedure and the whole neuroimaging picture is pulled out of shape. Might it be that investigators have simply rushed to make proclamations about nature of the elephant of creativity after managing to grab only a piece of the trunk – if that, I hastily add, given the problems with divergent thinking tests for neuroscience research?

All this doesn't preclude that subtypes of creativity, or subtypes of subtypes, will eventually be localizable. If we go small enough, subprocesses responsible for generating ideational combinations must be located somewhere, albeit in different places for different mental domains. After all, they can't float in mid-synapse. Underline the phrase *small enough* here, though, because proper localization necessitates that we start breaking down creativity into cognitive subcomponents that represent valid divisions and distribute them, right at the outset, throughout the information-processing system. This we have yet to do.

We have come to the end of our demolition project. Its aim was to disabuse anyone of the residual validity of the simplistic ideas about creativity that currently dominate the airwaves and the amorphous creativity tests that spring from them. The only way to be creative about the brain mechanisms of creative thinking is to ignore all this noise and explore more promising directions. A great many people may not thank me in the short term for nudging them out of their epistemological safe zone. But the next generation may thank me in the long term if I succeed. I must give it a proper try. So, let's open the front door and begin.

Recommended readings

Dietrich, A. (2004b). The cognitive neuroscience of creativity. *Psychonomic Bulletin & Review, 11*, 1011–1026.

Dietrich, A. (2007a). *Introduction to consciousness*. London: Palgrave Macmillan.

Dietrich, A. (2007b). Who is afraid of a cognitive neuroscience of creativity? *Methods, 42*, 22–27.

Dietrich, A., & Kanso, R. (2010). A review of EEG, ERP and neuroimaging studies of creativity and insight. *Psychological Bulletin, 136*, 822–848.

Fink, A., & Benedek, M. (2014). EEG alpha power and creative ideation. *Neuroscience and Biobehavioral Reviews, 44*, 111–123.

Gazzaniga, M. S. (2000). *The mind's past*. Berkeley, CA: California University Press.

Lehrer, J. (2008). The eureka hunt. *The New Yorker*, July 28.

Runco, M. A. (Ed.). (1991). *Divergent thinking*. Norwood, NJ: Ablex Publishing Corporation.

Uttall, W. R. (2001). *The new phrenology*. Cambridge, MA: MIT Press.

Weisberg, R. W. (2013). On the demystification of insight: A critique of neuroimaging studies of insight. *Creativity Research Journal, 25*, 1–14.

3
You're Gonna Need a Bigger Boat

The chapter's title is taken from a famous line in the movie *Jaws*. Brody, a local police chief played by Roy Schneider, is charged with hunting down a giant great white shark that attacks swimmers in a beach resort. He enlists the help of Quint, a grizzled and experienced shark hunter played by Robert Shaw. Together they set out aboard the old seafarer's aging vessel, the Orca. It is Brody who catches a glimpse of the great white first. Visibly in shock over its size, he takes a few steps back, turns to Quint, and stumbles: "You're gonna need a bigger boat."

Neuroscience is unkind to common sense. This is not a particular difficult idea to accept, one would think. Much of science would seem to fly in the face – indeed, *does* fly in the face – of what philosophers call, not without a touch of smugness, folk physics. The most arresting example of this is certainly the strange subatomic world of quantum physics but, in fact, all of the well-won triumphs of science escape our best efforts of introspective detection. But somehow, this seems harder to accept for folk psychology. To begin with, we are being asked to imagine that a three-pound, mushy pile of electrified biochemistry can hope for the best, rethink a decision, or be bored to tears. We must then come to the realization that we are not just wrong about something but that we are wrong about ourselves. All this is much easier said than done. Even people at ease with the gospel of modern neuroscience assume that the up close and personal experience we have of our own mind connects seamlessly with the deeper reality of the brain's inner workings. It doesn't. Many also think that creativity would break down into mechanistic explanations we can grasp with common sense. It wouldn't. Evidently, to capture the mechanisms of creative thinking, we're gonna need a bigger boat.

Exorcising the ghost in the machine

To see what I mean, let me caricature the instinctive belief about how the mind works that we all have but seldom, if ever, examine. Before we can make any progress on the question of how brains compute creative ideas, we must drive out this deep-seated but ultimately misbegotten impression. It goes something like this: I experience myself as being somewhere inside my own head. I look out at the world through the peepholes that are my eyes, catching the sights that are out there. Information enters through my senses and is built up, by my brain, into mental images that are then displayed in their full glory on a virtual mental screen, or some kind of theatrical stage, for me, the audience, to see and appreciate. From my little cranial command post, the place inside where "I" am, I can then order my brain to move my body. This is how it feels like to have a mind, isn't it? Putting the matter this comically helps – I hope – to see that it is an amusingly deluded belief, to put it in the most charitable terms possible. You will notice that all this implies that there is a special place – a stage or screen – that is brightly lit, where information is displayed for the Mind to be acted upon.

But – and here's the troubling point – none of this exists. You will soon discover in these pages that, no matter how intuitive it strikes you, there is no central place anywhere in the brain; no dazzling show reeling off specially selected conscious information; and no Higher Executive who inhabits the brain and to whom consciousness, or a creative thought, happens.

The philosopher Daniel Dennett has attacked this most intuitive of conception of the mind with both barrels (Dennett, 1991). He dubs it the Cartesian theater, after Rene Descartes whose name is forever attached to it for the simple reason that he went through great lengths to sharpen it to a formal philosophical theory. Cartesian dualism is the thesis that there are two kinds of stuff in the universe: mind (immaterial and immortal clumps of soulstuff) and matter (tables, chairs, and airplanes). There are endless difficulties attached to keeping these two worlds categorically apart. Consider just one. Suppose you are hit in the head by an aberrant baseball and feel dozy for a few moments as a result. Why? According to Cartesian dualism, brains are entirely unnecessary for minds. How do baseballs change thoughts? How can we accept that a few milligrams of a drug, say, Prozac, can make us feel peachy and maintain, in one and the same breath, the existence of some non-physical, eternal Godstuff that is separate from it in kind. The bare fact that a chemical can change our belief system is sufficient grounds for outright refutation of Cartesian dualism. Perhaps nothing speaks more clearly to the patent absurdity of this theory than the philosopher Gilbert Ryle's dead-on phrase "ghost in the machine."

Of all the cognitive illusions that warp reality around our own self-importance, the Cartesian theater is the granddaddy of them all. It's a pernicious fallacy of thinking that we must identify and consciously abandon because it's not a benign crutch for the imagination but a hopeful monster that, as long as we keep it, sabotages all of our attempts to find the brain mechanisms that make us so creative.

To appreciate the Cartesian ghost's various manifestations, and bring its churning to a halt, it is worth drawing it out from yet another angle. Sensory information comes in and motor commands go out. There must be a middle, mustn't there, a place or time in-between, where information – however briefly – enters and exits the conscious mind. This is the classic sandwich conception in which consciousness occurs between sensory and motor processes. Well, the trouble with brains, it seems, is that if we carefully trace sensory input through the pathways all the way until we arrive at a motor neuron, we find that there is no middle, no special place or time somewhere along the way, where *in*bound information is pooled and catapulted into the magic spotlight of consciousness for the benefit of a commander in-chief, who then generates *out*bound information.

Suppose you are open to, even comfortable with, a material theory of consciousness in general and bought this book in the hope of learning something about how creativity works in the brain. What's the danger, apart from the dualism inherent in it, to cling on to this convenient metaphor? Why do I insist that you must flip your thinking and fully let go of the Cartesian theater? For one thing, neuroscientists agree that there is no such pivotal place in the brain where it all comes together. Nor is there a Central Experiencer, an Ego or Self, separate from the hubbub in the brain. The brain, so much is clear, is a massive, parallel processing system. Its representations are widely distributed in multiple, independent streams of activity, that are, at no time, synthesized in one central location, or into one coherent picture, for the mind's eye. So, at the minimum, the Cartesian theater image is factually mistaken. And here's the thing. Neuroscientists know this, of course, and waste no time explicitly renouncing any allegiance to it. Which is why it is all the more remarkable that even otherwise good materialists continue to be seduced by the siren songs of this powerful illusion. It is a disarming reflection of its intuitive appeal that knowing its secrets does little to diminish its misleading effects. For the record, Cartesian materialism, another Dennett term, is the expression philosophers use to describe this unfortunate intrusion of Cartesian thinking into materialism.

The full predicament doesn't come into clear view until we consider the consequences. Once we enter the Cartesian theater and re-represent the input that has been already nicely and completely analyzed by our sensory systems, we must also conjure up a fully conscious homunculus, a little man inside the head, who marvels at the show, controls the consoles and gauges, and eventually pulls the strings of the motor system. This is when matters go from bad to worse. Now we are stuck explaining the innards of this homunculus and an infinite regress immediately looms. Not just that. The homunculus – conveniently enough – just happens to have the right kind of powers and abilities to explain what needs to be explained in the first place (Dennett, 1991). In hacker circles, this known as a spoofing attack. The homunculus program impersonates the real mechanism and thwarts the very job a theory of creativity is supposed to do, providing a mechanistic account of how new insights come into existence.

This is a deadly trap! We make some progress for a while, explaining this and that aspect of creative thinking, and right when the going gets tough we take shelter in the Cartesian theater by inventing – sim sam sum – an internal agent who handles all the bits still missing. The trouble is that this lures us into thinking that we've done the job, that we can stop, when, in fact, we have solved nothing. All we've really done is kick the can down the road. We are no better off resorting to miracles on the tenth step than – like Descartes – on the first.

Cartesian materialism is easier to spot than you might think. The tell-tale sign is when a neuroscientist captivates an audience with fluctuating sodium-potassium currents, spike trains in the central nucleus of the amygdala, or dopamine binding sites, and then ends the heady demonstration by declaring that the information "reaches" or "enters" consciousness. By now you will recognize the lumbering problem and the reason why I insist on right and proper exorcism. The story implies that there must be some other, further place where the mind is. And no sooner is the Cartesian ghost in the machine, the creative Designer comes back into the design process, and we are tangled up in the infinity loops of dualism.

If you have trouble breaking the back of this cognitive illusion, you are not alone. Information is either "in" or "out" of consciousness, isn't it? There has to be a difference, a place that marks the middle, a crucial moment in time when the information changes its status from unconscious to conscious and a Higher Self confers the meaning. Don't worry.

Assistance is on the way. In this chapter, we will equip ourselves with a few corrective devices that will help us think more clearly about the brain and the way its networks operate.

Until that time, a two-step exercise in imagination-shifting might go a long way to defeat this false image. To start, we can remind ourselves that the Cartesian theater is flat wrong. If that doesn't do the trick, we can, whenever we think we have done all the explanatory work that can be done, ask ourselves the logical next question: What, exactly, is it we are pointing to? Who is this "me" reading the neurological record? What we will find is not some fully conscious Designer, but something that, upon further inspection, can itself be decomposed into subcomponents and embedded into the operation of the brain. It is at this point, when we insist on going all way, that even the hardiest materialists cringe in horror at the full realization that there really is nobody home and that those special moments of creative insight, when the sparks of inspiration fly, could be fully reverse-engineered.

We can also opt for a more formal approach and defeat the homuncularism the way an infinite regress is usually defeated in philosophy – right at the beginning. This occurs via two steps. First, we break down consciousness into infinitely small pieces and distribute them throughout the brain right at the outset. This avoids the tactical error of getting hold of the problem from the wrong end. Second, we turn the nesting of homunculi on its head and make higher homunculi less powerful than their hosts. In this way, the homuncular regress becomes finite, bottoming out with homunculi so simple that we can replace them with neurons, each itself as unconscious as a silicon switch.

This leaves us with a lot of pesky questions. Just, how else should we think about the mind and understand, at an intuitive level, what's going on? And: where do creative insights come from?

Linearizing pandemonium

If you are interested in finding out how and where creative ideas happen, a good first step, it would seem, is to get a handle on how conscious thoughts emerge in general. To do this, I will introduce and combine the evidence and theorizing from various disciplines. This is harder to do than you might think. Keeping up with the literature on consciousness is a little like trying to outrun a tidal wave. And if the sheer amount of information doesn't get to you, the dense jargon of brainspeak surely will. Throw in, for good measure, the neck-breaking mental gymnastics one must perform to understand the oodles of seriously twisted ideas from people whose only obvious talent is to make very delicate maneuvers of logic sound terribly important and quantum physics begins to look positively self-evident. It is all a bit of a challenge.

To bring you a very brief (and rough) primer of what we know, or think we know, about consciousness in the brain requires that we use a few flag-waving oversimplifications in the form of toy models that illustrate key features of the brain's connectionist architecture and the way neurons go about conducting their business. This will do more than just help us reach escape velocity from the Cartesian theater. It will help us to get to know the creative mind as it is.

Suppose a friend asks you what you were doing on your birthday ten years ago. Where did you spend it? Who was with you that day? What did you do? If you have ever wondered how your memory works, and at some point you must have, you will know that there is no formal logic to it.

Library databases are decidedly more structured affairs in comparison. They come in several types but all are based on a tidy indexing scheme that carefully labels and catalogs our accumulated wisdom, and a systematic application of rules that retrieves it. The need to bring order to the things we know is as old as knowledge production itself. The classical world codified its knowledge into seven subjects, the seven liberal arts. It is probably not too much to say that this classification system, and in much the same shape, remained the basis for libraries and curricula for over a thousand years in large part because the prevailing ecclesiastical wind of the Dark Ages had put a screeching halt to the inquisitory ways of the ancient Greeks. With the explosion of knowledge since, more complex systems had to be developed. The Library of Congress, for instance, employs a multi-part system of classes and subclasses. The logic behind the scheme, however, is the same. As long as you understand the method, you can find anything you want with it. What's more, cross-indexing will tell you how all items in the Library are related to all others. Such are the complexities, information science is now itself a science.

Things get more interesting with the Internet. Looking for information in the vast network of the world's intertubes needs a different approach. This is because the information out there is not structured in neat and logically adjacent categories. Nor is it ordered alphabetically or by size. The bits and pieces are scattered and disjointed. To find anything in the disorderly fabric of reality requires a search algorithm of a specific sort, the sort that can make some people in Silicon Valley very rich indeed.

To return to your birthday of ten years ago, how, and where, does the brain represent knowledge? What underlying organization holds it all together? And how does it keep track of which piece goes with which? These are important questions, it would seem, if we want to trace creative ideas to their source. What we need to assist us in getting clear about these complex matters is a toy version of the brain's organization. As it happens, the internet's semi-organic makeup provides just such a toy version. We will use this more familiar friend to great advantage as we shift our perspective about the brain's inner workings.

Connectionism represents human memory in experienced-based clusters or concepts that are interconnected in a network-like structure (Anderson, 1996). These clusters break down further into individual nodes or neurons. Just as every computer linked to the Internet has its preferred channels of communication, in the brain, every node is connected to other nodes through previous associations – in time, space, or semantic meaning. It is for this reason that we encounter such trouble when recalling information that cuts across well-trotted connections. Try to list, for instance, the months of the year in alphabetical order.

All nodes operate at their own individual pace and intensity, a baseline activation rate that signifies the weight they have in the network. This is also known as the frequency-of-occurrence value, an apt name to describe how often a node flares up when the network is buzzing with activity. Some of the node values to the network are rather permanently set. These hardwired parts change little, if at all, over a person's lifetime and reflect the more stable dimensions of our personality and behavior. Other nodes have frequency-of-occurrence values that are optional or more flexible. The ability of some nodes to shift their weight assignment, and the strength of their relationship to other nodes, means a great deal to you and me. In the words of William James (1880): "There is very little difference between one man and another, but what there is, is very important." It is these flexible parts that individualize the network configuration, making a brain come to embody, over time, a person's unique past experience, opinions, preferences, and expertise. The overall tuning also determines how information is recalled. When we remember a past event, the activation of a concept in the knowledge structure spreads along the path of the strongest connections. This spreading activation, to use the term in the trade, is rather like lightning following the path of least resistance. To translate this into Internet speak, think of neurons as users and their links as strength of their friendship and you have a useful image to structure your thinking about the brain's architecture. Now, hold that thought for a bit. We will come back to the calibration of flexible weights because this influences how specific information flows through the network, and hence might generate creative ideas.

Like all complex systems, the brain has a unique problem. At any one time, it must track a massive amount of information and perform a multitude of chores, trivial and complicated. It can carry out these computations in parallel because it delegates each task to one of a vast number of specialized and independent modules, often branded hordes of demons, that has evolved to handle exactly that task. For this reason we speak of a massive, parallel-processing system. So, here then is the unique problem. You will have noticed that conscious thoughts and bodily movements are serial phenomena. We don't have two streams of consciousness, two selves, or make two separate movements to lift a cup of coffee. We experience the world, including ourselves, as an integrated whole, not composed of bits and pieces. But why, given the brain's many independent agents? How does a super complex, multi-unit system come up, in a reasonable amount of time, with one, single decision?

It takes some strenuous exercise of thought to get comfortable with this perspective, but the brain isn't the monolithic and unified entity our conscious experience tells us it is. In truth, it is a diverse society comprised of umpteen individual subsystems and units, each with its own duties and responsibilities. But this understanding only takes us half way. A consequence of this architecture of the mind is that there must also be a number of well-defined operating rules that determine which of the many demons rises from the depths and takes up temporary residence in consciousness. In point of fact, there is just one: competition. This one simple interaction rule is the brain's fundamental mode of operation. Put another way, the *raison d'être* of any node – or module or demon – in the brain is to beat others to the only prize that counts: to gain access either to consciousness or to muscles. Actually, the former, ascendency to consciousness, is just a roundabout way to get to muscles. In the end, the ultimate goal is to determine the organism's next move, and this is just easier to do when you are in the driver seat of consciousness. This shouldn't entirely surprise us. Competition lies at the heart of all interactions in the biosphere.

The notion of cerebral anarchy, hordes of demons struggling for control, is initially counterintuitive, not to mention discomforting, but it grows on you once you see how it enlightens some otherwise puzzling phenomena. Incidentally, the basic idea of neural competition is almost always presented as a recent discovery, but in fact it was the mathematician Oliver Selfridge (1959) who hit the solution first. The only recent thing about it is neuroscientists paying any attention to it. Selfridge's pandemonium model solves the problem we posed earlier. It is a computer program in which hordes of independent demons are locked into an internal struggle for supremacy. But – and here's the thing – competition between them guarantees that the whole system eventually settles on a single output.

The best way of understanding just what this means for the brain's internal dynamics is to adopt another simplifying toy version: a parliamentary democracy (Crick & Koch, 2003). Replace competition with elections, neurons with politicians, hordes of demons with parties, and the strength of their associations with, well, the strength of their associations. To gain access to power, individuals in a democracy join parties, campaign for support, make deals, and form passing alliances, all in a fierce tug-of-war to attain a better starting position. Election day comes and brings about a winning coalition that forms, temporarily, the next government. For the time this new administration holds power, it determines, singlehandedly, the country's course of action. Note that this process, based exclusively on competitive interactions, results in a single output decision – a single foreign policy, for instance – from a society, to take the United States, of hundreds of millions of people, all with their own opinions and ideas. The case is similar in the domain of neurons, except that the brain lacks many simplifying features, such as orderly and regular elections.

Much like people, neurons are profusely interconnected in sets of networks. And much like people, they can use the tangled web of their connections to form groups and assemblies in very flexible, distributed, and transient ways. Neuroscientists speak of neuronal coalitions when neurons team up in a brief but stable partnership. These coalitions endlessly compete; they fall apart or join together or change allegiance in endless arrangements, but every competition has a winner, and these winners grow stronger as they go. The physiological mechanisms that strengthen the internal stability of such widely distributed representations in the brain are the subject of a great many studies in neuroscience these days. There is no need to get all technical about it, but to give you a flavor, a list of top candidates includes: number of neurons in the coalition, strength of activation, temporal synchronization of spike trains, oscillatory stability, and dopamine activation. Whether they recruit more neurons, or better entrench their individual firing pattern, local winners eventually become global players and bond in transient super-coalitions that compete, brain-wide, with other hopeful contenders that have done the same. A winning coalition finally emerges whose representation is temporarily active in consciousness. The brain, in other words, settles on a singular output in play-off fashion, on the basis of nonstop, head-to-head competitions. This winner-takes-it-all strategy also explains the fact that access to consciousness is all-or-none, despite being built up from the messy, graded processing in the knowledge structure underneath. The losers of the competition, the neuronal coalitions that did not muster enough clout, dissipate into oblivion, leaving no room for a powerful semifinalist to compromise purposeful movement or the single stream of consciousness. The unity of consciousness, and the unity of action, is the result of a scrupulous elimination tournament.

Notice that this construal of competing cell-assemblies flips the arrow of causation in our thinking about agency from top-down to bottom-up. It does away, in one stroke, with the lethal infinite regress, a homunculus watching the happenings in the brain, because consciousness becomes, to use Abraham Lincoln's words, "government of the people, by the people, for the people."

Another usefully simple and vivid analogy, even if a bit of a stretcher, is fame (Dennett, 1995). As with many things in life, what most people want, few achieve. There are, of course, any number of ways to reach celebrity status – including the most arresting variety: being famous for being famous – but, for the most part, the bottleneck to the glitzy top of stardom must be negotiated by way of competition. The main feature of being famous is, needless to say, that others know about you. This, in turn, means access. Provided you have a broadcasting platform of some kind – television, for instance – your message can reach many people in an instant, without going door-to-door. We can think of consciousness as having the same property, or, more to the point, the same purpose. Information in the brain that is conscious is famous in the sense that it is widely known among other demons. By virtue of being famous, conscious demons can assert greater influence over how the system, as a whole, functions.

You may think that fame in the brain is taking it too far. That it may be. But it would be a mistake to snub the central ideas of access and power, because they lie at the heart of perhaps the most widely accepted model of consciousness, the grandly named global workspace theory, or GWT for short. If a hypothetical poll were to ask neuroscientists and philosophers what theory of mind they are prepared to defend, GWT would be voted among the front-runners, probably even into pole position. First pitched by the psychologist Bernard Baars in the late 1980s, it's a connectionist model that provides an infrastructure for conscious thought. The core concept, according to Baars (1988, p. 42), is that consciousness is seen as a "distributed society of specialists that is equipped with a working memory, called a global workspace, whose content can be broadcast to the system as a whole." GWT is designed, in short, for the fast and efficient exchange and dissemination of information. By postulating the existence of a virtual space in the brain, demons can post their messages that are then temporarily available to the rest of the system. It works like a blackboard to quickly tell everyone what the overall plan is. Going global this way is simply the best way to spread information fast through a very large number of autonomous, individual processors. It's this global availability, Baars says, that renders information conscious.

GWT has two very attractive features. One is that the global neuronal workspace has no single, central location. It is a moving target comprised of a continually changing set of large, interconnected networks. The other is no less appealing. It is the plain fact that evidence from neuroscience bears out exactly this notion (Dehaene & Naccache, 2001). Conscious thoughts in the brain indeed know no sharp anatomical boundaries. This neither-here-nor-there property of consciousness alone should bring to a grinding halt the quest to locate creative ideas someplace specific in the brain. A new ideational combination of information, a flash of insight, posted on the global blackboard by a strongly interacting super-coalition of demons is a distributed entity.

Now it is time to add to this developing view of the mind one key feature I have kept on the sidelines so far. Since Selfridge's pandemonium model, theories based on a connectionist architecture of flexible networks have always assumed that interactions between different representations are governed by bottom-up competition. But top-down processing comes into it, too. In the brain, the competition in the knowledge structure below is strongly biased by upper brain structures, a fact that is appreciated by nearly all recent theorizing on the subject.

This is easily confirmed by experience. Suppose you turn your attention from reading this book to answering your phone, this would also change the thoughts you hold in consciousness, wouldn't it? Attention, in other words, affects how the competition in the knowledge structure plays out. In the most general terms, cognition in the brain is organized in a functional hierarchy, with, roughly, inflexible brainstem circuits at the bottom, basic learning and memory processes in mid-level regions and higher mental faculties in the cerebral cortex at the top. The most highly priced piece of real estate in the cerebral cortex is the prefrontal cortex which carries out very advanced cognitive functions, such as working memory and directed attention. From their position at the top, these computations feed back to lower layers of the hierarchy, providing integrative input in the process. Another way of putting this is that the bottom-up competition is strongly influenced by attentional processes via top-down projections from the prefrontal cortex, which selectively enhance some representations over others (Dehaene & Changeux, 2011).

But, I must quickly interject, attention here is not meant to substitute for some kind of Cartesian King or cranial Supervisor who appoints the next government. This false friend itself dissolves into functions that themselves need no supervision. Remember the two-step exercise in your defense against the clutches of the Cartesian theater. A sound mechanism of creativity demands from us that we dethrone the Designer in us. Fitting top-down control into our toy version of the connectionist brain might provide some propulsive help. For in a parliamentary democracy, this nudging from higher levels happens all the time, yet no one would argue that a supernatural force is at work. It may be a sizable cash donation to a political campaign or the backing of the president by a celebrity, but such top-down influences are generated from within the system, and their intent is to rig the competition going on below. To convert this back into brain talk, these top-down projections shift the frequency-of-occurrence weights in the knowledge structure, lowering the values of some nodes while increasing those of others.

This might be a good place to take stock of the concepts we have encountered so far. Insights from connectionist modeling and cognitive neuroscience have converged on the view that the brain is a network of individually operating units and that consciousness is the outcome of large-scale competition among them. The competition is strongly biased by attentional processes via top-down projections from the prefrontal cortex, which selectively enhances some network activity over others. Seen from this corrected perspective, the stream of consciousness is nothing but a cute cover story that filters the underlying mentalese into a narrative stream that acts as a decent indicator of what the organism, as a whole, is doing. Or if you like it in more mechanical language, our phenomenology, the content in consciousness, is not the continuous, integrated flow we experience but the outcome of a series of discrete representations, sequenced together on the fly from different, endlessly competing, parallel streams of computation, each consisting of continuously shifting coalitions of neurons. From this emerges, at the phenomenal level of conscious experience, the story we tell ourselves, though this is not what's really going on underneath. In other words, the conscious mind is a sort of user-friendly interface of the vastly more complex brain in the same way Windows is a user-friendly interface of the vastly more complex computer. It linearizes the myriads of parallel neural processes into an interface that makes the brain seems to work as if it were a serial processor. The upshot is that we can tell others a coherent story, a quick summary of what is going on, at the level of the whole organism.

Like so much of modern neuroscience, the account I have sketched out till now doesn't map easily onto experience. And things will get less intuitive still as we build the bigger boat we need to capture the mechanisms of creativity.

The brain's multiple system levels

The study of memory has always taken center stage in psychology and neuroscience, which makes it all the remarkable that it wasn't until the early 1990s that the notion of multiple memory systems became fully part and parcel of neuroscience's conceptual toolbox. Fueled by patients suffering from strikingly selective amnesia and a better grasp of mental processes in general, theorists realized that the brain has two distinct systems for knowledge representation, one implicit and one explicit. This fact casts a long shadow on the study of creativity, and in this section we will develop some of the conceptual foundation that we need later on to understand the different types of creative behaviors that exist.

The explicit and implicit systems are both part of the brain's overall connectionist architecture but they operate independently of each other. Each system, for instance, handles its own acquisition, storage, transformation, and usage of knowledge. The key differences are often summarized as follows. The explicit system is rule-based, its content can be expressed by verbal communication, and it is tied to consciousness. The implicit system is skill or experience based, its content is not verbalizable and it can only be conveyed through task performance, and it is inaccessible to consciousness (Haider & French, 2005; Reber, 1993; Schacter & Buckner, 1998). All this needs further unpacking.

The existence of two distinct systems that acquire and represent information indicates that each must be specialized in some way. This is indeed so. The explicit system has evolved for flexibility while the purpose of the implicit system is efficiency (Dienes & Perner, 2002). Both systems also differ in terms of anatomy, and a mountain of research has been done to map them onto their respective brain regions. The brain circuits underlying the explicit system are critically dependent on, as might be expected, the prefrontal cortex, but abundant evidence also shows that regions of the so-called medial temporal lobe, such as the hippocampus or parts of the parietal cortex, play a role. The neural substrates of the implicit system are somewhat less clear, but structures that are closely linked to the brain's motor system have been implicated most often. They include the basal ganglia, the cerebellum, and a part of the cortex called the supplementary motor area.

The dual architecture of the mind is a book in itself. Psychologists have been working intensively on our two modes of thinking and decision-making, and several excellent books have appeared in recent years that should be read by anyone interested in the topic. Perhaps the best known is by the psychologist Daniel Kahneman (2011), who adopted the labels System 1 and System 2 for this division. While System 1 is automatic, quick and works with no perceived mental effort, System 2 is associated with attention, deliberate effort, subjective experience as well as a sense of self and agency. Although the meaning of System 1 and System 2 overlaps with, respectively, implicit and explicit, they are not the same. As a quick example to illustrate this, many operations of System 1 are not implicit in the same sense the term is used in cognitive neuroscience; the rule-of-thumb judgments System 1 makes are neither inaccessible to consciousness nor can they only be conveyed through motor execution. For our purposes, these differences in meaning can be largely ignored, however. What matters is the fact that the mind has two levels that differ radically in the way they engage the world. In this book, I will use the implicit–explicit taxonomy. The reason is simple. Since cognitive psychologists and neuroscientists describe their findings using this implicit–explicit division, and since we are looking for brain mechanisms, it is easier to connect to this terminology.

Before we plunge into a few demonstrations that will help us think more clearly about these matters, I will introduce one more level of complexity in the explicit information-processing system. This system is further subdivided into two main components, long-term memory and working memory. While long-term memory refers to all information we hold in the knowledge structure, those representations temporarily active in working memory are the phenomenal content of consciousness, the here and now of our immediate experience if you like. A useful, if distorted, oversimplification is that they correspond to, respectively, a computer's hard drive and RAM memory. Working memory, then,

54

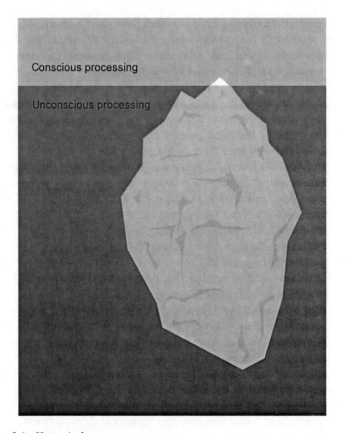

Figure 3.1 Heavy iceberg

The brain has evolved two anatomically and functionally separate cognitive systems that have evolved for fundamentally different purposes. The explicit system is a sophisticated system that represents knowledge in a higher-order format and can, thanks mostly to the computational infrastructure in the prefrontal cortex, use it in a conscious and flexible manner. That is not to say that explicit knowledge is conscious. Only the tiny amount temporarily active in working memory is. The implicit system is a more primitive and evolutionarily ancient system that does not form these fancy higher-order representations. Implicit knowledge is embedded into the procedure which renders it always unavailable for conscious processing. Recall Freud's famous iceberg metaphor of the mind that compares consciousness to the one-tenth of the iceberg floating above water and the unconscious to the much larger, nine-tenth submerged portion. Freud gets some points for the right direction but the iceberg image is still off by a wide margin. It is surely closer to the truth to say that 99 percent plus of all the brain's computations occur in the ill-lit basement of the unconscious.

describes the ability to process information online. It is a monitoring system of on-going events that momentarily keeps in mind knowledge that is relevant to the situation, so that we can work with it. It is in working memory that you are holding the information you read at the beginning of this sentence so that the end still makes sense to you. This used to be called short-term memory, a phrase that has fallen out of favor because this kind of memory buffer is not really limited by duration. Although we think of active representations in working memory as those that are conscious, it would be a mistake to conclude that working memory is the seat of consciousness. You will remember global workspace theory and the idea of victorious coalitions. Active representations, to be fully conscious and globally accessible, must be in working memory, but these representations emanate from nodes and networks that are distributed all over the brain (see Figure 3.1).

With this minimal bit of theoretical bedrock established, we can now shed some light on a few quirks of everyday behavior. By drawing these out in the open, we put ourselves in a position later on to make sense of the experience of flow, a distinct state of mind that many creative people seek out in order to enhance creative expression.

Unlike the explicit system, the implicit system is a simple all-in-one system. It isn't further divided into subcomponents and a single brain structure can handle all information-processing stages. As said, implicit knowledge is not verbalizable and remains inaccessible to consciousness. The working memory buffer in the explicit system – holding currently conscious content – can only know of the existence of knowledge imprinted in the implicit system when we express it through movement. This leads to the curious but rather common situation that we often cannot explain why we do what we do or how we know what we know. I often ask my students to imagine a standard keyboard and tell me the letters, from right to left, that make up the middle row. The task's only other instruction is that all finger movements are disallowed, even twitching. Try it. You will see right away what a surprisingly tricky task this is, even if you are a good typist. What's more, you probably cheated and solved the task by imagining how your fingers would move across the keyboard. Or suppose I ask you to explain, again without the use of your hands, how to tie shoelaces? These are examples of bits of implicit knowledge that you can perform but cannot put in words.

Although probably an uncommon situation in the real world, information can be acquired exclusively by either the explicit or implicit system. The standard example of pure implicit learning is language acquisition in children. It takes place largely independently of conscious attempts to learn and largely in the absence of explicit knowledge about what was acquired. Implicit learning can also be demonstrated in adults, however. Take, for instance, the Tower of Hanoi, a game in which three rings that are stacked according to size on a pole have to be moved, one by one, over an intermediate pole to a third pole without ever putting a larger ring on top of a smaller one. The optimal solution involves seven steps and students learn this task in short order. Yet, it is virtually impossible for them to give an accurate explanation of the rules they followed. If the verbal account of how they did it is translated into a computer program, the machine is unable to repeat it. In contrast, explicit knowledge isn't learning-by-doing, but occurs through the conscious application of a set of rules. In the process, the explicit system forms a mental representation that includes not only what to do with the information but also knowledge about what, and the fact that, it was acquired. The standard example here is the acquisition of a second language in adulthood.

A more common scenario is that learning engages both systems simultaneously, which means that the brain forms two distinct mental representations, one explicit and one implicit. Because each system subserves different functions, it is unlikely that either representation alone is a complete characterization of the learned task. While some information may be represented in both systems, other information may reside in one system but not the other. For instance, cooking a multi-course dinner requires tasks that are exclusively explicit, such as mixing ingredients according to instruction, while other tasks, such as deciding when the vegetables are done, are largely implicit.

The degree to which either system has a complete mental image of what's going on depends largely on the amount of practice. A native language acquired at infancy is, as said, entirely learned and largely represented in the implicit system. But with considerable study the explicit system can develop its own (explicit) representation of the phonology, semantics, and grammar. This isn't easy, as any English major will tell you, and an essential requirement to be able teach a native language to others. Learning a second language in adulthood is a decidedly different affair. This is because it engages the explicit system which, by way of formal rules, builds a mental representation of the language with no intuitive feel for it. But with extensive practice, often nothing short of total immersion into the linguistic environment, the knowledge can also become represented in the implicit system. We commonly speak of *internalizing* or becoming *second nature* when we build an implicit representation of a task though practice. We are right to expect true experts to have both kinds of knowledge, for which they would need two fairly detailed but different representations of the same task. In general, knowledge of a task can be explicit and/or implicit, but neither is likely to be a complete representation of the task.

Mindsets and their aftershocks

In planking our bigger boat, we will acquaint ourselves next with a couple of concepts that are standard thinking tools in cognitive psychology: task sets and the related idea of task-set inertia. Scientists use them to explain all sorts of fascinating effects that pop up when people in a psychology lab switch from one mental task to another. We will also use them to great advantage in our quest, because they can tell us how we initially perceive a creative task and how we configure possible solution spaces.

In everyday life, we perform countless tasks and must constantly switch from one to the next. Take cooking pasta, presumably a straightforward task that most people handle in cruise control. You probably think there's not much to it, but the complexity of pasta cooking would quickly dawn on you if you had to explain it to someone who has never done it. More striking still, suppose you are being asked to program a robot to do it. Since robots lack any kind of common sense about the world, you would even have to specify minuscule details, such as the force vector of a single digit in one finger of the hand that would grip the salt shaker, let alone lifting it, positioning it over the water, turning it over, or a million other tidbits of implicit knowledge. The point here is that even the smallest task consists of a complex array of sub-components and demands that we execute numerous, mostly implicit sub-routines, only to change everything when we go on to one of life's next little challenges. In response to these demands, brains don't simply make mental resources available in a generic sort of way but configure them to suit a task's unique set of requirements. That means that the brain must also reconfigure these resources when switching from one task to another.

A task set denotes the configuration of mental resources that goes with a task (Allport et al., 1994; Monsell, 2003). For our intents and purposes, we can also use the word mindset to mean the same thing. This move would probably be considered a sin in the professional circles in which I travel because mindset is a broader term that isn't bound to a specific task. I am conservative and vote Republican is a mindset but not a task set, for instance. But we can ride roughshod over these differences, because they don't come into play in our context.

A task set has two key elements. First, it defines those aspects of a task to which we selectively attend. When we try to solve a problem, we cannot turn all the possible knobs of the problem at once. We start by turning some knobs and when they fail to yield a solution, we shift our focus to others. Someone with a different mindset might hit upon the solution faster, or slower, simply by focusing on different features of the task. A task set also defines the dimensions of the response that are bound to specific aspects of the task (Hommel, 2004). For instance, playing a video game on a touch screen requires exact finger-pointing movements. Playing the same game with a console, the player must perform side-to-side hand movements. The term in the field for this binding is stimulus-response mapping, and it plays an important role in the smooth perception-action sequences of flow experiences we will take up in Chapter 8. Framed in connectionist language, a task set details all the operational parameters a neural network is set to – initial default settings of the nodes, the influence a node asserts on the knowledge structure, control processes, permissible transformations, category boundaries, expectations, and troubleshooting instructions among rather many others. The construct was first formulated in the early 1990s in response to experiments requiring subjects to shift frequently between different tasks. The central finding is that task-switching produces substantial performance costs. Subjects respond substantially slower and make more errors.

A task set is specified to astonishing detail. It may stipulate, for instance, how long it should take for an elevator to move after we press the call button, or it tells you what shape a cake would have after you bite off a piece, a matter of some social importance if you balance it in your hand. We can think of it as a kind of preparedness plan that contains the elements and their values that are tagged as temporarily belonging together in the network because they played a role in completing the task in the past. By facilitating certain task-relevant cognitive operations and inhibiting others, the implementation of a task set in the brain affects the processing of all stimuli associated with that task. Another way of saying this is that task sets fix the angle from which we see, approach, and respond to a creative problem. The general point of a task set is, of course, efficiency. Since the network is also tuned to perform the right input–output mapping, a task set, when in force, prepares us to perform a task in a particular, and more effective, way. Note that all these configuration settings and operating directives are essentially predictions that are contained in the processing pathways. Violating them would surprise us and trigger us to search for the cause (Haider & Rose, 2007).

We cannot perform a task until the cognitive system is properly attuned and organized. Like a tabula-rasa robot, we would not even know how to approach it. Should the task change, the task set that goes with it must first be uploaded, so to speak (Mayr & Kliegl, 2000). Task-set reconfiguration, or TSR for short, costs time and mental resources because a new task brings about the activation of the entire task set associated it. All nodes in the knowledge structure that are part of the new coalition must shift their weights and the strength of their connections must be recalibrated. The upshot is of course that, so-primed, the spreading activation in the network is biased in such a way that we can respond faster and more accurately to the task at hand. These distributed activity patterns are then stored as whole entities in memory. When you prepare to drive your car, the network is specifically enabled for that very task, as opposed to, say, playing tennis or ironing a shirt.

Task-set switching occurs voluntarily and involuntarily. It can be triggered by an event demanding our attention – the smell of coffee or a red traffic light. In fact, some stimuli so strongly activate a task set that the tendency to perform the task is irresistible and unintentional. Reading road signs or cereal boxes during breakfast are good examples. A task set turnover can also occur because we decide to shift our focus to something else. As a friendly reminder, beware of the siren songs of dualism here. This "we decide" does not ride above the fray. It is also a broad coalition of neurons that simply helps nudge the current government from power. In either case, the change ripples through the network, altering coalition membership and weight configurations, which results in the re-setting of the cognitive system.

A mindset can be activated more or less strongly. In fact, the brain must constantly perform a balancing act to guarantee effective cognition. To maintain our attentional focus, a task set must have some internal strength and stability to keep the ongoing task free from interference and disruption by other task sets. Without this shielding of the cognitive system against irrelevant and intruding information, we wouldn't be able to focus on one task for long. Many brain scientists think that the main effort of a reigning task set, apart from grappling with the actual task, might well go into strongly inhibiting other, competing task sets (Dreisbach & Haider, 2009). For a parallel, we turn again to our toy version of democracy. A president or prime minister also devotes seemingly endless amounts of time to dealing with the opposition or campaigning for re-election. Failing to suppress hopeful contenders would lead to swift loss in power. One reason for the high cost of inhibition stems from the fact that networks are not discrete entities. Since any given knowledge node can belong to any number of task sets, it can simply shift allegiance and send ongoing spreading activation down a different path. At the same time, task-set activation must also allow enough flexibility for mental gear changing so that we can adjust should the context necessitate it. This delicate stability-flexibility trade-off requires a great deal of endogenous control; weak task sets fall easily from the stream of consciousness, strong ones lead to perseverance and mental rigidity.

The concepts of task sets put us into a better position later on to shed light on the brain mechanism of creative thinking. For reasons that are not entirely clear, the notion of task sets, although commonplace in cognitive psychology, is not yet the good idea mill it must become in the neuroscience of creativity. This is somewhat odd. One would think that the relevance of mindsets to creativity is immediately self-evident. The brain's task representation governs a whole stack of mental operations. It determines how we initially approach a problem-solving task and specifies those aspects of the problem that we think are most likely to hold the key to a solution (Öllinger et al., 2013). It also maps the shape of the solution space and establishes search parameters that are, in effect, predictions about the kinds of solutions that are likely and the form they might take. The strength of the task set also determines the degree of functional fixedness, the extent to which we are stuck on a certain, and often false, solution path. Finally, all these network factors that are likely mediated by age, mental state, level of expertise, and a whole host of personality traits. We will do justice to some of them in later chapters.

One prominent feature of creative ideas that cannot be explained by task sets is the experience of being hit by a sudden flash of insight while the mind is miles away on some beach. After all, we no longer work on the task. To appreciate how such Eureka moments occur, we need to turn our attention to one final tool cognitive psychologists use to think about the mind. Suppose you are stuck on a problem and decide to take a break. The task you will take on next – whatever it is – sets off a task-set reconfiguration that re-calibrates all the network's nodes to suit the new assignment. But this is not to say that the problem disappears from the network's activity. What happens to it during the incubation period?

To find some preliminary answers, we return to our toy world of electoral politics to illustrate what we know about the toppling of a ruling task-set coalition in the brain. If you can bear the unavoidable simpli-fications for a moment, there seem to be three possibilities. The first is a coup d'état, in which a new and powerful federation of brain cells overthrows the old mindset. The most obvious cause for a coup d'état is a sudden change in the environment that requires our immediate attention. Take reading, the task set that is presumably holding sway in your mind right now. It stands little chance to stay in power when, say, the fire alarm goes off. The second is dictatorship, in which we uphold the current task set by the sheer force of concentration. Recall that such top-down amplifications rig the competition among neurons at the base, in this case in favor of the incumbent task set. It's not unlike bailing out the teetering government by throwing resources at it. Matters take a different – and highly fascinating – turn with possi-bility three. As every schoolchild knows, paying attention has limits. Even the strongest task set cannot be propped up indefinitely. Suppose then a reigning mindset disintegrates all on its own. Perhaps it can-not maintain the internal strength among its loosely assembled motley crew of neurons and simply self-destructs. Or the costs of running the inhibitory control processes become prohibitive. Suppose further there isn't a willing, or able, replacement standing by to fill the impending power vacuum – think Fall of Rome, not Russian Revolution. In such a state of daydreaming, no task predominates in the mind and conscious thinking careens pinball-style from one imaginary scenario to another.

We got into the finer points of power politics in the first place, you will remember, to shed light on the role of incubation in the forma-tion of creative insights. So, irrespective of which of the three options transpires – coup d'état, dictatorship, or daydreaming – the burning question as to how, exactly, incubation facilitates creativity, is this. What happens to the old task set?

Once we put the question like this, we are on our way to a sci-entifically sound explanation. The proposal that has received the most experimental support to date is the aptly-named task-set inertia (Allport et al., 1994). It was introduced to explain an unexpected asym-metry in task-switching studies that could not be accounted for with task-set reconfiguration alone. When subjects were asked to switch from a less familiar task, which naturally evokes a weaker task set, to a more familiar one, which evokes a stronger task set, the switch costs were larger. Why would it take more time to recalibrate the cognitive system for a task that is more familiar?

Bits of the task-set inertia story are known, many details are not, mak-ing a few generalizations of what we can say about it unavoidable.

Neural networks, so much is clear, are not binary on/off switches. So there is no principled reason to assume that expulsion from working memory spells instant death for a neuronal assembly. Like everything else going at full tilt, a strongly interacting coalition of neurons would need time to decay back to baseline condition. The task-switching costs psychologists observed in their studies could only emanate from such network aftershocks. The critical difference would be that this residual activation hovers at intensity levels below the threshold of consciousness. The case for such aftershocks in the knowledge structure isn't exactly ironclad but there are enough indications that we can assume that it is happening. Incidentally, the transient persistence of an old task set is also the answer to the curious asymmetry in switching experiments. A new task set would be subjected to some interference from the old one.

Discussion in the scientific literature on how strong this inertia might be or how long it could last is curiously absent. So we must exercise interpretive caution when we want to extend the aftershock theory, as we might call it, to creative thinking. But this is a matter of obvious relevance, one would think, for coming to terms with the emergence of flashes of insights while the conscious mind is otherwise applied. Clearly, the fact that the removal of a problem from the limelight of conscious awareness can break the impasse that often frustrates the conscious search process shows that the task-set coalition associated with the problem continues to reverberate with purpose.

But of course it is never going to be as simple as that. The aftershock theory relies solely on residual activity in the knowledge network, and it is unlikely that a single mechanism is at play here. There are at least two considerations that suggest that a comprehensive explanation needs more work. For starters, there is the obvious snag that creative insights have a way of popping up long after we last worked on a problem. It is hard to see how transient task-set inertia could linger for days or weeks. Trickier still is the issue of a goal state. The fact that there's still a problem in need of a solution cannot be embedded at the level of the knowledge structure itself. Goal representation in the brain is the business of higher-order brain structures like the prefrontal cortex.

One way to address these complications, and put together a more inclusive explanation of the incubation effect, involves the idea of fringe working memory (Cowan, 2005). Working memory is thought to have both, a focal center and a fringe, with the fringe containing information that still has some conscious properties or is relegated to a lower priority. Nothing illustrates fringe working memory more vividly than the annoying tip-of-tongue feeling. We know that we know but this metacognitive clue alone cannot ignite the associated knowledge network. This is because fringe working memory lacks qualitative content; it is a sort of index that only represents *that* something is represented, but not what that something is. This indexing function of fringe working memory provides a coherent account for the persistence of the intention to find a solution, although we no longer consciously pursue the problem.

If we are right about task-set inertia and fringe working memory, the reshuffling of bits of information into ideational combinations during incubation might work like this. Recall that conscious thinking also takes place on several system levels. Working memory, operating at the higher organizational level, maintains the motivational focus to find a solution, and organizes, at the lower level of the knowledge structure, the rearrangement of information in long-term memory to do so. Suppose now we switch tasks from, say, creative writing to cooking pasta. This decision moves the active goal state representation from the focal center of attention to the fringe of working memory and thus dethrones the task set from prime time to a lingering afterthought. Naturally, neither would have much oomph once exiled to the mind's hinterland. Still, a fringe goal representation of unfinished business somewhere out there would continue to provide some organizational control and might steer the spreading activation of the fading mindset toward a resolution.

You may have noticed that this account only gets us half way. It doesn't yet answer the core question we set out to answer. How do insights occur during incubation? What seems to be missing is an appraisal of some kind. Residual rumbling in the brain's networks sounds all very well but how does the mind recognize the right solution from among all the combinatorial activity occurring in its knowledge base? There must be someone who assigns meaning, someone who watches the trial-and-error process, picks the correct solution and decides to catapult it into the brightly lit working memory buffer. Who thinks all this through? This line of questioning, doggedly returned, is a tactical error because one gets hold of the problem from the wrong end and embarks on a direction that leads straight into the dead end of the Cartesian theater. To stop the infinite regress before it starts, and prevent our boat from shipwrecking on the shores of dualism, we must flip our thinking and look for an explanation in deeper and lower levels of the brain's engine room.

One strong candidate is the speed of processing (Whittlesea, 2004). Let me explain. A pre-calibrated and weighted network creates processing speed differentials for different kinds of information that is run on it. Depending on the specific configuration of the nodes, some information is processed more expediently than others. That information is simply a better fit for the preset processing pathways of the task set. The speed-of-processing parameter can serve as a strengthening mechanism in the following way. Recall that the brain settles all its business by way of competition. Suppose that the shuffling of informational units in the knowledge structure yields a particular ideational combination that ripples through it with great ease. The neuronal coalition computing this representation would gather internal strength as a result. Whether this momentum suffices for ascendency to consciousness depends largely on the other neuronal coalitions it must compete against. Individual differences enter the picture here, too. A person with different network settings – for whatever reason: upbringing, genes, expertise, or past experience – may process the same potential solution at a lower speed and not get a creative insight.

The Cartesian ghost is so persuasive and the opportunities for surrendering to it so abundant that you may feel yet again the instinctive tug to ask just how the speed of processing increases for the right solution. Who determines that? Don't do this to yourself. Once you succumb to this powerful seduction and let the Designer back into the design process, you might as well stop reading the book right here.

Recommended readings

Allport, A., Styles, E. A., & Hsieh, S. (1994). Shifting intentional set: Exploring the dynamic control of tasks. In C. Umiltà & M. Moscovitch (Eds.), *Attention and performance 15: Conscious and nonconscious information processing* (pp. 421–452). Cambridge, MA: MIT Press.

Baars, B. J. (1988). *A cognitive theory of consciousness*. Cambridge: Cambridge University Press.

Cowan, N. (2005). *Working memory capacity*. Hove, East Sussex: Psychological Press.

Dehaene, S., & Naccache, L. (2001). Towards a cognitive science of consciousness: Basic evidence and a workspace framework. *Cognition, 79*, 1–37.

Dennett, D. C. (1991). *Consciousness explained*. Boston: Little, Brown & Co.

Dietrich, A. (2007a). *Introduction to consciousness*. London: Palgrave Macmillan.

Dienes, Z., & Perner, J. (1999). A theory of implicit and explicit knowledge. *Behavioral and Brain Sciences, 5*, 735–808.

Helie, S., & Sun, R. (2010). Incubation, insight, and creative problem solving: A unified theory and a connectionist model. *Psychological Review, 117*, 994–1024.

Kahneman, D. (2011). *Thinking fast and slow*. London: Penguin Books.
Monsell, S. (2003). Task switching. *Trends on Cognitive Science, 7*, 134–140.
Selfridge, O. (1959). Pandemonium: A paradigm for learning. In *Proceedings of the Symposium on the mechanization of thought processes held at the National Physics Laboratory, November 1958*. London: HM Stationary Office.

4
The Cogwheels of Culture

Culture evolves; in at least this much, there is agreement. The vexed question is how. We pass on cultural units – things, skills, beliefs, and so on – which leave behind a trail of gradual and cumulative changes. The sticking point is this: Is cultural evolution Darwinian? This hot-button topic is long on sneering and short on substance with people digging in for the long haul. Champions of Darwinism in culture like to describe their opponents as mushy humanists and soft-headed poets who, having overdosed on postmodernism, are prone to panic attacks whenever they hear the rattling of the saber of science. Not to be outdone, the opponents heap scorn on the entire enterprise of Darwinizing the social sciences and humanities and like to depict their rivals as overzealous scientists and pigheaded technophiles who, having overdosed on positivism, erratically swing the club of Darwinism at everything in sight. Amidst all the pugnacious hyperbole, writing about it makes you want to wear a safety helmet.

For the first few billion years, organic evolution has been the primary mechanism of change on our planet. By around 50,000 years ago, it had even created culture. An explosion of new ideas and technologies followed that would radically transform our lifestyle. In just a few thousand years, an evolutionary eye blink by all measures, we catapulted ourselves from cave-dwelling hunter-gatherers to our high-tech world of skyscrapers, cybernetics, telecommunications, nanotechnology, and genetic engineering. Biological evolution, operating at a glacial pace orders of magnitude slower than this, had little, if anything, to do with it. Cultural evolution has turned the tables on biological evolution and has taken over as the primary agent of change on Earth. By way of books, songs, or movies, humans can transmit and accumulate information non-genetically. This chapter takes a look at how the cogwheels of culture turn over.

The Cogwheels of Culture 67

The origins of our creative ideas, and how they arise, have been a prominent and long-standing showcase in this debate on cultural evolution. More than half a century ago, Donald Campbell (1960) proposed that creative thoughts result from the twofold process of blind variation (BV) followed by selective retention (SR), or BVSR. The idea that human creativity is based, in part or whole, on blind generation has been stated, with further embellishments, by a number of authors since, most notably Karl Popper (1974), Donald Campbell (1974) and, more recently, Colin Martindale (1990), Dean Simonton (1999, 2011), and Daniel Dennett (1995, 2004). Most of the work fleshing out the details has been done by Dean Simonton who has insisted until recently, as did Campbell and Popper, that the variation processes is fundamentally blind. As might be expected, these proposals have provoked a blast wave of criticism. The attack has been aimed at two levels. One has been directed against the idea of any type of Darwinian analysis of human creativity (Dasgupta, 2004; Russ, 1999; Sternberg, 1998, 1999), a move that has been flanked by a more targeted critique aimed specifically at the issue of blindness (Kronfeldner, 2010; Martindale, 1999; Richerson & Boyd, 2005; Schooler & Dougal, 1999).

When handling difficult or counterintuitive ideas, keeping things lined up properly is good policy. For just this reason, let me take stock of where we stand. We saw in Chapter 2 that for all its prominence at the apex of human mental faculties, we know next to nothing about how brains generate creative ideas. With all previous attempts to tighten the screws on this matter aborted, the neuroscientific study of creativity finds itself in a theoretical void that is unique in the brain sciences. Although there are undoubtedly several reasons for this malaise, two stand out. One is the profoundly mistaken way of thinking most of us have, neuroscientists included, about how brains work. So, in Chapter 3, we first had to upend the Cartesian theater and replace it with ideas that can bear the load we need to find some real answers.

With the ground cleared, and a few corrective thinking devices in hand, we are now in a better position to pursue the second reason for neuroscience's failure to make progress on creativity. The curious fact is that we already know of a sound mechanism for creativity, namely the variation-selection process that does all the creating and designing in the biosphere. Oddly, this point is underappreciated, so it is worth stressing. All sides in the debate concur that culture is an evolutionary system and that the copying and transmitting of cultural information happens in brains. Yet, almost no neuroscience study has used the rationale of the evolutionary two-step to set up empirical protocols. Apart from closet dualism, which we will continue to smoke out in this chapter, a contributing factor to this calamity is a largely irrelevant and obstructive debate over how far Darwinism extends upward into culture and, by extension, human creativity. This exchange neither bears on the essential Darwinian rationale necessary to apply a generate-and-test framework in neuroscientific studies of creativity nor do we need to foreclose this approach because differences exist to how exactly this mechanism operates in biological creativity.

This brings us to the main objective of the chapter: to x-ray the core issues of the cultural evolution debate for the purpose of distilling from it a single conclusion, a common denominator that, though universally accepted, still has not found its way to the neurocognition lab. There are three core issues making up this common denominator and each gets its own section here. In "Patterns of change", we highlight how change comes about in different evolutionary systems: variational for Darwin, transformational for Lamarck. We then dissect, in "The units of mentalese", how heredity occurs, either by particulating units of information – Darwin's case – or by blending them – Lamarck's case. The final section takes on the matter of blindness. This is the most barbed issue because it rolls a whole host of widespread confusions into one big conceptual muddle. But to anticipate the main point, the weight of the evidence in psychology and anthropology is that creative thinking appears to be partially directed and hence fits, strictly speaking, neither into the rigid category requirements of Neo-Darwinian (total) blindness nor Lamarckian (total) directedness. By showing how easy it is to interpret the facts to suit one's theoretical taste – inflating a category boundary here, redefining a term there – this acrimonious debate is exposed as a case of scientific grandstanding. Classifying culture as either definitely Darwinian or undoubtedly non-Darwinian, then, is either a case of much ado about nothing or a tectonic shift in thinking, depending on whether you are a lumper or a splitter.

History of a logjam

In the biosphere, all products – from mitochondria to the floor plan of the duck billed platypus – are created by the process of evolution by natural selection. Before Darwin, people could not imagine how complex design comes to be without a designer. Biologists, back then, needed a skyhook, a term Daniel Dennett (1995) uses to refer to a miracle, such as God or some other divine intervention. The underlying basic error in thinking here is that this presupposes that it takes a big fancy thing to make a less fancy thing. By this logic, we fall into the trap of explaining a puzzle by invoking a larger one, a move that forces us, sooner or later, to appeal to a skyhook that comes from on high. You may recognize this as the same kind of infinite regress we encountered with the Cartesian homunculus. The great inversion of reasoning Darwin made was that a big fancy thing like us can be made by a mindless, purposeless process that works itself up from below. Given sufficient time, cranes, Dennett's term for a bottom-up process like evolution, can do the designing work just fine.

In an often quoted letter to Charles Lyell, Darwin wrote: "If I were convinced that I required such additions to the theory of natural selection, I would reject it as rubbish ... I would give nothing for the theory of natural selection, if it requires a miraculous addition at any one stage of descent." Science, indeed, has never accomplished much of anything by resorting to miracles when things got tricky. But without an inversion of reasoning, from top-down to bottom-up, a theory, any theory, that attempts to explain complex design gets backed up into a corner where the only recourse left is a heavenly force of some kind. Following biology, neuroscience must also do an inversion of reasoning and – you will remember the mantra – take the Designer out of the design process, replacing it, through and through, with a mechanical process that looks at the artifacts of culture with no miraculous addition at any one stage. A Cartesian ghost cannot do the explanatory work we require.

Let us now take a closer look at evolutionary systems. Stripped to its essentials, evolution is a process that takes place whenever three conditions are met: (1) replication: there must exist some sort of unit capable of making copies of itself; (2) variation, which occurs when error creeps in the copying mechanism; and (3) selection, which determines the differential fitness of the variant copies (Dawkins, 1976). Darwin's theory of evolution by natural selection is a specific instantiation of this. But from a mathematical point of view, it is only one example of what is actually a whole class of evolutionary algorithms that ratchets on these three requirements.

We know evolution as a theory that explains life on Earth. But, in principle, evolution need not involve genes, life, or ecosystems. As long as something, anything, shows mutation, differential survival, and inheritance that something, mindless or not, evolves. Evolution, then, is a general method for change. It is this abstraction that allows Darwinism to diffuse out from its home base in biology and ignite the current debate in culture. Though still a radical shift in perspective for many, the underlying mathematical language of algorithms is key. Any system fulfilling the three requirements of replication, variation and selection, is considered a member of the class of Darwinian algorithms. Accordingly, Darwin's theory of evolution by natural selection is a specific instance of that larger class. Neo-Darwinism, or the modern synthesis, which incorporates additional parameters in its algorithmic function – Weismann barrier, digital inheritance, blindness, genetic drift, sexual selection, epigenetic inheritance, etc. – is another member of it. This algorithm also happens to be the best portrayal we currently have of the one moving organic evolution here on Earth. Of course, we can lift Lamarckian evolution from its biological roots just as easily. Lamarck's theory (Lamarck, 1809), however, belongs to an entirely different class of evolutionary algorithms, which, as we shall see shortly, is fixed to a different set of parameters (Lewontin, 1970). To paint with this broader brush of algorithms, we must disregard the historical fact that we happen first upon the concept of evolution in the realm of biology. By holding the specifics of how the process works in biology to be the gold standard, we miss the fact that it is but one example of how an evolutionary algorithm could work.

All this, and more, got started when Darwin (1859/1968) published the *Origin of Species* in 1859. Gallons of ink have been spilled over evolutionary issues since, filling shelves of books, articles, and TED programs. Darwinian thinking in culture has never been a topic that lends itself naturally to sober, scholarly discourse. But recently people have turned up the heat another notch still. To isolate the wedge issues, permit me first to present a mini sketch of the historical highlights in this transfixing saga. Of course, the reader should recognize that such a high-speed flight over vast expanses of intellectual history cannot but do violence to nuances.

Herbert Spencer was the most famous of the early promoters of Darwinism in culture. His brand of social Darwinism, however, is now the canonical example of how not to extend Darwin's theory to the social realm. It was a false start, the repercussions of which are still felt in the field today. For one thing, it wasn't, actually, Darwinian but a Lamarckian version of social change, a point not lost on his contemporaries. For reasons that will become apparent soon, it wasn't easy back then to tell Lamarck's from Darwin's theory. Evolutionary systems have many complications hidden in their cogwheels and most of them simply hadn't been worked out yet at the time. Perhaps nothing speaks more clearly to this than Darwin's support for the core idea of Lamarck's theory, the inheritance of acquired characteristics. Darwin, you could say, was not a particularly good Darwinist. How much more difficult then to lift evolutionary theories out of their home base in biology and make them do explanatory work elsewhere. A wide scope for confusion is as good as guaranteed.

Darwinism to most people is the Darwinism of Darwin. This sounds like an obscure statement of the obvious but, as it happens, it isn't. No sooner did Darwin hoist the flag of evolution, legions of biologists went to work on the nitty-gritty details of how this variation-selection drivetrain works. Darwinism as we know it now has become a much more restrictive and precise theory and is no longer the Darwinism of Darwin. This simple truth continues to be overlooked in even some of the most erudite and scrupulous writing on cultural evolution.

Darwin's theory was barely a few decades old when the first of the legions of biologists entered the picture and supplied the first major twist in this tale. In the late 1900s, August Weismann showed that only one cell type – the germ cells (egg and sperm) – carry hereditary information; all other cells of the body – somatic cells – are not agents of heredity. We know this as the genotype-phenotype distinction today, the difference between the inherited basis of a trait and its observable expression. The clincher was that the effect is strictly one-way. Since the germline holds the instructions to build somatic cells (and other germ cells), changes to them can ripple through to the next generation of somatic cells. Not so in reverse. Having no means of making copies of themselves, bodily cells, neurons included, take any modification acquired in life into their molecular grave. Culture, in short, is not heritable, at least not biologically. The route: phenotype to genotype, and on to the next generation, is impossible. The Weismann barrier, as this is known, had two immediate effects. One, it put an end to Lamarck in biology. Duly sharpened like this, the inheritance of acquired characteristics was consigned into the ever-fuller dustbin of biology's history. Two, it also put an end – wrongly, in this case – to Darwin in culture. Culture became seen *on top* of nature and any influence of biological processes on it – causal or otherwise – was flatly negated. This had consequences. For at this point, biologists and social scientists parted ways and stopped talking to one another, exceptions aside, for nearly 100 years.

If Weismann was pillar one, then Gregor Mendel was pillar two. Hereditary information can be passed on in one of two ways, either in entities that blend, like colored paint, or remain distinct, like tones in an accord. Blending inheritance was widely accepted in Darwin's time, even by Darwin. It was an inadequate model, however, and people knew it. It failed to explain, for instance, the simple matter of how some traits – blue eyes, say – can disappear for several generations only to re-emerge down the line unaltered. In addition, blending dilutes variation, eroding the differences for natural selection to work on. Only a discontinuous copy mechanism could account for these phenomena, which is where Mendel's laws of heredity, rediscovered around the turn of the century, come in. In particulate Mendelian inheritance, genes from the parents stay as they are in the offspring; they do not mix. This is also called hard inheritance and contrasted with Lamarckian-style blending or soft inheritance. Genetics is, in a word, digital. Famously, Darwin didn't know of Mendel's work.

These giant leaps, the genotype-phenotype distinction and the discrete mechanism of heredity, clarified two important components of the evolutionary system that propels the biosphere. In the 1930s, population genetics became the third major amendment to Darwin's original idea. The integration of all three improvements with Darwin's theory is known as the modern synthesis or, alternatively, Neo-Darwinism (Fisher, 1930; Huxley, 1942). The fact that Darwin's Darwinism is quite different from today's understanding of Neo-Darwinism, with all the added bells and whistles of the modern synthesis, is a major source of confusion that plagues the modern debate on how far Darwinism extends upward into culture. All too often both sides in this face-off feed one another arrant hyperbole because they have a different take on Darwinism.

All right, back to the story. The Weismann barrier was quickly pushed into service to mark the new fault line separating the biological and mental worlds. True to the long, Cartesian tradition of dualism so endemic in Western thinking, the individual was dismembered into two distinct, non-overlapping categories, nature and culture. Because, it was reasoned, there is no causal flow from phenotype to genotype, culture cannot become nature. Whatever we learn in life is not transmitted genetically and, it seemed to follow, cannot contribute to the survival of the lineage. This proved to be a first-rate airbag for the bad ideas popping up everywhere at the time – social determinism, racism, fascism, eugenics, and other dystopian fantasies. As it happens, Weismann himself made use of it – to knee-cap Spencer.

Meanwhile, in a case that turned out to be a case of greedy overextension, cultural separatists went to work to fix the one problem that still remained. To make culture fully sovereign of biology, an entity in its own right, the Weismann barrier had to be sealed shut also from the other side, for this prospect was not eliminated from the matrix of causation by the Weismann barrier. Nature could still become culture, that is to say, the specific architecture of the brain could still determine how the mind works. It may sound difficult to pull off a gambit like this but all it took was to revive an idea that had been collecting dust, update it a bit and Darwinism could be safely bottled up within biology. This idea was nothing other than John Locke's tabula rasa, the presumption that our minds were blank slates at birth on to which the rules of culture were written. If the brain is indeed a general-purpose device – to use the modern term – then cultural phenomena can obviously not come from biology. So, culture can only be explained by references to culture. No sooner was this proclaimed, the banner of independence was hoisted by a growing battalion of thinkers around the turn of the century. Emile Durkheim was a key spokesperson of this movement, along with Max Weber and Karl Marx. They hoped to remove from the concept of human nature all context in order to set up an indomitable *raison d'être* for the social sciences and humanities. In what Tooby and Cosmides (1992), two leaders of the opposing pack, dubbed the Standard Social Sciences Model, or SSSM, the division of labor was neat, clean, and convenient: a content-free biology is balanced out by the content-supplying disciplines of anthropology, sociology, and the humanities.

This take on culture grew large, and malignant, with postmodernism, a tradition that went whole hog and adopted the additional, and divisive, step to attribute the causes of culture, solely and exclusively, to social processes. The individual, in that view, ceased to exist. Holding the group, and not the individual, to be the maker of all things cultural forced the postmodernist to endorse the following, rather perplexing position. If content doesn't come from the individual, but emerges from interactions between them, the mind could not possibly be the wellspring of culture. Mind-creates-culture would be exactly backward to a postmodernist. Instead, it is culture that creates the mind. This judo-like move converted the mind into an empty bucket, waiting to be filled by social constructions that materialize out of the thin air of social exchanges. The postmodernism program had the net effect of setting the social sciences adrift, away from the scientifically analyzable landscape of causation that is home to the natural sciences.

Efforts to protect the mind from being a full member of the canon of science are nothing new. But hopes of halting the perpetual advance of science by erecting an unbreachable barrier – even if sensible at the time – have a sorry history. Such attempts have backfired with such predictable regularity, forcing retreat after retreat, that anyone must feel deeply uneasy about adopting such a tactic. Given this, it shouldn't come as a surprise that the next twist in the story is the inevitable push back. Rebellious undercurrents to SSSM orthodoxies existed already during its heyday but a counterculture – if that's the right phrase to use – didn't reach escape velocity from its gravity well in cognitive science until the final decades of the twentieth century. Richard Dawkins famous book *The Selfish Gene*, published in 1976, was a key turning point that swung the pendulum back toward integration between the biological and social sciences. In it, Dawkins proposed a cultural replicator unit, the meme, which functions like the replicating unit in the biosphere, DNA, did more than just make Darwinian overtones. Dawkins suggested that culture *is* a Darwinian evolutionary system.

This prompted a panicked hustle back to the line of scrimmage, with rumors about a hostile takeover abundant. Having appropriated content to their own disciplines, Darwinian thinking has been stubbornly resisted with the charge of territorial imperialism by those in the social sciences and humanities whose territory is being invaded. To admit that Darwinism, a foreign theory, could better explain the facts and observation than home-grown theories was paramount to filing for disciplinary insolvency. But something was afoot and the weight-bearing pillars holding up the roof of the SSSM have long collapsed. A gigantic pile of evidence from psychology and neuroscience had already tumbled down on it showing that brains are not some amorphous flubber at birth but instead come with a host of highly evolved capacities that shape our daily thoughts and behaviors. In retrospect, the idea that it is all nurture seems bizarre.

Despite this, there is little sign that this kettle is going off the boil. It's not uncommon, even today, to see otherwise calm folk – the sort of Type-B personality you wouldn't want ahead of you in traffic – grow incandescent with rage defending a version of the SSSM. One would be mistaken to brand all of it confused science bashing, a sort of knee-jerk biophobia unencumbered by the thought process. Of course there are those who regularly go into orbit denouncing Darwin outright – creationists, believers in intelligent design, etc. – but people who have gone off the reservation and away with the pixies must be taken up elsewhere. We shall focus on two other groups here.

The first are best dubbed closet dualists, and they constitute the overwhelming bulk of the antagonism against the upward spread of Darwinism into culture and, by extension, a fully scientific approach to creative thinking. Closet dualists waste no time telling you that they have no qualms with Darwinism in biology. But after they cede the brain to be the product of a bottom-up, evolutionary process, they make a stance there and reject as absurd the application of the same grammar and logic to psychology, especially for the mind's fancier arsenal of tricks – consciousness, free will, creativity, that sort of thing. This is perhaps because they can dimly see that if the tug-of-war is lost here, at this line, there is nothing, save for pixie dust, that protects the creative Designer from being subjected to the same bottom-up analysis. It is powerful proof that it is one thing to commit yourself to a view, it is quite another to accept all the logical consequences that come along with it. We all grow up with the warm blanket of dualism, the combination of instinctive charm and spiritual comfort that can only come from leaving your intuitions unexamined. In the end, we all want to believe in the magic spark of inspiration. But to get a handle on the mechanism that has made the human brain the single boldest invention machine that has ever existed, we have to throw a grenade into the well-cocooned pocket of ignorance in which we keep our fluffy, mystical view of creative thinking.

Exactly where a closet dualist draws the line can differ greatly from one to the next but, eventually, if one presses hard enough, there is a line. The snag is, of course, that this requires, beyond said line, a miraculous force, a skyhook to make it all work. This is a Faustian pact. Remember that we solve nothing by kicking the can down the road. All we do is replace our problem with a bigger one. Closet dualism is extraordinarily resilient to logic, but once it is properly smoked out, it must give way to its true nature: plain and simple dualism. And thus tied to mysticism, it is a throwaway not worth discussing in a scientific arena.

The other group applies the principles of evolution all the way down, but rejects the notion of culture being Darwinian in nature. The gist of it is this. Culture has evolved, from its Darwinian origins, into an evolutionary system so different from biological evolution that it cannot be labeled Darwinian without misuse of the term. This gene-culture co-evolution approach isn't so much based on knock-down philosophical arguments or the prospect of future breakthroughs in brain science, but rather on the reality that we require different mathematical procedures to analyze cultural data sets. This fact clearly implies that we are dealing with a process that is different to organic evolution. Cultural evolution, as proponents of this view put it, doesn't obey the laws of population genetics, a claim that we will examine a little further on. If this is even close to accurate, we should stop trying to fit square pegs into round holes and accept that we are dealing with a different beast. Boyd and Richerson (1985, 2005) are two of the founding fathers of this dual inheritance theory. Their target is not Darwinism *per se* but the attempt to lift it out of biology – and here comes the key point – without adequate modification. Co-evolutionists are opposed by people who might best be dubbed Darwinian fundamentalists – Daniel Dennett and Richard Dawkins, most prominently – who consider this line of thinking as confused. In the end, the difference, as we will see, comes down to one's definition of Darwinism.

Patterns of change

So what kind of evolutionary system is culture? To get to the bottom of this, we dissect three issues on the way to a single, uncontested conclusion. In securing this bare consensus, we gain a better vantage point from which to look for the brain mechanisms that can explain the kind of evolutionary change we are seeing in culture.

We start here with the difference between a Darwinian variational pattern of change and a Lamarckian transformational one. The next section then deals with heredity. In Darwinian evolution, information is passed on in a digital format; in Lamarckian evolution it is blended. Debates on this issue can take two forms, and we will briefly examine both. One is over the pros and cons of memetics; the other is over the structure of causal relationship that exists between original cultural items and their copies. This sounds more complicated than it is. The crux is this. Based on a stable replicating unit, a digital transmission format yields a vertical flow chart because items pass, in their entirety, only down the line, from one generation to the next. The flow chart in a blending process, by contrast, shows a more horizontal structure because items, in whole or in part, spread also within a generation. The third section is concerned with blindness. It is probably not too much to say that this feature of evolutionary algorithms tops the list of explosive powder kegs in the already illustrious annals of science. Darwinism is blind; Lamarckism is directed. It is not difficult to see why the utter lack of foresight and direction inherent in the Darwinian method causes existential vertigo in short order. It shouldn't come as much of a surprise then that many objections raised against cultural Darwinism mirror those historically mooted against biological Darwinism. Culture cannot be Darwinian, runs the argument, because the skillfully crafted designs of human artificers – books, bridges, ballads – are thoughtful, meaningful, and purposeful; they are planned and not the mindless ticking away of a mechanical and insipid procedure. But there is every reason to suppose that we also need to press the kill button on this intuition.

What we will find at the end of this road is not uncharted territory. Darwinism is variational, discrete, and blind. Lamarckism is transformational, continuous, and directed. What is seldom realized, however, is that these bits need not come grouped together like this. The three issues of variational/transformational, discrete/continuous, and blind/directed are quite distinct from one another, and there is no reason an evolutionary system cannot consist of a different mix (Kronfeldner, 2007). Our single, uncontested conclusion flows from this. Bracketing the second issue of how units of information are copied, a matter that can only be settled by progress in neuroscience, it draws out the fact that culture is a variational evolutionary system that involves some directedness. I devote the rest of this chapter to lift these features out of the muddy waters in which many people prefer to keep them, because any lack of clarity here, at the level of evolutionary biology, is prone to lead to Cartesian danglers once we push for the analysis of creativity at the level of the brain.

The first issue, the pattern of change, isn't contentious. Culture is a variational system. The vantage point to help us understand this is the population level. How does a population, as a whole, change over time? To take the familiar Darwinian case first, a variational system is based on the variation-selection method. It is fair to say that this is Darwin's key insight. Individuals, or the constituent units of a population, vary naturally and a sorting process biases their survival. As a result, adaptive mutations spread in the population and, here is the main point, become dominant *relative to* the maladaptive ones. Darwinian evolution is a statistical change that shifts the proportions of the different variants over time (Lewontin, 1991). The reason why the population changes is because the statistical distribution changes.

A Lamarckian transformational system works in a different way. It is not based on naturally occurring variation but on adaptation-guaranteeing instruction. Variation exists but it is treated as noise and thus evolutionarily unimportant. The Lamarckian system includes no waste and no competition. We should underline the word waste here, because this is the telltale sign of a Darwinian system. Without variation, a selection process is obviously superfluous because there is nothing it could work on. All units of the population change together, at the same time, at the same rate. We can say that the reason why the population changes is because all its members are transformed, jointly, in the direction of adaptation.

We must add a note of caution here to not equate Lamarckian evolution with creationism. We can illustrate the difference by pursuing the question of how it is possible that change is automatically adaptive – always. What ensures adaptivity in this process? The answer is not a divine power but rather the environment. Lamarckian evolution is a lawful, instructive method of change that has no need for an intervening deity. Having said that, the system does include, as a built-in feature, the notion of inevitable progress, the idea that the human species undergoes automatic development toward greater complexity, or more to the point, perfection. Because change is directed, or rather instructed, by the environment, it is guaranteed to be adaptive. This imposes a definite direction to Lamarckian evolution and gives it a purpose that doubles up as a kind of *ersatz* for a Creator. So progress in this evolutionary system is guaranteed by always causing change in each and every individual toward increased complexity. This is obviously not a good description for culture. A Darwinian system can – but does not have to – lead to progress; it is certainly not built in. Darwinian algorithms simply do what they do; they are creative – one accidental move at a time – on their way to nowhere in particular.

The units of mentalese

This takes us to the second issue: the units of cultural heredity, or lack thereof, and the way they are transmitted. Unlike the variational nature of cultural change, this matter is positively controversial. The reason is simple. Nobody has the foggiest understanding how the brain copies information. Neuroscience, for all its might, cannot tell us the ins and outs of how ideas have sex. If truth be told, we don't even have the beginning of a framework. When hard evidence is scant, the next best thing to do is to wring the indirect evidence for what it's worth. This involves studying the mercurial, and often mysterious, ways in which cultural artifacts seem to multiply, propagate and wither away. And that, in a nutshell, is the main reason why the field is ablaze with heat and controversy. Indirect data, as everyone knows who has done time in an (educational) institution, are priceless gems in the academic ether. They are the fertilizer for a professor's favorite activity: be at loggerheads over some knotty theoretical puzzle that regular folk don't even know exist. Clearly, you are not getting tenure by agreeing with your colleague down the hall when this course of action can somehow be avoided.

Darwin also didn't have the faintest idea of the unit, or mechanism, of heredity. Little did Darwin know – how could he in 1859 – of the molecular machinery that lies underneath. It remained the single biggest hitch for the theory of natural selection until the 1930s when Ronald

Fisher incorporated the work of Mendel and population genetics into the modern synthesis. And, of course, until the DNA replicator itself was discovered by Watson and Crick in 1953. No wonder Darwin maintained his lifelong courtship with Lamarck's inheritance of acquired characteristics.

That biological evolution is digital is crucial. A digital format is substrate neutral because the replicating unit itself does not undergo changes, either in shape or constitution, during the copying. This renders the process of copying independent of the actual stuff doing the copying. A computer works this way, too. Here the digital format creates a separation between the CPU and memory, between hardware and software. In a Lamarckian blending process, by contrast, the supposed hereditary material itself is part of what is copied, making it more difficult to abstract the information from the medium that carries the information. As a result, the copying process in Lamarckian soft inheritance cannot readily be transferred to a vehicle consisting of a different kind of material.

Of all the ways one can frame the seesawing debate over culture, the most eye-catching has been without a doubt the meme (Dawkins, 1976). Recall that biological evolution is an instance of a more generic, algorithmic principle for change, an all-purpose engineering method, if you like. There are any number of ways in which mutation, selection, and heredity can interact to turn over the evolutionary quality crank. This insight led Richard Dawkins' to propose that our thoughts have some gene-like properties. They can be seen as virus-like chunks of information that are copied or imitated in a variation-selection process as they are passed from person to person. Brains continuously copy these memes with error and the fads and fashions of society determine their differential survival. If units of culture replicate in the same way as DNA molecules replicate, then cultural evolution is memetic evolution, and we are dealing with the differential fitness of memes.

Much is often made of all this. Memes are controversial, no doubt, both in highbrow and popular culture. Some people don't tire talking up memes *ad libitum* – meme machines here, meme-infested brains there – conveniently neglecting the minor matter that there is no proof of life for these elusive mental replicators. As Dawkins (1999) admits, "[m]emes have not yet found their Watson and Crick; they even lack their Mendel."

In what is surely a greater defect, no empirical science has sprung up around the meme concept to possibly change that. Not surprisingly, salvos of skepticism have descended on memes in a veritable explosion of passion and fury. One broadside comes from people that vaguely admit to an interesting half-analogy between genes and memes and quickly add that this is about as far as you can take it. Another, less charitable crowd, shreds the idea of self-replicating cultural particles altogether, ridiculing meme aficionados as squids who spray great clouds of ink at their opponents just to confuse them.

The gene-meme analogy indeed gets increasingly difficult to uphold the more one wishes to press it. The list of theoretical problems is formidable. For a start, memeticists don't agree where and what memes are. Those who hold a neural view say that they are patterns of activity in the brain's network that, like genes, carry instructions for making things. Others think of memes as the artifacts themselves, which implies that they are not only in the brain but also out in the world. Critics further point out that memes cannot be counted; they are not traceable; and they don't have boundaries the way genes do. And how can an entity without boundaries copy itself with high fidelity? Should we conclude, then, without further questions, that cultural evolution cannot be Darwinian?

What probably bothers anti-memeticists the most are the implications for our sense of agency. Since Darwin a central debate within the theory of evolution has been over the proper units of selection. The gene-centric view of biological evolution maintains that selection does not take place at the level of groups or even individuals since traits and characteristics at that level are not inheritable. The proper unit is the gene, because that is the unit that makes the copies. Bodies are just vehicles for them. Translated to memes, the units of selection in cultural evolution would be the meme. Like genes, they replicate for their own sake, not the sake of their hosts – our brains. It follows that culture exist for the survival of memes. An individual, then, is not a creator and selector of cultural units but just a bearer of them, a bearer of cultural units. We are not the agents of our own ideas in the same that bodies are not the agents of biological selection.

There are undoubtedly some exaggerations attached to memes, on both sides, but they do make for excellent thought experiments that can guide us to some of the debate's critical joints. We can simply think of them as units of imitation – bits worth plagiarizing – that have fuzzy and flexible boundaries. If dodging the bullet like this sounds evasive, consider genetics, a field that has flourished for decades without a decent definition of the word gene (Crick & Koch, 1998). In the biosphere, information is embodied in DNA and copied in discrete chunks of them – genes. Computers are digital machines, too. They symbolize information in a binary mode using electronic on-and-off switches.

To what extent all of these problems are indeed problems and thus provide a disanalogy between gene and meme is up for neuroscience to figure out. But ask for how the brain represents and copies information, and you will find even seasoned neuroscientists looking at their feet in utmost humility. Most prefer to repress it into the unconscious, along with other conundrums, such as consciousness or the meaning of life. If you insist many would probably go for some kind of electronic scheme. That does seem sensible. We know that neurons communicate by the rate of firing. Since neurons either fire an action potential or they don't – ones and zeros – this makes for a digital code to boost. Brain scientists at home in electrophysiology generally tell you that the behavior of individual neurons is unlikely to be the elementary unit of mentalese. A more hopeful candidate is, as William Calvin (1996) has proposed, a coordinated pattern of a whole array of brain cells. One might be forgiven to think that an aggregate signal comprised of millions of individual units must be analog, but this isn't necessarily so. Don't forget, the DNA polymer is also happily analog underneath. When the ragtag gang of organic bits is done joining, blending and binding to yield the DNA molecule, a stable unit is formed that can copy itself with high fidelity. Indeed, any analog signal can be treated in a digital manner with only a minimal loss of information. In precisely the same way, one can imagine that an ensemble of oscillating neurons must reach a high level of stability – in frequency, coherence, number of neurons, or some other parameter – before it can reliably act as a carrier for mental information. But that isn't to say that neuroscientists generally think of the brain as a digital computer – indeed, by all accounts, they'd probably bet on it being an analog computing machine.

Another way this debate has been framed is by examining the relationship between cultural items and their copies. Without a science of, for a lack of a better word, neuromemetics, anthropologists – and nearly everyone else in the field of cultural evolution – have turned their attention to the indirect evidence. And of that, there is plenty. From cooking recipes over architectural styles to sports games, cultures are awash with clues about how traits, habits, and quirks are assimilated, amalgamated, and attenuated. What emerges from this detective work is that the discrete-bullet theory of heredity begins to look a trifle flimsy. The diffusion of cultural artifacts bears only scant resemblance to the vertical, straight-down structure we'd expect to find with hard, digital inheritance.

This is complicated further by the fact that the object of the copying bonanza seems to be the cultural artifact itself. So far we have talked of memes but quite another issue is whether there is an equivalent to the Weismann barrier in the brain. Recall that in biological evolution the phenotypic interactor (with the environment) doesn't alter the genotypic replicator so that acquired characteristics, which operate on phenotypes, are not heritable – at least not through genes. Suppose, for the sake of argument, that memes exist and are stored in brains – somehow. If we follow this line of thinking, a specific meme would represent the blueprint for a cultural artifact, say, the instructions for using chopsticks. Now, a phenotype is made of this by someone explaining to you how to eat with chopsticks. What would have to happen next simply can't occur in biological evolution. You would have to reconstruct the memotype from the phenotype by representing that behavior in your brain. The Weismann barrier tells you that the phenotype cannot make the genotype, however. What's more, there is no causal relationship between memes and their phenotypic expression. The idea of the sun, for instance, does not make the sun come up. Memeticists typically take the relationship of meme to phenotype as a semantic one. Indeed they go further and admit that the Weismannian genotype-phenotype distinction is best not used for memes.

At this point, we must acknowledge, and then set aside, certain complications. In what is known as epigenetic inheritance, biology has recently woken up to the fact that heritable transmission can also occur by non-genetic means – parent to daughter cells, as in the cytoplasm of an egg, for instance (Jablonka & Lamb, 2005). The general view is that this is compatible with Darwinism. The central dogma of Darwinism doesn't rule out the inheritance of acquired characteristics *per se*; what it excludes is the inheritance of acquired characteristics *through genes*. Thus, the Weismann barrier remains, and so does the genotype-phenotype distinction with its no-return causal arrow. Epigenetic inheritance means simply that genes are not the only hereditary material. If you subscribe to the substance neutrality view of Darwinian evolutionary algorithms, this isn't much of a surprise anyway, let alone threatens the Darwinian bedrock of biology. It is just another way the Darwinian ratchet of generate-and-test passes on information.

To come back to the main issue, Darwinian algorithms, as we will see in more detail in the next section, consist of the discontinuous, twin sub-processes of variation and selection in which selection occurs *ex post facto*, that is, after the fact of the variation. But that doesn't seem to apply to culture. The development of ideas, skills, and beliefs, some theorists are quick to throw in, cannot be divorced from environmental factors. The argument, in other words, is that modifications at the phenotype level alter the meme replicator.

Cultural documents, as a rule, brim over with signs of cross-lineage blending (Collard et al., 2006). Many people take these pliable effects to mean that cultural evolution must be an evolutionary process based on Lamarckian soft inheritance (Gould, 1979). It goes without saying that meme supporters will have none of this. Too fast, too fast, they interject and there are at least two considerations that suggest that this argument indeed needs further work. First, viruses, bacteria, and plants happily mingle and mix as well and, just to complicate things, "cultural" data from animals – beaver dams, hunting skills, etc. – all show signs of merging like watercolor left in the rain (Abbott et al., 2003). By this reasoning, we should also herald the end of Darwinism in biology.

We also mustn't forget the circumstantial character of the evidence. Recall again Darwin's fix. The essential mechanism of heredity was an intractable problem in his time. Without knowledge of particulate Mendelian genetics, Darwin couldn't draw conclusions from looking at the phenotypic manifestations of body height or nest-building ability. From one level up, all inheritance looks like blending. This is why he couldn't purge Lamarckian-style soft inheritance from his thinking. To infer the ground rules of a lower level from a higher level is a non sequitur. All sorts of different patterns could emerge. There is a serious lesson to be extracted from this. Anthropology has been struggling for a long time, without tangible success, to identify and define units of culture. But the underlying neural mechanism of cultural heredity cannot be gleaned from indirect anthropological evidence because any pattern of transmission can arise from any number of neural mechanisms.

Memes may indeed turn out to be the wrong way to think about cultural transmission but we cannot go there from here. Some people defend the meme perspective by showing how well it explains the evolution of a soup recipe over time (Blackmore, 1999). Others take a different example – how the craft of making a clay pot is passed down from teacher to apprentice – to build an equally persuasive case for blending (Kronfeldner, 2007). Judging from the sheer number of published papers on his work habits, the poster boy of this premature gnashing of teeth is Picasso. What has made Picasso the *Escherichia coli* of cultural evolution was his fondness for not only making many preliminary sketches for his paintings but also of keeping them – actually, signing and selling them. In fact, the National Museum Centro de Arte Reina Sophia in Madrid, which houses his most famous work of art, El Guernica, displays a fair number of them right next to the final thing. Analyze them carefully and you will find a singular fact. Picasso's thinking evolved over time. He tried, tweaked and tested many ideas before settling on one that pleased him sufficiently to stay with it. These sketches have become the center of a back-and-forth pitting the role of chance in creativity against a more systematic process that is heavily directed by expertise (Simonton, 2007; Weisberg, 2004). Similar exchanges of fire over how creativity works have erupted over Kekulé's famous benzene ring discovery, Edison's many inventions, or Poincaré's introspective reflections. But, without repeating the argument, these pontifications cannot tell us about the grammar and logic of the neural mechanism lying underneath. Only the neuroscientific counterpart of genetics can tell us how information is copied. The interwoven nature of culture does not, by itself, invalidate memetics. We need to know more about how humans hold ideas in their heads and how the ideas in your head influence the ideas in my head. All this would seem to suggest that the venom, on both sides, has been discharged too early.

But for gene-culture co-evolutionists this will not do. There is so much crisscrossing and traversing going on, they contend, the smoking gun isn't the existence of horizontal diffusion. It's the quantity and extent of it. Recall their claim that cultural data sets don't obey the rules of population genetics. This is not a minor matter because population genetics is considered the theoretical cornerstone of Neo-Darwinism. Population genetics is a tool that describes how the composition of biological populations, including their horizontal diffusion, should change over time on the basis of the diverse forces acting on them – mutation rates, selection pressures, and so on. This takes some fancy footwork, or as they'd put it, abstract mathematical modeling. And why is this important? Population genetics takes all the moving pieces of biological evolution, plus their dynamic interplay, and spits out broad patterns of how the process of evolution transpires in a population. Now take the word "biological" and substitute it for the word "cultural" and we can start appreciating the co-evolutionist's key point. If cultural evolution is digital, and hence Neo-Darwinian, the tools of population genetics should give us robust generalizations for cultural change the way they do for biological change. And yes, you guessed it: they don't. Never mind our ignorance of the brain's inner workings. Seen from this angle, there must be differences between nature and culture – irrespective of where they lie.

The yin-yang of all this is brought to a kind of glorious consummation when Darwinian fundamentalists calmly concede this point without a fight only to insist, in one and the same breath, that this doesn't justify the label of Lamarckianism. Culture, they'd claim, is still a Darwinian system, one with a few clever improvements no doubt, but calling it or treating it as a separate thing that then independently co-evolves alongside nature is a profound mischaracterization of the basic crank mechanism that propels culture. At a minimum, it is a tactical error that feeds the hopeful monster of closet dualism. Naturally, co-evolutionists object. But of course these are nothing more than opinions, and, as is the way with other people's opinions, they are generally dismissed as irrelevant. But to underscore the point I was on about earlier, this rancorous clash has had the ghastly side effect of ignoring evolutionary thinking in the search for the neural mechanisms of creativity.

The small matter of blindness

The matter of blindness, the third issue on our way to a common denominator, actually hits the same spot but from a slightly different angle. Of course it has been the reason for Darwinism's noisy run-in with religion. I am guessing you've heard about that. Fearing dire repercussions for spirituality, morality, and meaning, the many efforts to restore to evolution a guiding hand of higher wisdom in the variation component – directed mutation, notably – and the selection component – a force from above that hand-picks winning variants – are testimony to just how hard it is to go all the way with a theory of creation that lacks a teleological safety net. These last-gasp holdouts against Darwinism went bang in biology soon after Darwin published his theory and are now routinely taught in science classes as exemplary cases of fatuous thinking, laid bare. Darwinian algorithms simply do what they do; they are creative, one uninformed move at a time.

In biological evolution, this conclusion is nothing new of course. Everyone accepts it. But the possibility that cultural evolution also isn't directed toward a final end, an ultimate cause, is still greeted with cries of despair and alarm. Once in a while one finds precious instances of joined-up thinking, but much of even the most meticulous writing on the topic is bedeviled by a curious error in distinguishing between two meanings of blind. While some people take it to mean random, others freely use it as a stand-in for undirected. Sometimes you can find authors make use of both meanings in the same sentence. This can cause immense confusion.

The term random, attached to Darwinism in particular, has been particularly hit and miss. Take Hoyle's fallacy, the most infamous example. In it, Fred Hoyle (1984), a distinguished astronomer by all evidence, estimated the probability of life occurring on Earth to be about as likely as a hurricane sweeping through a scrapyard and assembling a ready-to-fly Boeing 747. Some readers might recognize this junkyard tornado example as a warmed over version of the infinite monkey theorem, the odds of Shakespeare's Hamlet being written by a monkey thrashing away at a keyboard. What drives both of these duds is the common but false presumption that complexity must arise from a single, random step. If so, this would indeed be a vastly improbable event, though not infinitely so. What this ignores is, of course, the fact that evolution is a cumulative builder that rigorously field-tests its designs every step of the way. The result of many iterations isn't random at all but replete with functional reasons for why the design features exist as they do. The endless number of different renderings of this incoherent line of thinking is a disarming reflection of the determination, almost at any cost to logicality, to find reprieve from the perception of genetic determinism. To bring this to a point, variation is blind but selection isn't (Dawkins, 1986).

Such massive blind spots aside, the term random, in a variation-selection process, is usually taken to express the idea that all mutations should occur with equally likelihood. On the merits of this definition we must conclude that neither biological nor cultural evolution is random. While it is obvious that human creators don't generate possible solutions to a problem in a random manner, you could be excused for not knowing that this isn't the case for biological creativity either. But, contrary to widespread belief, it is. Take, for example, the phenomenon of adaptive mutation (Foster, 2004). Each gene has its own mutation rate, which can vary according to such factors as physical events, radiation, chromosome location, or a dozen other factors. Some genes have so high a mutation rate that they are referred to as hot spots. Mutation rates can even intensify in times of stress, which makes good mutations more plentiful. Strong selection, in the parlance of biology, can increase the mutation pressure. This is not directed mutation but nonetheless a clear anticipation of need. So, to drop the first hint, mutations are blind (unguided) with respect to subsequent selection but not blind (random) with respect to rate. There are also developmental constraints to consider. Certain mutations simply cannot arise given the evolutionary trajectory a species has already taken – no spontaneous wings for elephants. From this, we can readily see that randomness is not required for an evolutionary system to be Darwinian (Hull, 2001).

Having identified, and broken off, that weary piece, we can saccade to the center of the volcano. What can we say about the term undirected or, to use the word biologists prefer, unguided? That is harder to answer than you might think. Not in biology, mind you. Here the matter is, again, uncontested. The variation process is undirected as far as adaptive consequences are concerned; it churns out mutations with no general bias in the direction of good. This utter lack of foresight in terms of adaptation is a central tenet of Darwinism: In the biosphere, evolution is a discontinuous two-step process, mutation first, selection second, causal reverse flow excluded. That selection occurs *ex post facto* means that there is no (or zero) statistical correlation between the factors causing novelty and those that sort it. Another way of saying this is that variation and selection are totally uncoupled, 100 percent independent of one another. Now, contrast this with its opposite, Lamarckian evolution. Recall that change in a Lamarckian evolutionary system is not based on variation and selection, so blindness plays no role in it. The system is an instructional or transformational one in which adaptation is certain, from the start. This amounts to a probability of 1; change is totally directed, a coupling of 100 percent.

The instant we ask the same question about culture, we find ourselves in a morass as thick and hot as lava. The irony is that almost everyone agrees on the key point: creative thinking is neither totally blind nor totally guided. The general probability of variants being adaptive is neither zero nor one. In addition to the fact that cultural data sets don't obey the rules of population genetics, we have arrived at this inference because of what psychologists and computer scientists call expert systems. In a typical experiment of this kind the problem-solving habits of novices are compared to those of experts. After even a cursory glimpse at the results of such a study, it is hard to escape the conclusion that the occurrence of novel ideas (variation) is influenced by the kind of problem (selection). Experts have acquired knowledge that allows them to generate guesses that are informed by the characteristics of the problem. This favoring of adaptability is a cognitive coupling between variation and selection. Even Simonton, the most forceful proponent of blindness in recent decades, had to retreat from the position of blindness and concede degrees of blindness. He now places creativity on a blindness-sightedness continuum but continues to insist calling it the BVSR model (Simonton, 2013). But this just backward, as it should be degrees of sightedness. As Kronfeldner (2010) points out "there cannot be more or less blindness . . . since undirectedness is defined as the absence of any coupling. Either a process is undirected or it is more or less directed." For our purposes, the result is the same. There is now universal agreement that human idea formation is directed to some degree. Our main task in the chapters to come is to shed light on how, exactly, the brain manages to gain this bit of sightedness.

We can now appreciate more clearly the single conclusion I want to bring to the fore. Because the class variational/transformational is different from the class blind/directed, the total elimination of directedness is simply not necessary for a variational system. An evolutionary system can be a variational one yet involve some coupling. Based on what we know, this seems to be the case for culture (Kronfeldner, 2010).

Are you a lumper or a splitter?

What is less agreed on is how to classify this seemingly highly combustible fact. Is culture still Darwinian? Or is Lamarck staging a comeback? Some indication of the strength of feeling attached to this matter is given by the fact that there are whole issues of journals in which this controversy is watered, fertilized, and hot-housed. I take a more salutary route. By injecting a heavy dose of common sense and goodwill into this incendiary issue, I hope to highlight the fact that there is a great deal made out of very little.

We must clear this up before we can proceed, because all the hooting and pouncing concerns additional features of how exactly the generate-and-test algorithm plays itself out in organic evolution, which need not be settled to continue with the basic principles of evolution in neuroscience. You will remember from Chapter 2 that no currently circulating theory on creative thinking – divergent thinking, defocused attention, or right brains – holds water. The main reason for this disciplinary bankruptcy is the simple fact that neuroscience has failed to ground its studies in the most obvious of paradigms, the variation-selection process of change that does all creating and designing in the biosphere. It seems as if the mere existence of the general debate over cultural Darwinism leads neuroscientists to think that the jury is still out as to whether the essential Darwinian rationale of generate-and-test is useful *at all* in the search for the mechanisms that compute creative ideas. For neuroscience, the broader debate has become a decoy, willfully ballyhooed by some for ideological reasons and carelessly misread by others, who wrongly believe that all the bells and whistles of the modern synthesis must correspond to the cultural version of the evolutionary algorithm before neuroscientists should play with it in the domain of human creative processes.

If you take a categorical, Kantian-style approach to your definitions, neither Neo-Darwinism nor Lamarckism describes the crank mechanism driving cultural change. Should you feel the urgent itch to take sides nonetheless, here is how you can do it.

If you are a splitter by temperament, you could take the data from horizontal transmission in culture and conclude with heavy confidence that the cognitive coupling evident in human creative thinking is a breach of Darwinism as we know it today – Neo-Darwinism, to be exact. After all, the matter of blindness isn't some minor add-on but a central organizing dogma of modern Darwinism. All you have to do to pull this off is to take zero coupling to be the lone member of one class, with all other possibilities squeezed into the other class of directedness (Kronfeldner, 2010). Coiled up like this, you can now sling-shoot past all the unsuspecting Darwin-aficionados with ease, offering up a stream of clever commentaries avowing that cultural evolution, and by extension human creativity, is not Darwinian. Plus, you can draw comfort and support from finding yourself in much esteemed company. Stephen J. Gould was a prominent ringleader in this group, but other famous people maintaining that all aspects of Neo-Darwinian must be satisfied are Richard Lewontin, Steven Pinker, Noam Chomsky, Robert Boyd, Peter Richardson, among rather countless others. For them, biological and cultural evolution are different systems. Here is how Gould (1979) put it: "Human cultural evolution, in strong opposition to our biological history, is Lamarckian in character." All share the objection to the Darwinism label for human creativity and designing. I won't sway you from this position (I haven't got the energy, for one thing).

This being academia, it doesn't end there. It only takes a moment's reflection to realize that you can also fly a kite for the reverse position. So, suppose you are a lumper instead. Armed with a more elastic, bigger-picture take on Darwinism, you strip the definition to the essential core of a variation-selection process that designs from the ground up. Lest we forget, this inversion of reasoning, that creation as the handiwork of cranes, not skyhooks, was Darwin's key insight. There is no principled reason, apart from civility, making this a verboten move. So, you forget all the other paraphernalia of the modern synthesis and define Darwinian the way Darwin himself understood it. To carry this off, you reboot the discussion and simply insist that a process is either directed, making Lamarck the sole constituent of one class, or it is more or less undirected, which lumps all degrees of blindness into the other class, and you can start running victory laps shouting that Lamarckian is obviously the wrong label for cultural evolution. Should this, minimalist Darwinian view appeal to you, you can also get plenty of philosophical tailwind from academia's glitterati, such as Richard Dawkins or Daniel

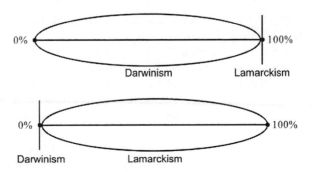

Figure 4.1 The sightedness continuum

Unlike its Eastern counterparts, Western philosophy has left us ill-prepared to grapple with continuums. We seem to prefer a categorical dichotomy over smooth gradualism and fuzzy sets any day. Suppose your gut tells you that cultural Darwinism is wrong – somehow. But, to your indignation, people actually demand a rational argument from you. Not to be caught empty-handed, you split the blind-directedness spectrum into two, mutually exclusive categories. One, which you call Darwinism, you fill with the outlier from the extreme low end of the continuum of 0 percent directedness, that is to say, zero coupling between variation and selection. The other, which you call Lamarckian, you fill with all other cases that are directed to some degree. Once set up like this, you can let off a battering ram against the suffocating excess of your opponents' position who think – falsely, as is now clear for everyone to see – that culture is Darwinian. Needless to say, having attended the odd philosophy class in college themselves, your rivals respond in kind, by performing the same trick. They mash around the categories lines so that Lamarckism is the lone outlier at the high end and Darwinism encompasses the rest of the spectrum. They then hold forth on the merits of their own astute analysis while declaring yours to be densely ignorant or absurd on the grounds that it misconstrues the real issue. And by such means did the controversy grow.

Dennett, among many others. I won't sway you from this position either, for the same reason (see Figure 4.1).

Both positions are abusive. Although this doesn't make me any new friends on either side of this contentious divide, the matter comes down to how you understand and define Darwinism. All parties agree that culture is something in its own right in the sense that it cannot be explained by Neo-Darwinian evolution the way it operates in the biosphere. It is something added to our biological equipment. If you demand that organic evolution must map on to culture in every single aspect of the modern synthesis, that is, be completely analogous to cultural evolution, it is easy to defeat the thesis of cultural Darwinism. Culture and nature are different processes. If, on the other hand, you are a minimalist and redefine your terms so as to focus on Darwin's core idea, culture is obviously – by definitional feat, almost – a Darwinian system. In all events, culture and nature can be described using slightly different parameters of fitness functions but they both fall under the umbrella of evolutionary algorithms. Calling the extension of biological evolution to culture an analogy betrays only our knowledge of the historical fact that the basic algorithmic process was discovered in the biosphere first. If you are a splitter, you see the difference between biology and culture as evidence for two systems; if you are a lumper, you see culture as an improved version of essentially the same system. Evidently, Darwinian fundamentalist are lumpers; co-evolutionists are splitters.

It is well known that books are easier to understand when authors are frank and candid about their positions. So, for the record, my own bias is toward lumping. Here is why. It would be odd, I'd think, if the biospheric version of this mechanism, using the most basic – blind – of Darwinian algorithms, would not find, sooner or later, a way to improve on itself, to bootstrap so to speak. The partial coupling in creative thinking, the ability to look ahead a few steps, is not only compatible with Darwinism, but an entirely predictable outcome of a system that relentlessly turns the quality crank. It is of such obvious adaptive value that any Darwinian algorithm would eventually hit on a way to evolve better, more sophisticated Darwinian algorithms. And nothing would be more adaptive than making a computational machine – the brain – that is a tad bit less blind.

The same cannot be said about Lamarckian evolution. Cultural evolution is not, to turn the argument on its head, a watered-down version of a Lamarckian algorithm. Change in culture doesn't come to each individual in the same way. And as soon as change works on only some individuals but not others, we immediately have an evolutionary system that fulfills the three Darwinian requirements of variation, fitness differences, and inheritance. Culture didn't evolve from the 100 percent end of the continuum, from an adaptive guaranteeing instructional process. It is not a Lamarckian system with a bit of variation; it is a Darwinian system with a bit of coupling. Emphasizing that culture originates from the zero end of the sightedness continuum also has the additional benefit of counteracting the ever-present seductive hunch of closet dualism. Or to help ourselves once more to Dennett's clever metaphor, the mind is a collection of cranes and, over time, some of them have specialized in the tasks of making better cranes, leaving us with supercranes that can see a bit farther and do some extraordinary lifting in the creativity department. So, to return to the question we posed at the beginning of this chapter, I'd opt for calling culture a Darwinian system. But if you are allergic to the word, I wouldn't mind some other label either.

One of the main themes in the chapters ahead is to answer the question thrown up by this conclusion. What is the neural mechanism the brain uses to gain partial sightedness? Obviously, creative people are not a special class of prophets.

Recommended readings

Darwin, C. (1859/1968). *The origin of species*. London: Penguin.

Dawkins, R. (1976). *The selfish gene*. Oxford: Oxford University Press.

Dawkins, R. (1986). *The blind watchmaker*. New York: W.W. Norton.

Dennett, D. C. (1995). *Darwin's' dangerous idea*. New York: Simon & Schuster.

Gould, S. J. (1979). Shades of Lamarck. *Natural History, 88*, 22–28.

Huxley, J. (1942). *Evolution: The modern synthesis*. London: Allen & Unwin.

Kronfeldner, M. E. (2010). Darwinian "blind" hypothesis formation revisited. *Synthese, 175*, 193–218.

Lewontin, R. C. (1970). The units of selection. *Annual Review of Ecology and Systematics, 1*, 1–18.

Mesoudi, A., Whiten, A., & Laland, K. N. (2006). Towards a unified science of cultural evolution. *Behavioral and Brain Sciences, 29*, 329–347.

Pinker, S. (2002). *The blank slate: The modern denial of human nature*. New York: Penguin.

Richerson, P. J., & Boyd, R. (2005). *Not by genes alone: How culture transformed human evolution*. Chicago: University of Chicago Press.

Simonton, D. K. (2007). The creative process in Picasso's Guernica sketches: Monotonic improvements or nonmonotonic variation. *Creativity Research Journal, 19*, 329–344.

Tooby, J., & Cosmides, L. (1992). The psychological foundations of culture. In J. Barkow, L. Cosmides, & J. Tooby (Eds.), *The adapted mind: Evolutionary psychology and the generation of culture*. New York: Oxford University Press.

5
The Mind's New Tricks

In the spring of 2008, I was invited to participate in a National Science Foundation workshop on creative designing in Aix-en-Provence. Right at the beginning of the meeting, I experienced a vivid and arresting example of the deep-seated angst about keeping evolutionary thinking, in any form, out of creativity and away from the mind. It was also my crisis point that finally convinced me that I can no longer put off engaging with this issue. The workshop was to identify future directions in creativity research and design science, bringing together people from all relevant disciplines. Engineers mingled with cognitive psychologists, neuroscientist, designers, and people from artificial intelligence. But scientists from one discipline were, conspicuously, missing. When I put the question to John Gero, the workshop's organizer, why there were no evolutionary biologists present at the meeting, he told me, without a whiff of reservation, that they have nothing to do with the field of creativity and design thinking. I responded by asking the following: If you want to know how pots with handles are made, wouldn't you want to talk to people who can tell you how pots are made? Tragically, this was not an academic armchair discussion in which a lumper realizes he is talking to a splitter, or perhaps a closet dualist. The workshop was to make recommendations about future funding priorities for one of the biggest funding agencies in the world: it was to report on where things are heading with creativity research and what would be needed to get there. Yet the entire underlying bedrock of the only mechanistic explanation of creativity we know of – the theory of evolution – was thrown out before things got started.

This is not uncommon. Spend enough time talking to people about the brain mechanisms of creative thinking and you will encounter a paradox. Virtually everyone working on this issue tells you right away that they disown any commitment to mystical muses or crude light-bulb-in-brain type schemes. Dig a bit deeper and this seemingly enlightened opener quickly gives way to a wall of resistance against the idea that creativity can be fully understood scientifically and formalized *all the way down*. Something magical about the inspired genius, they'd say, will always remain. The full force of this submerged position is perhaps best measured by the headwind facing evolutionary approaches to creativity. The natural tug toward believing that we are special and somehow don't fit into the natural order gets the better of them.

The sharp end of the stick has been a – typically hot and overheated – debate over how far Darwinism reaches upward into culture and, by extension, human creative thought. Despite the bruising rhetoric of ridicule and contempt on both sides, all parties agree that culture cannot be reduced to genetic (or epigenetic) inheritance. Similar but different seems to be the motto. Except that those who see biological and cultural evolution to be different processes, or at least different enough to warrant discrete treatment, underline the word different, while those stressing that both are members of a common supercategory (variational evolutionary systems), with culture being a sort of two-point-0 version, underline the word similar.

Things have reached such a pitch that the emergence of substantial common ground in the theoretical landscape has largely gone unnoticed. I brought you a long way to bring the existence of this consensus into clear focus. In organic evolution, the twin sub-processes of variation and selection are discontinuous with selection imposing a direction on evolution after the variation is done. While blindness in the variation process is a feature of the biological version of evolution, it doesn't appear to be part of the cultural one. In other words, the coupling parameter of the evolutionary algorithm in the biosphere is set to zero. In a Lamarckian evolutionary algorithm, on the other hand, this parameter is set to one. To reiterate the main point, creative thinking appears to be partially sighted and thus fits neither into the rigid category requirements of Neo-Darwinian (total) blindness nor Lamarckian (total) sightedness. Once we understand that the elimination of directedness is simply not necessary for a variational system, we can appreciate just what a pointless exercise this back-and-forth over the Darwinian label is. Name it what you like, cultural evolution is a variational system that involves some coupling. Remember that Darwin didn't know about this blind, *ex post facto* quirk of his theory. All his life, he accommodated Lamarck's idea of acquired characteristics and relied in his thinking in part on directed generation of novelty. It is fair to say, then, that Darwin didn't think variation was totally blind. Ironically, those who demand that the evolutionary algorithm of the biosphere must be completely analogous to the one in the infosphere before we can legitimately apply Darwinian thinking to culture must, by the same token, be prepared to also defend the somewhat odd thesis that Darwin, believing as he did in blending and coupling, was not a Darwinist.

Remember also that we are bracketing the nature of the replicating process in cultural evolution. In biological evolution, this plays itself out in a digital format, using a (DNA) replicator that has evolved to make copies of itself in high-fidelity. In cultural evolution, we don't know how inheritance works. This is to say, to leave no room for confusion, the brain proceeds via the evolutionary generate-and-test crank alright, we just don't know how the copying is done. Luckily, with neuroscience being nowhere near its Watson-and-Crick moment, we don't have to insist on the specifics to continue here.

Neuroscientists working on creativity have dealt with the debate over cultural evolution by not thinking about it. Search through the literature as you will, and you won't find many experiments in neuroscience that make use of the basic Darwinian rationale. That the existence of this common denominator has been universally overlooked, like one would a tic, is as crazy as it is amazing. For what other than the brain causes all the cultural artifacts around us?

Unified design space

Disciplines have their traditions. What makes interdisciplinary work so fertile at times is that concepts from one discipline can do wonders once imported into another. In a single swoop, they can do more good than years of honest and hard intellectual labor. Unified design space is just such a concept (Dennett, 1995), and it is a mystery that it remains largely unabsorbed into research on creativity and problem-solving. It is now time to properly introduce this more powerful parable because it can dislodge false intuitions about human creativity that are nearly impossible to shake otherwise. Nesting all creative products, all designs, actual *and* potential, into their specific niches in design space, is an ideal base camp from which to explore the tracks creators made in the conceptual space they find themselves in. Mathematics, philosophy, biology, and artificial intelligence are all disciplines with strong traditions of talking about topographies that frame questions in terms of multi-dimensional coordinates in a fitness landscape. In psychology, even if we allow for the odd mentioning in passing, this isn't so. In the field of creativity especially, the very place where this seems a sensible thing to do, there is little serious use of it.

The most famous exposition of this concept is Jorge Luis Borges' (1956) iconic short story *The Library of Babel*. Building on the ancient notion of the world as a book, Borges tells of people who inhabit a "universe (which others call the Library)" that is shaped in an apparently endless honeycomb of interlocking hexagonal rooms separated by vast air shafts. Hallways connect to other rooms on the same level and a spiral staircase connects to rooms above and below. All walls of all rooms are stacked with books. "Like all men of the Library," Borges' narrator tells us, "I have traveled in my youth; I have wandered in search of a book, perhaps the catalogue of catalogues...", but all the books, certainly every book every traveler through the Library has ever seen, seems to contain nothing but complete nonsense. Apart from a few tantalizing hints of sense here and there, which are, one can easily imagine, the source of much discussion among the people of the Library, the books are filled with nothing but pages upon pages of random combinations of letters, spaces, and punctuation. From their explorations, the people of the Library finally did manage to deduce the nature of their world based on two observations. First, every book makes use of only the same 25 symbols. Second, there are no two identical books. The Library, then, these people realized, contains *all possible books* – all actual ones and all potential future ones anyone could ever write.

The full measure of Borges' literary thought experiment does not come into clear view until it is fleshed out, since all the usual descriptors of very large numbers – astronomical, drop in the ocean, etc. – are comically inadequate here. The imagination also isn't lifted to suitable heights by an intellectual approach, say, by stating that the Library of Babel contains more books than there are subatomic particles in the universe (which it does, with no trouble) or by properly quantifying the number of volumes in the Library with a 10 raised to the power of a number with lots of zeros.

The chances of finding a book with so much as a single sentence of meaning in it is unlikely to the extreme. As Borges notes: "...nonsense is normal in the Library and...the reasonable (and even the humble and pure coherence) is an almost miraculous exception." To get a fix on how vast the Library is, Daniel Dennett (1995) used Herman Melville's novel *Moby Dick* as an example. Borges stacks the books in random order but such is the scale of the Library of Babel that an alphabetical organization would not help in locating Moby Dick either. There is an immense number of books that differ from the canonical version in just one – or two or three or ten – places. The part of the Library that contains all possible permutations of changes in any of, say, 5,347 characters is so vast that it can only be described as a galaxy of books and any one of those is readily recognizable as Moby Dick. In fact, if you can imagine this (and of course you can't), the Moby Dick galaxy alone is vastly larger than the entire physical universe. There are volumes in which the first ten pages are correct and the remainder is nothing but question marks, or punctuation marks, or Ns, or any combination thereof. You might find the book in which only the 42nd page is correct and the rest is gibberish, except for the last page with lists the top ten reasons for why you should believe in the tooth fairy. The Library must also contain your biography that describes the events of your life accurately up to the present day – or yesterday, or October 10 of last year, and so on – only to end over the last hundred pages with the repeating string GJR Q?WS. But there are also, in-between the vast reaches of utter nonsense, galaxies of comprehensible and semi comprehensible endings, and one book for every possible ever-bifurcating future scenario of your life. And then there are all those magnificent translations of all of these books in all languages (or any combination of languages) and, of course, entire galaxies of shoddy translations that differ in any one number of typos from the magnificent ones. We also shouldn't pass over lightly all the books containing commentaries of these biographies, the interpretations of the commentaries, refutations of the interpretations, critiques of the refutations, and all their lower-grade versions that diverge in an infinite number of ways. Finally, one of the books is *Hamlet*, even if Borges' Library is the creation of a monkey hammering away on a typewriter. It is all something of a challenge to the imagination.

Richard Dawkins (1986) used a similar device to describe the space of all possible genomes. His Biomorph Land is actually a tiny subset of the vastly larger Library of Babel because all possible combinations of the DNA alphabet A, C, G, and T are already contained in it. Bracketing the issue of sequence length for now, all possible sequences of these DNA units make all possible biological creatures. The vast, vast majority don't spell out actually viable bauplans, as a simple change in a single locus might doom a design. But perched in-between these vast reaches of hopeful monsters are sequences that contain the blueprints for all the "good" designs, from cuttlefish to cockatoos. Needless to say, only an infinitesimally small subset of those workable organisms has ever come into existence in the 4.6-billion-year history of Earth. This readily explains, for instance, something people often find perplexing. Why are chimpanzees, which differ from us by only 1 percent in their

DNA sequence, so unlike us, given that the human population exhibits so much variation in its own genome? Think, by way of comparison, of the gazillions of books in the Moby Dick galaxy. All the different copies, despite their variability, are still immeasurably far away from all the versions in *The Old Man and the Sea* galaxy of books. Chimps and humans, in the vastness of Biomorph Land, still belong to different galaxies that are separated by an immense expanse of genetic space.

We can think of design space as the logical space that contains all possible permutations of information. All creations, every design that has been made and every design that might be made, complex or simple, actual or potential, biological or cultural, alive or artificial, have their proper place somewhere within it. To borrow from Dennett (1995) again: "There is only one design space, and everything actual in it is united with everything else."

The concept of design space brings into sharp focus that all fruits of our creative adventures are threads of actuality that emerge from a vastly larger set of possibilities. Anything or anyone making moves in an unknown fitness landscape, therefore, creates and designs. This is a shift in thinking that tightens the screws at the right end, because it allows us to see how tracks weave themselves through design space.

This move, to a topographical perspective, renders clear and robust important insights into creativity that are otherwise absent. Take accessibility, the idea that local constraints in any neighborhood of design space place limits on possible future trajectories (Ayers, 1968). Recall my earlier reference to the impossibility of spontaneous wings for elephants. Some designs can simply not evolve because they are unworkable from the current position in genetic space. This is true even if the necessary mutations were to appear. As a particular organism evolves in its niche, by the steady climbing of gradualism, its possible course through genetic space is ever more constrained. With each moment of modest creativity in one direction, other directions are progressively eliminated.

The game of chess illustrates this nicely. At the start, the match is wide open and most moves are actually possible moves, permitting a near infinite number of paths the game could take. As play unwinds, however, in its own peculiar way, many otherwise permissible moves become inaccessible from the actual position of the figures on the board. This precludes, in turn, countless trajectories from being actualized that are entirely possible trajectories in chess. At some point, often toward the end of play, the configuration is so twisted that a player has but one move if she is to stay alive. This is called a forced move. It is not the best move; it is the only one left to make. All other options are instantly suicidal. An exhaustive, brute Darwinian search algorithm let loose on this design problem is sure to find that winning move in short order, irrespective of whether the first move is maximally lucky or maximally stupid, in which case it only takes a bit longer. Of course in the game of life these search algorithms work on a whole population of organisms, the equivalent of a large number of simultaneous chess games all played forward from exactly the same position. One version, though, is going to keep the lineage in play.

Examples abound in evolution of organisms passing through such highly contingent bottlenecks in design space. They are simply a function of the actual trajectory already taken and the local constraints of the design space topography. Eyes are the canonical example. They have evolved independently several times – as many as 30, according to some sources – because they represent such an elegant adaptation given, first, the properties of light on Earth and, second, the fact that your predator is presently evolving a similar sensory gadget. But in hindsight, forced moves look to us for all the world like precognition – the work of a Mindful Planner. For, how could an inadvertent process that is allegedly blind know exactly what to do in this instance? Given the odds, hitting on the ingenious solution – the only one possible to boost – seems so improbable, so out of the question, that it must be, um, miraculous. Hindsight, as they say, is 20–20.

Even if we have trouble fathoming how this could be, by framing the problem as we did, in terms of actuality and possibility, the error in thinking is vividly exposed. This ill-fated deliberation can only occur if we ignore all the other routes the algorithm also tried, and failed, to find the saving move. Seen from this angle, you don't need to stretch your imagination to see that the mere fact that we humans are an actuality has anything to do with intentional planning or inevitability. If we rewind the tape, even if we keep the exact same constraints, the likelihood of us showing up again is vanishingly small, vastly more so in fact than the likelihood of the exact same chess game reoccurring. This is because massively contingent situations limiting play to just a few forward moves are uncommon in the immensity of design space. At every turn, there is an array of good moves, even in a species' end game, and each can open up new paths leading to totally new regions of genetic space. There is an important lesson to be learned from this. As we shall see shortly, it is in large part the casual oversight of not counting in all the cul-de-sacs, coupled with the retrospective glorious coronation of the winning design, that seduces people into believing that the case is different for human creators; that they create top-down, with Intention or Intrinsic Intelligence. Always remember the mantra, we must take the Designer out of the design process and parse out its tasks among the hordes of demons in the brain, none of which is, or shelters, an angelical muse.

The magic wand theory

It is time for a sanity check. Before continuing with my efforts to shed light on the brain mechanisms of creativity, let us pause for a moment and consider what would constitute a different mechanism for human creativity. What sort of alternative theory would we need to refute the Darwinian project once and for all? If we wish to deny the bottom up direction of evolutionary algorithms outright, perhaps because we think that mechanical trial and error runs – however refined – is repugnant and beneath the dignity of the human mind, let alone the creative genius, we must come at it from on high. This, and only this, if true, would be the downfall of the Darwinism paradigm for human creativity. Let's take this idea for a test drive so we are crystal clear about what this view would actually commit us to.

By inverting the basic reasoning, we can approach the matter of how creative achievements come into existence from the opposite, top-down direction. You don't need to put on your mental running shoes to see that this direction catapults the mind into the lofty position of a miracle maker, a skyhook. Consider what it entails. For a start, it renders variation-selection explorations superfluous. Instead of generate-and-test thought trials, of any kind, this position dictates that we must be able – somehow – to hit the clever solution outright, in a single shot, with 100 percent accuracy. Although hardly ever drawn out like this, it isn't at all uncommon, in spite of its obvious consequences, to hear some version of this adamantly defended, even by scientists amply trained in empirical thinking. Putting emotion before reason, they go all out and flatly assert that the mind, during those fleeting glimpses into the Platonic world beyond, can transcend the machinery of the brain that does all the ordinary, day-to-day mental chores. If we wish to ride behind this flag, we'd be following intellectual giants of the first order. The mathematician Roger Penrose (1989), for instance, comes to mind. Creative insights, he says, are revealed to you. In a scientific arena, we are safe in dismissing this as airy-fairy nonsense.

We could, of course, always go for a softer version that doesn't give us this unsavory feeling of falling off the edge of our intellectual universe. One option would be directed mutation. Here we'd at least preserve the need for a variation-selection mechanism of some sort. Many find this idea instantly attractive; after all, the magic-wand theory does sound a bit fantastic and, besides, it cannot be right because otherwise thinking wouldn't be necessary to begin with. Directed mutation does have a more gratifying feel to it, and many people have been taken in. But it is nothing but protracted agony. The position quickly goes boom because it merely postpones the place at which we must smuggle in the gift from the Gods. As you will be aware by now, this isn't a good thing if you are interested in brain mechanisms. Directed by whom? The Mind? How? The answer is obvious once the question is put like this. The only way to keep the Cartesian ghost at bay is to nest homunculi into ever smaller homunculi until the process bottoms out at actual mechanisms. As long as the Designer is in the picture, we don't have a mechanism. All it does is bring us back to square one. Let Darwin's words be our guide again: there cannot be "a miraculous addition at any one stage of descent." Incidentally, this also makes the question of whodunnit – who does all the clever designing – fall expediently, and somewhat unceremoniously, by the wayside.

The trouble with closet dualism is so pervasive and possibilities for flummoxing so extensive that flushing out any tacit resistance to a Darwinian analysis of creativity is good policy. One particularly common last-ditch effort is to hide behind proximate explanations and hope for the best. It involves a bait-and-switch tactic that is difficult to spot, not the least because it is often employed by psychologists and neuroscientists who have no qualms with Darwinism in general. To understand it, we must first distinguish between two types of explanations. So-called proximate explanations are those that tell us *how* something works; they refer to the immediate causes of behavior. Task set and task-set inertia, for instance, two cognitive mechanisms that we encountered in Chapter 3 are examples of proximate explanations. Ultimate explanations, on the other hand, are those that answer *why* a behavior exist in the first place; they are evolutionary explanations that tell us about ultimate function and purpose.

We can now appreciate the bait-and-switch tactic that parades proximate mechanisms of creativity as ultimate causes, preparatory to proclaiming the Darwinian approach as failed. The argument has the following structure: (1) start by explicitly renouncing any vulnerability to miraculous intrusions from above – just so everyone knows that you are allied with the armies of progress; (2) put forth a clever-sounding explanation for creative thinking at the level of psychological processes – creators have expert knowledge and don't do trial-and-error is a popular one; (3) convince yourself – and here comes the sleight of hand – that this actually works as an ultimate, rather than a proximate, cause; and (4) retreat to the safety of your ontological comfort zone until the pesky challenge from Darwinists subsides. In the event it persists, go over to (5) intellectual stonewalling by simply switching to a new proximate explanation – intention or foresight, maybe. The goal is to present a moving target, to yourself and others, that keeps the Darwinian grenade from detonating inside the well-protected pocket of ignorance in which you cherish your sense of creative agency.

When you hear the siren song of the Cartesian ghost in the form of a proximate explanation, and think that you have explained creativity in the brain, remember the two-step exercise from Chapter 3. First, remind yourself that the Cartesian theater ends in a deadly infinite regress, a fact that should help you in initiating the second step: going back to work. Look at the proximate explanation – expertise, intentions, or foresight – and ask yourself how you can break it down further. What, exactly, are the neural processes that make up intentions? How does the brain compute foresight? What cognitive mechanisms underlie expert knowledge, and how do they facilitate creative thinking? A proximate (neural) explanation that ignores ultimate (evolutionary) causation solves nothing. You can run but you can't hide, as they say. Still, many people hold on like grim death to any proximate explanation for creativity that they think could be pitted against the variation-selection method in the misguided hope of alleviating the bad case of jitters Darwinism induces in them. It's a teddy bear for grownups, nothing else.

Recall that an adaptive fit gives, in hindsight, the appearance of being designed for a purpose, especially when the situation called for a forced move. There must have been a guiding hand, somewhere, somehow. For, what are the odds, in the vast ocean of possibilities, that a blind process stumbles on the clever solution by chance alone? So absurd is this suggestion to some people that they dismiss it as patently wrong. Recall also that this intuition is pumped, in part, by the notorious failure to see actuality as a subset of potentiality. Coupled with our tendency to venerate the actual, this is a potent cocktail of self-deceit. Daniel Kahneman (2011) has coined the rather unwieldy acronym WYSIATI – what you see is all there is – for the fact that we don't keep track of alternatives, or even that there are alternatives, and solely rely on the evidence in front of us. Kahneman has shown that WYSIATI is the source of several cognitive biases underlying everyday decision-making. This is also true for creativity. Only if we give ourselves to flights of editorializing out the errors, almosts, half-rights, or anything else potentially ego-deflating, can we cling on to the false impression that creative thinking is a top-down process. And it is here that we see the full power of casting creativity into a mathematical space that includes both, all the actualized designs and all the potential ones.

Throwing sand into this illusion generator is made the more difficult by the fact that our crashes, false starts, and near triumphs are not, for the most part, made in public. They even escape our own efforts of introspective detection, as many transpire in the shadowy basement of the unconscious mind. This leads to the perverse situation that we join the rest of the world in believing that our own creative ideas come from a single stroke of the magic wand. With all but the start and end points of the problem-solving process inaccessible to conscious reflection, we come to feel that there is no way that all the other potential solution, which seem now so abortive in retrospect, could have possibly occurred to us. How much more difficult, then, to explode this fairy tale of the single-shot design. And this brings us rather neatly to the next topic.

Bring out yer dead

The betraying sign of a variation-selection mechanism at work is waste. We can nudge a bit closer to seeing the Darwinian drivetrain behind human creativity by looking at the forensic evidence it would have to leave behind in the career paths of creative people; things like splendid failures, messy zigzagging, serendipitous finds, descent with modification, dumb luck, useless contraptions, false theories, unsold paintings, or awful compositions. In doing this, we keep in mind that it isn't strictly necessary that the fundamental nature of a mechanism manifest at one level of a phenomenon (neural processes) is discernable at a higher level (behavior of individuals), but sober evidence to that effect helps greatly with conceiving of the possibility. And that is all we need at this point to break the back of the magic-wand intuition. The question we can ask, then, is this. Do the biographies of creators, their actual trajectories through design space, betray the signature of generate-and-test trials?

Historiometric studies, the somewhat lifeless name for this field of psychology, have come to exactly this conclusion (Simonton, 1999). As it happens, the waste is everywhere. By examining the historical records of hundreds of individual creators in the arts and sciences, psychologists have been able to demonstrate something that is, given our inflated view of the creative genius, quite counterintuitive at first encounter. For any creator, the relationship between the number of total works and the number of works society has deemed over time as first rate – regardless of how greatness is operationally defined – for any time period during a creator's career, is constant. Huh? Let me explain. The equal-odds rule, as it is known, shows that the period in which a creator's most major works appear is also the period that sees the most flops, and thus the highest, overall quantity (Simonton, 1997). Take, by way of example, Thomas Edison, one of those rare creators honest – or obsessed – enough to document all his failures in minute detail. The study of his original notebooks shows that Edison employed a small number of basic, commonsense problem-solving strategies to increase the likelihood of striking inventive gold. "Simultaneously pursue multiple lines of investigation" was one of them. "Repeat components in multiple inventions" was another. The engineer Nikola Tesla mockingly called Edison's method the empirical dragnet. "I was a sorry witness to such doings" he wrote. "A little theory . . . would have saved him ninety percent of his labor." But Edison's grind-it-out algorithm did yield a total of 1,093 patents, still the record. It is apparent to anyone who cares to look at the issue, the creative process, even for geniuses, is a hit-and-miss affair in which the odds of success remain stable over a creator's lifetime. If you still have trouble letting go off the top-down direction, think of it this way: Who would regularly, *with intention and purpose*, pump out duds and fizzers? But all creative geniuses have.

Another way of expressing the equal-odds rule is to say that quality is a probabilistic function of quantity. This leads to the unexpected consequence that quantity is a predictor of quality – which it is, in fact, the best besides. If this sounds not quite right to you, you can take some comfort in knowing that most people I tell this to are skeptical. Indeed, it is revealing that one rarely finds students, or colleagues, who don't respond to this by denouncing it on the spot as rank nonsense. I once made the tactical – and professional – mistake at a faculty meeting in my university to propose, judiciously citing the equal-odds rule, to use quantity as a criterion for promotion and tenure decisions *when other evidence is sparse*. The exact wording of my colleagues' response cannot, for aesthetic reasons, be reported here nor was it deemed suitable, apparently, to be recorded in the meeting's minutes.

The specifics of the equal-odds rule has recently been called into question because it focuses on finished products rather than individual thought trials but the generalization remains valid. The psychologist Dean Simonton (2003) has found it to hold for longitudinal as well as for cross-sectional data, although recent work has shown that this holds better for the sciences than the arts (Simonton, 2011). A cursory look at the history of technological change confirms this easily. Inventors, or their contemporaries, regularly fail to recognize the applications of their discoveries, never mind foresee how their devices would be put to use by the next generation of inventors. Who, for instance, could have guessed at the time that Alessandro Volta's spark gun, which he invented to detect the bad air thought to cause malaria, would end up as a carburetor in a car engine (Burke, 1995)? The history of technology is full of twists and turns, a rollercoaster ride that is more like the bouncing of a pinball rather than a straight line. It is easy to overlook the fact that for every artist, scientist, and engineer the road to success is littered with theoretical and empirical blunders.

Scientists discover; artists create. No one disputes, of course, that scientists are not creative but whatever it is that they discover was, in a very real sense, already there to be discovered, wasn't it? One just had to look at it in the right way. In this view, scientists are mere path-finders of the truth. Artists, on the other hand, are path-creators, aren't they? They conjure up fantasy worlds from nothing but their imagination that would not exist were it not for their creative inspiration.

This intuition, too, is an accounting error and the design space perspective makes clear why. Here the misreading of the record doesn't stem from editing out the dead but from the failure to see the interplay between actuality and potentiality. In science, a creative product has to be functional. With such an uncompromising fitness criterion for upward moves, creators more quickly zero in on certain privileged regions in design space. These favored places exist because the laws of the universe generate a highly structured topography that contains more bottlenecks and forced moves. These peaks of the landscape act like beacons of light – obvious solutions to common problems – that can be reached from a number of different starting points. If a design is good enough to evolve once, the same design, given the fitness function doesn't change, is good enough to evolve another time. The evolution of eyes is the example I used earlier. Sometimes there is just one way things can be done. We'd expect, for instance, that any intelligent beings, anywhere in the universe, to sooner or later hit upon Euclidian geometry, gravity, the periodic table, or, for that matter, Darwinian natural selection.

This overstates the case a bit. Scientists, for their part, care deeply about the actual trajectories taken. And for good reasons. Newtonian physics is a case in point. It explained the visible universe so completely, so comprehensively, that one might be forgiven for thinking that its discovery was inevitable, just a matter of time. If Newton hadn't done it surely someone else would have. This argument suffers from two problems. First, it assumes that scientific knowledge is right, in an absolute sense, rather than what it really is, an approximation of the truth. Seen from a topographical perspective, the view supposes that there must be a single summit in design space and that this summit has one, and only one, route up it. Einstein's theory of relativity, which superseded the Newtonian paradigm, certainly undermines the specifics of that claim. At a minimum, keep in mind that our knowledge of the world depends utterly on the kind of quirky consciousness we happen to have, as it is "in there" that we understand the universe. Other beings, with different kinds of on-board computers, would surely *create* different representations of reality.

Second, if someone other than Newton had made the final few clever moves up to this particular plateau in design space, the details of the theory would have certainly been different, even if ever so slightly. However, tiny fluctuations like that are known to have big effects on future trajectories. Perhaps the demise of classical mechanics would have happened sooner – or later – than it did had we a slightly modified version of the theory. This we will never know. Ironically, this is often said about the theory of relativity. It's such an eccentric piece of reductionism that physics, without the historical accident of Einstein, might have run straight past this particular beacon of light in favor of some other, further, but nevertheless temporary, paradigm. And, who knows, perhaps that place might have provided better accessibility to the holy grail of physics, a final theory of everything. This, too, we will never know.

Contrast this with the far less rugged artistic region of design space. Here the fitness function has other sources: our sense of aesthetics, harmony, symmetry, or beauty. Thanks largely to cultural differences, this adaptive landscape is more amorphous, but it does contain forced moves, or at least massively contingent bottlenecks, leading to a few beacons of light. Wouldn't you think, for instance, that Beethoven's fifth was just a matter of time? Still, it would strike us as odd to hear an artist say: "I discovered this painting." But the painting was contained in the larger space of all possible paintings and thus, in some sense, already there, waiting to be discovered. Pablo Picasso apparently knew this when he said: "Je ne cherche pas; je trouve." Lewis Carroll, too, had a suspicion about this when he wrote in *Sylvie and Bruno* that in the near future, writers will no longer ask, "What book shall I write?" but, "Which book shall I write?" In the same vein, wouldn't it also strike us as odd to hear someone say: "Newton created gravity?"

What makes our intuition misfire by such a wide margin? Seeing the world through our own warped force field is standard operating procedure of course. Psychologists have long accepted the sobering fact that our mind comes with a whole stack of cognitive biases preloaded and pre-installed. The one doing most of the dopamine squirting here is the failure to do proper bookkeeping of the pluses and minuses. But without it, we cannot appreciate Exhibit A of the Darwinian argument: the waste that didn't make it through the selection process.

Four upgrades to biological creativity

We now have a clear way forward. Once we accept the variation-selection nature of creative thinking, and turn our back on the blind alleys offering no hope of progress or improvement, we can ask more constructive and competent questions about the brain mechanism of creativity. Our starting point in this quest is the common denominator of cultural evolution we distilled in the last chapter, namely that culture is a variational system that involves some coupling. This raises the following, most obvious questions. How do brains manage to accomplish this partial coupling of variation to selection? At the conceptual level, the question has a deceptively simple answer: Brains produce representations of the world that can inform – give direction to – the search process. That is to say, brains produce mental models that simulate the consequences of generate-and-test trials that are then fed into the variation process. But this doesn't even begin to tell the story of what happens in neural networks during creative thinking. How does this work exactly? Which parameters of the infospheric evolutionary algorithm are changed, and to which values? And why does this give us the feeling of foresight and purpose when we think creatively?

In the remainder of this book, I will provide some surprising answers to these pressing questions. We start this journey by getting clear about what the upgrades to the evolutionary algorithms running on brains are exactly. What properties do cultural evolutionary algorithms possess that are not part of their biological cousins? We can simplify this task by restricting ourselves to four features that readily distinguish evolutionary algorithms occurring in brains from those transforming nature, as it is these features that are most in need of a neural explanation. They are: (1) heuristics, which provide a causal arrow from selection back to variation conferring degrees of sightedness; (2) the establishment of fitness criteria for selection processes that are necessarily hypothetical; (3) cognitive scaffolding that enable multistep thought trials; and

(4) the experiences of foresight and intention that accompany human creativity.

To begin with heuristic algorithms, we must first clear the ground of an odd perception of what is and what isn't an algorithm. Our thinking is pulled out of shape by the tradition that algorithms supposedly differ from other search methods in fundamental ways. Standard textbooks typically divide problem-solving strategies into three kinds. The first is trial and error, which the book tells us is only really useful for problems that have a limited number of solutions. The second strategy is an algorithm, which is a method that produces a solution through the strict application of a set of rules. Algorithms are foolproof if correctly executed, but they are also inefficient and require time. Suppose you lose your keys somewhere in your house. If you look for them using the algorithmic method, you would search the house square by square. Of course, this is guaranteed to work but you may also go mad before finding them. The obvious, and misleading, conclusion the student should draw from this example is that humans don't use algorithms in daily life, because we have to solve our problems in real time. But luckily for us, there is a third method, heuristics. This is a rule-of-thumb, a sort of quick and dirty way of doing things, in which you first look for the keys in the most likely places. It removes from the search a lot of seemingly foolish choices, leading to a speedier end of the search.

I am piling on the drama a bit but it goes without saying, I hope, that all three methods are instances of algorithms. The trouble with this is that this seemingly harmless way of illustrating the issue invites the mistaken view that we are dealing with fundamentally different categories. This ceases to be a minor matter of teaching strategy when we read in the same textbook that computers, being the mindless things they are, use mere algorithms to arrive at solutions while we are blessed with the gift of clever – meaning, heuristic – thinking. Unless you subscribe to the belief that your mind is made from small clumps of heavenly goo, or turns over on quantum fuel, you must concede that your brain runs algorithms on its neural infrastructure.

Being blind, evolutionary algorithms in nature explore problem spaces by running brute, uneducated searches. This kind of exploration contains no speculation as to where in design space an up ramp may be located. The algorithm relies on the brute power and time, not clever short cuts, which renders it neither particularly fast nor efficient. But the XXL size of the real world, to say nothing of the sheer unlimited supply of test subjects, has kept biological evolution from grinding to a halt.

Not that the algorithm did run out of time in umpteen cases, relegating the respective species back to the mere potential side of Biomorph Land.

The human mind is such a heavy lifter in design space, zooming ahead in leaps and bounds, because we don't approach unknown solution spaces the way biological evolution does, with brute, search algorithms. Instead of treating all directions as equally likely to harbor improvements, heuristic algorithms contain hypotheses that focus the search. Actually, a more accurate way of saying this is that heuristics ignore parts of the solution space and, in that way, limit the search from the outset (Gigerenzer & Gaissmaier, 2011). With the long shots out of the picture, the algorithm can then comb through a more bite size portion of possibilities. Smelling the chance to insert a Cartesian Designer with Special Powers here, how did we come by this neat little trick, you might feel compelled to ask? Who makes these guesses if it isn't me? Apart from the fact that the mindless chess program on your computer does *that*, too, you will hopefully recognize this as a hospital pass, a reference to rugby in which a player has no choice but to catch a pass from a teammate despite the inevitable and instant hard tackle of a fast-approaching opponent. The answer to this ill-conceived line of inquiry is simple. The capacity to constrain the search *a priori* arises from two sources. First, brains have extracted good design principles – folk physics, folk psychology, linear logic, etc. – from the common stock of design elements and feed them into search functions exploring the infosphere (Dennett, 1995). This causes a coupling effect; the occurrence of novel ideas (variation) is informed in advance by the kind of problem (selection). That is to say, adaptive variants crop up more readily *because* the environment (the nature of the question) helps guide the novelty-generating process. Since these common solutions to common problems yield, effectively, a bit of sightedness with respect to adaptation, they have accumulated over time, becoming integrated into the neural hardware as a result.

Once again, Dennett (1995) helps us to cast this into more vivid language. Heuristic algorithms are not skyhooks but simply better cranes. He invites us to think of the mind is a collection of cranes and, over time, some of these cranes have specialized in the tasks of making more powerful cranes. Again, this doesn't change the nature of the creative process itself. Once we identify a favorable region, the journey of discovery proceed the same. We generate variants, test them for beauty, functionality, or some other fitness criterion, and enter those that pass muster into the next round of thought trials. At each waystation, the search is reset and the expedition continues its course.

As outstanding as this array of hardwired pruning techniques is, it doesn't cover the ground we need. What really puts the quality crank in the brain into high gear isn't heuristics from hardwired folk physics or folk psychology. We share these adaptations with many of our animal relatives and, at any rate, they cannot account for creative feats that are counterintuitive – the theory of relativity, for instance. The capacity to constrain the search *a priori* has a second source. It arises from the brain's prediction machinery, and it is this mechanism that really boosts the algorithm's sightedness by orders of magnitude. But we are getting ahead of ourselves, as this is the subject of the next chapter.

For the mind's second upgrade, we first need to describe a complication inherent in dry runs. Evolutionary algorithms require a fitness function. Darwin's phrase "evolution by natural selection" denotes the fact that selection occurs in the real world, on individuals made flesh. The differential rates of survival are determined by causal factors present in the environment. But in thought trials, concrete gives way to hypothetical. Here the selection process depends on merit criteria that must also be modeled. But on what basis is this done? Since the very essence of creative thinking is to go into uncharted territory, how do we establish what *would be* adaptive in that unknown topography? This, too, must necessarily be driven via predictive processes (Dietrich & Haider, 2015).

A third adaptation enhancing organic evolution is scaffolding, the temporarily support of design features that could otherwise not be part of the final design. This upgrade brings about cognitive coupling in a different way. Nature doesn't do future positive effects. It is a shortsighted selection by hindsight. Every single variation-selection cycle in a species' trajectory is actualized and must, in its own right, be a viable form. If a mutation doesn't confer a fitness advantage right there right then, it cannot spread through a population. The algorithm, in other words, cannot jump over impossible intermediates, making the basic move in Darwinian evolution one of generate-and-field-test. This instant pay-off requirement means that a design needing a temporary scaffold on the way to a superior one is unreachable by this kind of evolutionary algorithm. This is true even if suitable mutations were to arise. Not being able to look down the road, not even a single step, nature punishes arriving at the wrong time in the wrong place.

Not so for brains. They can short-circuit instantiation and breed multiple generations of ideas in a hypothetical manner. This produces an effect so striking that it has left many proponents of cultural Darwinism scratching their heads for an explanation. Clearly, since some designs require elements that cannot be realized without a temporary scaffold, a mechanism that requires fitness at every iteration, such as biological evolution, can also not build them. But thanks to the capacity for representation, brains can bypass transitional stages that are sterile and evolve a thing of beauty even if all the intervening steps are ugly contraptions. This makes the basic move in cultural evolution one of generate-and-hypothesis-test, enabling a plethora of higher-order, discontinuous design solutions. In the same way multiple-cell organisms, once evolved, made a whole new array of designs possible that cannot be made from single-cell organisms, the scaffolding adaptation has opened up regions of design space that are off limits to biological evolution. While some animals might come equipped with the first upgrade of heuristics, cognitive scaffolding is likely to be present in our brains only. But like heuristic guesses, it must have limits. The ability to see beyond the immediate cannot be absolute otherwise we'd be dealing with clairvoyance.

We can draw out this difference in another way. It has been said that evolution is a tinkerer. It must build using only those components that are already there. Thus, it can only modify existing designs. It cannot make a completely new one. For this reason, evolved designs are rarely best possible designs, since they must keep all the twist and turns of earlier design work. Quite often a device that evolved to do a specific job gets co-opted, with all its quirks, to serve a quite different function at a later stage. But we, this argument continues, can create from scratch, using components as they fit. Refracted through the light of the mind's scaffolding upgrade, however, our creativity is tinkering, too. Higher-order tinkering perhaps, but tinkering nonetheless. The illusion of a discontinuity is created by a scaffold removing the optimizing process a few steps from its direct predecessor. Like fireworks falling from the sky, this gives the appearance of creative inspiration coming from on high, lest we forget that it was originally shot up there from down below.

In introducing this scaffolding adaptation, we must acknowledge and then set aside one theoretical possibility that has given life to those who argue that human creativity is, like biological creativity, fundamentally blind. Given scaffolding, it's entirely possible that the cognitive coupling manifest at the conscious level of creativity is an artifact caused by cumulativity (Simonton, 2011). Several iterations of thought trials could give the appearance of directedness in ideational thinking when it could be instead the *cumulative* outcome of a series of blind variation-selection trials at the unconscious level. To be exact, the central point has been that there only needs to be blindness somewhere in the hierarchy. This idea of multiple selection levels within the brain has already received some air time in the field. So has the suggestion that it may mask blind variation at the level at which we experience our thoughts. Remember in this context that neuroscientists are completely in the dark about the brain's copying mechanism. For this reason, there is little support for this idea. For the same reasons, there is also little evidence against it. At any rate, it's a hail-mary argument that is unnecessary. Brains, as we have been and will be seeing, have overcome blindness without resorting to crystal balls.

Finally, for the mind's fourth trick, we consider the experience of foresight and intention accompanying creative behavior. I hardly need to point out that the creative process in the biosphere isn't teleological. It serves no end, and its designs are neither premeditated nor deliberately initiated in response to a perceived need. That would be evolutionary precognition. Human creators, by contrast, act on purpose; they have an objective in mind and thus create with intent. Although one might expect such improvements in a method that inexorably bootstraps, the argument from foresight is typically framed in psychology in terms of expert knowledge and presented as if at odds with evolutionary models of creativity (Dasgupta, 2004; Russ, 1999; Schooler & Dougal, 1999; Sternberg, 1998, 1999). In fact, the usually calm waters of academe notwithstanding, people have gone nuts over this point, with some people claiming it to be clear evidence for runaway Darwinism while others charge them with not seeing the forest for the trees. Because the feeling of foresight and intention is the most commonly used objection raised by Darwin-dreaders to argue for a categorical difference between human creativity and the creativity in the biosphere or artificial intelligence, it gets its own section, the next.

The foresight fallacy

If psychologists and neuroscientists are asked to put their finger on the defining difference between the creativity of Mother Nature and ours, nine out of ten would probably use the words foresight or intentions, wouldn't they? Others might prefer terms such as planning, purpose, premeditated, intentional, or mindful, but they all target essentially the same idea. What is often imparted in this formulation – sometime more, sometimes less – is that this is a categorical distinction. We have it, organic evolution doesn't. It certainly *seems* to be a sensible position. Isn't it obvious that theoretical physicists and jazz musicians don't buzz about their respective domains like balloons rapidly losing air? Of course not. They navigate it in a deliberate, insightful and – in case you need another descriptor – goal-directed way. Above all else, they comprehend the meaning of their (cultural) creations. We might be forgiven for thinking that there is a difference here – because there actually is – it just isn't a categorical one, not in a teleological sense anyway. Once again, then, your point of view on this matter greatly depends on whether you are a lumper or a splitter.

Irrespective of your preference on this, the belief in a fundamental line separating foresightful creativity from mere tinkering needs to be defused. Recall the earlier (and loud) noise I made about masquerading proximate (neural) mechanisms as ultimate (evolutionary) ones. Closet dualists often use the foresight argument as a treatment against the existential angst that comes from a theory of (cultural) creation without a Designer. If we give into this hunch, we simply exchange the skyhook fallacy for the foresight fallacy.

The argument from foresight careens through three stages. The first is straightforward. In biological evolution, there is no foresight in producing variants and no foresight in selecting them. The algorithm is accidental and blind with no general bias in the direction of good. So far so good, although we will have to quibble with this point as well. Stage two is no less obvious to the casual observer. It celebrates the human mind as an intentional agent by establishing that variation in cultural evolution is structured in a non-random manner, and so emerges, in the mind, in anticipation of subsequent selection. As evident by the occurrence of disproportionally fewer maladaptive variants, cultural innovation is biased toward systematic design improvements. From this setup, stage three is a no-brainer. Rising to a victorious crescendo, it declares the Darwinian campaign in culture a reductionist fantasy.

There are several ways we could go from here. One is to press on and demand specifics. As long as we don't fall for the bait-and-switch tactic, the position will explode all by itself because it runs, full bore, into some version of the magic-wand theory. Let us try to take a more scholarly route instead. The first cracks in this line of defense appear quickly as soon as we place the capacity to plan ahead along a continuum of sightedness, with total blindness on one extreme and prophetical vision on the other. We then nibble away at it from both sides. One broadside we aim at inflating the blindness of nature, a move we flank with equal gusto by deflating the almighty Designer.

At the low end of the continuum, we find the phenomenon of adaptive mutation. Recall from the last chapter that mutation, although random (blind) with respect to selection, isn't random with respect to rate. Strong selection pressure can increase the mutation rate, making the appearance of good mutations more likely. Such a faster turnover rate has an obvious adaptive advantage in times of sudden environmental changes. Granted, adaptive mutation isn't foresight *per se* but it does demonstrate a clear anticipation of need. From this very modest bit of proactive action, we can climb up the continuum to more interesting examples of nature's capacity to look ahead. Take for instance an animal's ability to actively restructure its environments. The technical term for this is niche construction and nothing epitomizes this more than the beaver dam (Laland & Sterelny, 2006). A few people wouldn't agree with the notion that the beaver constructs its dam for a purpose, and with at least a bit of foresight of what the dam will do for its survival. And what are we to make of all the other instances of prospective and goal-directed behavior in the animal kingdom? The "proto-culture" of chimpanzees, for instance. Doesn't some of that behavior strike you as intentional and purposeful? Evidently, foresight exists in biological evolution (Mesoudi, 2008). As for the other end, deflating the Designer, we have been on that project ever since we started, and the thread will continue to weave itself through the remaining chapters. In sum, although in some sense the brain is a foresightful machine – for a few steps, at least – but when it comes to ulterior purpose, it is still blind. The brain doesn't have a magic wand.

Once we blur the line like this, the simplistic dichotomy that fuels the foresight fallacy becomes manifestly indefensible. What's more, forcibly sorting all instances into this kind of all-or-nothing thinking – Hoover dam yes, beaver dam no – mischaracterizes the true avenues of causation. One could still hold out for a big jump from beavers to humans but this is a far cry from the original position of a categorical difference between organic and cultural evolution.

We turn next to the newly emerging prediction paradigm of neuroscience. One of the most exciting yet completely unmapped aspects of this framework is the prospect of a brain mechanism that drives these four upgrades to the mind's evolutionary algorithms and hence our understanding of the neural basis of creativity.

Recommended readings

Borges, J. L. (1956). La biblioteca de Babel. In *Ficciones*. Buenos Aires: Emece Editors.

Burke, J. (1995). *Connections*. New York: Little Brown & Co.

Dasgupta, S. (2004). Is creativity a Darwinian process? *Creativity Research Journal*, *16*, 403–413.

Dawkins, R. (1986). *The blind watchmaker.* New York: W.W. Norton.

Dennett, D. C. (1995). *Darwin's' dangerous idea.* New York: Simon & Schuster.

Dietrich , A., & Haider, H. (2015). Human creativity, evolutionary algorithms, and predictive representations: The mechanics of thought trials. *Psychonomic Bulletin & Review, 22,* 1011–1026.

Ingold, T. (2007). The trouble with "evolutionary biology." *Anthropology Today, 23,* 3–7.

Kronfeldner, M. E. (2010). Darwinian "blind" hypothesis formation revisited. *Synthese, 175,* 193–218.

Mesoudi, A. (2008). Foresight in cultural evolution. *Biological Philosophy, 23,* 243–255.

Penrose, R. (1989). *The emperor's new mind.* Oxford: Oxford University Press.

Simonton, D. K. (1997). Creative productivity: A predictive and explanatory model of career trajectories and landmarks. *Psychological Review, 104,* 66–89.

Sternberg, R. J. (1999). Darwinian creativity as a conventional religious faith. *Psychological Inquiry, 10,* 357–359.

6
Prophets of Design Space

The last half century has seen a veritable explosion of knowledge about the mind and how it works. With a pace that would leave anyone gasping for air, the mind sciences have developed solid theoretical foundations for our mental faculties and mountains of data to bear them out. Perhaps the single most glaring exception in this success story is creative thinking. It is hard to think of a mental phenomenon so central to the human condition that we understand so little. Even for consciousness, arguably a bigger problem, we have solid hypotheses – global working space, competing neuronal coalitions, higher-order thought, among rather many else – that have so far survived Popperian falsification. Not so for creativity. At the present moment, we have not a single cognitive or neural mechanism we can rely on for sure to explain the extraordinary creative achievements of a Galileo, Shakespeare, or Steve Jobs.

How did the neuroscience of creativity become the black sheep of psychology? We have seen that there is nothing to be gained from heating the brain with a no-good creativity test, picking up the buzzing electricity with crude neuroimaging technology, and proclaiming that creativity is located in some gyrus hidden in the folds of the cortex. Having foregone the hunt for real mechanisms for this kind of brainless neuroscience, the quest for creativity has been lost in the data compost of ill-conceived neuroimaging phrenology.

We have now landed in a place where we can escape this Kafka-loop. At least we are clear what needs to be explained first and foremost. So long as it is agreed that the common denominator of cultural evolution – a variational system with a small coupling upgrade – is the bedrock on which to anchor human creativity (and surely this much is unobjectionable), and we avoid getting suckered into the walled enclave of Cartesian materialism, we can start making theoretical hay. What a basic explanation calls for, then, are brain mechanisms that can account for the unique properties of cultural evolutionary algorithms that distinguish them from those in nature. We identified four such adaptations in the last chapter: (1) heuristics that provide degrees of sightedness, (2) fitness criteria for selection processes that must work in imaginary landscapes, (3) cognitive scaffolding that can pass over unviable forms, and (4) the much hyped feelings of foresight and intention that accompany human creativity. Once we have a handle on these pressing challenges, then we can go further and worry about the fiddly bits of the evolutionary algorithm that one might lump together under the heading of individual differences: a creator's expertise, personality characteristics, or motivation.

This chapter is about these four basic upgrades. Actually, it is about how brains implement them. This line of inquiry brings us in contact with one of the most exciting new developments in all of neuroscience, the brain's prediction imperative. Theorists have been converging from quite different quarters on the idea of prediction as a central purpose of brain function. The primacy of prediction in organizing neural computation revealingly synthesizes a host of new insights into the way brains carry out variation-selection thought trials. Our ability to run offline simulations of expected future environments and action outcomes informs this process both, at the level of variation and at the level of selection. But what prospective processing does above all else, is to give us a way to account for the seemingly paradoxical fact of how a process like biological evolution that is blind, clueless, and reactive can evolve a machine – the human brain – with processes that are (a tad bit) foresightful, purposeful, and proactive.

For the challenging task that lies ahead, it is paramount that we get a measure of the full force this new perspective holds for us. To cover that ground, I first take a few pages to describe the notion of a proactive brain by highlighting key cognitive domains that have recognized the central importance of prediction. My goal in this part is to extract the underlying computational principles of how neural emulators in the brain's motor system find solutions on a problem space. I then bring this to bear on creative thinking by applying the prediction framework to evolutionary algorithms. To anticipate the main conclusion, we'll see how internal representations of the emulated future provide a perfectly good account of the mind's four adaptations that make human creativity such a powerful force on this planet.

The prediction machine

An emerging organizing theme in neuroscience is that the brain has evolved, fundamentally, to make predictions (Bar, 2007; Grush, 2004). The claim here is not that the business of anticipating events is one of the brain's important chores, it is *the* main reason for having (big) brains in the first place. It's a perspective that seems counterintuitive at first, but you will warm up to it as soon as you see how it handles otherwise puzzling facts. The core idea is as follows. We can interact with the world in an infinite number of ways. Such complexity would quickly overwhelm us. So for behavior to be purposeful and timely in such a high-dimensional environment, the set of possible choices must be pruned. We accomplish this by continuously, automatically and, importantly, unconsciously generating expectations that meaningfully inform – constrain – perception and action at every moment in life (Llinás, 2009). Even when we daydream and don't engage in a specific activity the brain doesn't idle but actively produces predictions that anticipate future events.

That predictive computation is not an optional add-on comes into clear focus when we look at the timescales involved between sensory inputs and motor outputs (Wolpert et al., 1995). It is essential to account for sensorimotor timescales because the degrees of freedom in a dynamic integration of sensory and motor states is enormous, making it impossible for a plan of action to specify all possibilities *a priori*. To understand this, let me first describe the problem that needs to be solved by prediction. A large amount of neural tissue is devoted to the planning, programming, and execution of movement. There are two key concepts that are most central for the anatomical organization of the motor system. First, the motor system consists of a number of distributed regions, each making a unique contribution to skilled action. Second, the motor system is organized in a functional hierarchy with multiple levels of control. This is a highly efficient arrangement as higher-order structures need not be concerned with the details of the execution but delegate such tasks to lower-level components of the system. The whole motor system requires an appreciable amount of time to formulate a motor plan and send motor commands down to muscles. Sensory systems, for their part, take an equal amount of time to analyze perceptual input. If the interaction between the two is solely based on *actual* motor execution and *actual* sensory feedback, with one having to await the outcome of the other before initiating a response, the time delays would be huge. Neuroscientists know that a sensorimotor cycle that relies only on such direct engagement, and is limited to real-time neural processing, simply cannot keep pace with the rate of change between the actor and the environments. If this were so, our interactions with the world would happen much more slowly than they do.

The motor system solves this timing problem by relying on emulators. As soon as emulation is involved in the sensorimotor arc, the processing speed can increase beyond reality-based action and perception. This entails that the brain constructs, in addition to simply engaging with the body and the world, internal models that simulate the body and the world. This layer of coding in the brain can anticipate the sensory consequences of actions – so-called forward models – and invoke control processes that guide movement based on goal states, which are known as inverse models. It can also speed up perceptual processes by reducing the overall information load. This is possible because internal models of the world save us from having to decode all sensory information *de novo* every time. It streamlines perception to the much simpler computational task of resolving differences between the predicted and sensed environment (Wolpert et al., 2003).

The capacity to create expectations of the future is so central to our quest for a creativity mechanism that we must examine the role played by prospection in a few non-motor domains. A little sampler consisting of learning, memory, and attention will do the trick for us. For those interested in more, there is a broad literature on mental phenomena as diverse as observation, imitation, language, social interactions, and emotion.

The first field of psychology to recognize prediction as an essential driver of behavior was learning. Take classical conditioning. What determines conditioning in a standard Pavlovian paradigm is the discrepancy between the actual occurrence and the predicted occurrence of a reward. This difference of what we are expecting to get and what we are actually getting is dubbed the reward-prediction error. From this perspective, learning depends on the predictability of the reward or, to say it another way, the degree of unpredictability (surprise) governs the rate at which we learn. If this reward-prediction error is positive (we get more than we expected), learning occurs. If the error is negative (we get less than we expected), extinction takes place. It follows from this, somewhat surprisingly, that we don't learn anything at all if the reward-prediction error falls to zero, even if we are repeatedly confronted with the two paired stimuli. Without surprise, there is no change in behavior. This applies also to operant conditioning, except that there the difference signal is between expected and actual reinforcement. This places prediction at the heart of associative learning because it stresses the fact that learning occurs as a response to prediction errors. We could define learning, then, as a process aimed at updating emulation errors and optimizing prediction.

Memory, too, is for prediction. We think of memory as being about the past and prediction about the future. The new thinking turns this on its head. Contrary to what you might think is just plain old common sense, the point of memory is not to remember what was before but to be better at predicting what happens next. In other words, we form memories of the events in our lives to have information available with which to simulate the future (Clark, 2013; Fisher, 2006). Now this begins to sound disturbingly like the sort of talk that would make you edge away if told to you by a stranger on a park bench. But think about it in terms of adaptation. What else would memory be for? What good accrues to you by reminiscing about the past? Seen from this angle, memory is an epistemic device for simulation. What's more, psychologists have long known that memory is reconstructive and associative in nature, which makes it essentially the same process as imagination. It's a database that can be used to reconstruct the past. But, again, that's not its function; its function is to shuffle the information you possess so as to imagine the future. Memory, in short, serves to enable prediction based on prior experience.

This also applies to attention. We can all attest to the fact that we attend only to what we expect to see or hear, and psychologists have confirmed this in many carefully controlled experiments. Perception, it turns out, is not the result of a straightforward, bottom-up analysis of the world that takes in all of our surroundings in glorious detail. Rather, we select and chose what we perceive. Given the sheer amount of sensory information we are bombarded with, there is no other option. In consequence, visual perception is strongly influenced by top-down processing that contains – as you'd expect by now – predictions. Recall the blindspot exercise from your school-days. There is a place on the retina where the optic nerve leaves the eye to relay signals into the brain. No photoreceptors exist at that location. Why don't we experience blindspots in the corresponding visual scene? The answer lies with prediction. We construct internal models that temporarily label, rather than fully interpret, the outside world.

Although this new paradigm in neuroscience takes some getting used to, it is here to stay. So let's return to the concept's home base in motor neuroscience to flesh out some computational details that are important later on when we apply its explanatory power to the neural mechanisms of creativity. Specifically, we need to know how internal models of motor control, driven via efference copies, estimate the future sensory effects of different actions and how goal representations are used to guide them to their targets.

Predictive representation challenges the long-held view that information processing is serial, hierarchical, and one-way. Both paradigms that dominated twentieth-century psychology, behaviorism, and cognitive psychology, assumed so. The view took for granted that a process starts with the output of a lower-level process and terminates as soon as its output is passed to the next higher stage. The *ex post facto* variation-selection-inheritance sequence of biological evolution operates indeed in that way. However, the pervasiveness of feedforward information flow in cognition lays bare that this isn't a good model for neural processing. And that error carries over to the needless insistence on blind variation for human creativity.

Historically, the motivating insight was first introduced to psychology by one of the pioneers of psychology, William James. It is called the ideomotor principle, if you need to impress someone. It states that our own actions are represented like any other event, by way of perceptual inputs (Shin et al., 2010). Obviously, the motor system represents motor instructions in terms of joint and muscle positions. But brains understand motion in terms of perception, or changes in spatial location. So how do brains interpret motor plans that have motor coordinates, rather than the needed perceptual coordinates? The solution involves translating a joint-angle story into a retina-based story, so to speak. To represent upcoming motion in terms of changes to sensory systems, not motor systems, regions in the motor cortex, in addition to the actual motor plan, also make a copy of the motor plan. In neurolingo, this representation is known as an efference copy. And now comes the clever bit. The motor cortex then sends the efference copy to the brain's sensory regions – the posterior cortex, primarily – that co-registers the current motor instructions with sensory maps representing the body (Frith, 1992). By virtue of being a copy of the real deal, the efference copy can be used to predict what would happen to us if the motion is executed as planned. This process, also dubbed the forward model of the neural emulator, converts the motor plan into a representation predicting the sensory consequences of the planned action. Central is that the mapping occurs to regions processing sensations so that the nature of the predictive coding is not what we are about to do but what we are about to perceive.

An emulator also needs a second component, an inverse model that works the same problem backward. As noted earlier, given the degrees of freedom in a dynamic sensorimotor exchange, a motor plan cannot prepare upfront for all eventualities that might develop down the line. There are just too many possible bifurcations. Plus, actual sensory feedback is too slow to adjust for any in-flight modifications while the overall motor plan is put into action. This is actually a well-known problem in engineering. The solution to it is an inverse model, also known as a controller, that gets hold of the problem from the other end. It asks what motor coordinates I would need to realize a final outcome, say, to grasp the coffee mug on the table. The inverse model then makes a first pass at the problem by generating an efference copy. This efference copy goes back to the error-predicting forward model that computes, in turn, a preview of the sensory consequences. By running the efference copy on the brain's sensory maps of the body, error data is generated for the initial motor plan. That error, estimated by the two components of the neural emulator, is fed once more into the inverse model, updating its motor command, and thus the efference copy, is as a result (Wolpert et al., 2003). This optimizing proceeds as the motion unfolds letting both, the predictor and the controller, converge on the goal.

Some will recognize the computational principle involved here. It is known as Bayesian updating, after the eighteenth century mathematician Thomas Bayes. Bayesian updating is a method to improve a probability estimate as additional information about a situation becomes available. Bayes' theorem quantifies this honing procedure with the proper arithmetic, which even mathematicians find scary, I have been told. Any situation that requires a dynamic analysis of a sequence of incoming data can use Bayesian updating rules to optimize its approach to a target. The motor system is only one example how we make use of Bayesian inference. We also update our beliefs that way when we have to factor in new information. In the words of the motor neuroscientist Daniel Wolpert, we are Bayesian inference machines.

You might be relieved to know that this is the stop on the knowledge highway where we can get off. You are probably already wondering what all this fanciful talk about the computational principles involved in controlling movement has to do with creativity. A little spoiler might help us stay on track. You will have noticed that all these representations must occur unconsciously. After all, you aren't aware of elaborate computations making up internal models of the sensorimotor loop, are you? But this is not to say that this process has no phenomenological consequences. It turns out that it is precisely this advance knowledge of what we are about to do that we experience as an intention. Now, hold that thought for a moment, we'll come back to it a little further on to account for intentions in human creativity.

It is no surprise that the adaptation to represent the future appeared first in the motor system. Motricity must occur in real time and it is, a few exceptions aside, the only external manifestation of the brain's activity, making it also the only way we have of interacting with the world. It is also no surprise that the underlying computational solutions initially evolved for the control of movement have been exapted to address similar challenges of dynamic interactions arising in higher cognitive functions.

The co-registration of action plans to predicted sensory effects in the motor system is a form of implicit prediction. The brain, you may just recall from an earlier chapter, operates two independent cognitive systems to acquire and represent information. The explicit system is a sophisticated system that is capable, thanks mostly to the computational infrastructure in the prefrontal cortex, to represent knowledge in a higher-order format. In contrast, the implicit system is a more primitive, evolutionarily ancient system that doesn't form higher-order representations. These differences in computational competence also apply to the predictive machinery of each system. Neural emulators in the implicit system work "online," regulating ongoing and currently present behaviors, such as those concerned with immediate sensorimotor integration. Because of their inability to represent distant and hypothetical scenarios, prediction in the implicit system is limited to the range of a few seconds. Due to these short timescales, and the stepwise Bayesian updating, this type of emulation is quite accurate (Downing, 2009).

Our discussion has so far centered on this category of implicit predictors for the simple reason that the computational principles we needed to extract are best understood in this context. But complex strategies of prediction that exploit the same basic computational trick to represent the expected future can also be found in the explicit system. The difference is that explicit neural emulators can be run "offline," on problems that are abstract and that can be solved outside real time. Predictive representations in the explicit system are essential to higher cognition. They are involved in strategic planning, mental imagery, social interactions, and estimating the outcome of a series of decisions. Most important to our project, however, is that they are the type or representations that make brains so much more creative than Mother Nature because they are the wellspring of advanced information about the topography of potential alternate futures that have never before seen the light of day.

Ideational RPGs

Readers who accept the importance of the brain's prediction competence should have little trouble seeing its profound implications for the creative process. In point of fact, I have proposed that the prediction paradigm can cope with several complications that arise in partially sighted evolutionary algorithms that navigate abstract and unknown solution spaces, as is the case in human creating and designing. Together, the paradigms of evolution and prediction constitute the bedrock on which we must anchor the search for the neural basis of creativity. While the evolutionary approach – despite some support – hasn't been influential in this endeavor, the prediction perspective has yet to be applied to creativity at all. Indeed, it seems that either framework alone lacks the explanatory power to convincingly account for the phenomena of creative thinking. This changes, I hope to show, when one paradigm is considered through the lens of the other. In what follows, I outline in more detail how the evolutionary framework gains traction as a mechanistic explanation for human creativity through the application of prediction. The reverse also holds; the relevance of the prediction approach to creativity comes into clear view only when it is framed in terms of a generate-and-test paradigm.

I use the prediction perspective to ask several pointed questions about the nature of creative thought. And what better way to do this than to focus on the mind's four upgrades to the basic algorithm of biological evolution that has structured our discussion so far. So, we first examine how emulation causes partial sightedness in the variation process. We then work out how prediction impacts the creative process at the level of selection; specifically, we see how representations of a predicted goal can serve as merit criteria for a hypothetical fitness function. We follow this up by exploring how emulation chaining over many iterations underlies the scaffolding effect that enables thought trials to leap over unrealizable intermediates. And finally, in the last query, we make the case for predictive processing as the author of our feelings of foresight and intention.

Prediction mechanisms in the brain can direct the production of ideational combinations in a number of ways. To illustrate the basic process, I use the Bayesian updating rules of the motor system in which the forward model (predictor) and the inverse model (controller) converge on an answer. It also brings us back into contact with the principles of competing neuronal coalitions. Evidence from motor neuroscience suggests that there are multiple motor plans competing at any one time for access to muscles, so that the brain also runs simultaneously multiple forward models to predict the outcome of each motor plan. This means that each forward model emulating various sensory changes, and each update in the whole movement sequence, can be considered as a hypothesis tester for the context that it models (Wolpert et al., 2003). Cast into evolutionary language, I have proposed that we can regard the computational principle behind forward models as the neural analogue of a possible (partially sighted) variation process. For each predictor-controller pair trial, the efference copy with the smallest prediction error represents the best fit with respect to the desired goal state and is used to spawn the next generation of action commands.

But this gives us a problem. What determines fit here? The answer takes us back to the controller component of the neural emulator. You will remember that it is the inverse model that actually kicks off the entire process by computing a representation of the movement endpoint, the final body configuration to be reached. And therein lies the solution. In the terminology of evolutionary algorithms, we can think of the representation of this predicted goal state as the fitness function of the selection process, because it determines which movement commands are selected and eventually executed. It sorts each generation of efference copies according to their adaptive fit with respect to the target state.

One more step is needed to complete the basic idea, and it consists of drawing computational parallels between predictor-controller pair updating occurring in the motor system and offline emulation processes taking place in higher-order brain regions during creative thinking. Suppose now we take the different predictions of the various forward models to correspond to the variation component of idea generation. Suppose further we similarly equate the inverse model's representation of a goal state with the fitness function of the selection component. With the boundaries of a hypothetical solution space set up like this, we can start explorations in terra incognita without being totally blind. What's more, well-established Bayesian inference techniques could tell us how evolutionary search algorithms converge on creative solutions, even though the solution space' topography in that case is fundamentally unknown.

The key difference to biological creativity is the prediction of a target, a mental representation that takes an educated guess at a possible solution and exapts the computational principles that have first evolved for motor control to take aim at it. As we have seen, brains use predictive processing in all sorts of cognitive domains and there is no reason to suppose that it is different when we try to think creatively. Of course, we could always tread into the unknown blindly, letting ourselves be surprised by what might happen – Mother Nature's way to proceed. But how much better to have some idea of what might await us.

I call these predictive computations in the brain ideational RPGs – Representations of Predicted Goals. Some readers will know that RPG normally stands for rocket-propelled grenade, and I suspect that my choice of the acronym – to be honest, it's a backronym as I made the words to fit the abbreviation – has something to do with my many years of living in Beirut, Lebanon. But the analogy has some merit because these predictions are rather like a signal flare launched into the dark so we can get a glimpse of the territory ahead. Granted, real RPGs bring death, not light, but the meme is intended to denote the idea that ideational RPGs provide the means to advance on terrain by focusing further afield, rather than on the immediate next step.

The game-changing advantage of internalizing the selection process by way of ideational RPGs is not the ability to run simulation offline *per se*. It is that selection can now be coupled to the variation component, resulting in degrees of sightedness. It is by virtue of having both of the twin processes of the evolutionary algorithm operating in the same computational system that one, the ideational RPG, can be used to guide the other, the production of ideational variants. Recall that this isn't the case in biological evolution. There, the variation component is in the DNA, while the selection component is in the environment.

We noted in the last chapter that brains are such a creative force in design space because they use heuristic algorithms to focus their search functions. This ability has two sources. One is folk wisdom, hard-wired design principles that furnish the equations to constrain solution spaces *a priori*. We also noted that this set of pruning techniques probably isn't enough to account for the extraordinary creative capacities of the human species. What boost the blind, *ex post facto* search algorithms of the biosphere by orders of magnitude is the second source of heuristics, the predictive machinery of the brain's explicit system. The core idea of this mechanism is that higher-order executive processes in the prefrontal cortex configure the neural simulator with context, memory, or advanced expertise and compute, on that basis, highly informed RPGs that act like prospective beacons of light in a sea of possibilities.

Imaginary fitness landscapes

We now have an entirely new way of looking at creativity. My proposal of specific neural correlates for some components of the variation and selection process – forward models and ideational RPGs, respectively – opens up new avenues of investigations on how thought trials could proceed. This type of creativity – there are others, as we will see later on – would consist of generating a clever ideational RPG, finding the right kind of evolutionary algorithm that might cover the gap between the problem constellation and the ideational RPG and using Bayesian updating to emulate our way to it. If you hate reductionism, you surely won't be a fan of this reformulation of creativity. But it gives us new tools for thinking and a fresh attack on the brain mechanisms of creativity.

There are several complexities attached to an evolutionary variation-selection algorithm that has a coupling parameter greater than zero. None is as critical as the matter of how we impose a direction on the variation process at all. Where do we get the prudence to know beforehand what might count as adaptive? This issue doesn't arise for the creative process in the biosphere of course. There, the natural environment determines adaptivity, and it does so *ex post facto*. Nor, as we'll see soon, is this an issue for the creative process in the brain's implicit system. But in the virtual world of thought only the explicit system is able to conjure up, there is no real environment to test our ideas, on the ground so to speak. Here, the merit criteria for a selection process must also be modeled. On what basis is this done? Since the very essence of creative thinking is to go into uncharted territory, how do we establish what *would be* adaptive in an unknown region of design space.

The answer will be familiar to you by now. A hypothetical, foresightful selection process requires, for its successful wheeling, a fitness function that contains information about the future. Mind you, it doesn't have to be a prophecy, better-than-average guesses would do just fine in the long run. The mechanism for the mind's second adaptation, then, needs nothing more than an ideational RPG, because its specs would become, in this reasoning, the fitness function for the virtual variation-selection process. To establish promising fitness values, all neural emulators have to do is to take the accumulated knowledge stored in memory and generate a clever ideational RPG. This predictive representation can then equip the sorting process with the merit criteria it needs to ratchet through an imaginary landscape. A Bayesian joining-the-dots journey can do the rest.

Speaking of joining dots, it is time for a refresher of the brain's network operations. Before the Designer can rear its ugly head again and try to sneak back into the design process, it is a good idea at this point to link this account of creativity to our now familiar friends of task sets and the speed of processing. Recall from Chapter 3 that a task set details all the operational parameters a neural network is set to, such as the weights of the nodes or the strength of their connections. An ideational RPG would, essentially, operate like a task set, whether the goal state is held in working memory or only in fringe working memory. It preconfigures the knowledge network underneath to work in such a way as to optimize its computations with respect to the RPG. The speed of processing, on the other hand, could be the mechanism that might determine fitness values in such a network. A pre-calibrated, opinionated network creates processing speed differentials for different forward models that are run on it. Given the preset processing pathways established by the ideational RPG, fitness, in this view, is simply the ease and speed with which forward models make it through the network. A neural network then attaches probability values to the simulated variation and those items with the highest quality values or with the fastest speed of processing are kept for the next iteration.

It might be helpful at this point to think of a few real-world examples of ideational RPGs in the arts, sciences, and engineering. To engage these in reverse order, consider architecture, a case of creative behavior that can lean on a fairly well-defined goal state. Buildings come in all shapes and sizes but an architect commissioned to erect a new structure is likely heavily constrained in terms of space, price, or the building's purpose. These represent already a lot of data that can be used to configure the simulation process. The architect is further bound by a host of fixed parameters and specifications – gravity, behavior of building materials, and so on. Add to this, prior experiences, context, or special characteristics present in the environment and the churning of a neural simulator can already be highly informed. While this still leaves plenty of room for creative designing – fiddly bits in the evolutionary algorithm – an ideational RPG can now readily be generated. And as soon as it is launched, the exploratory activity can converge in a manner similar – computationally speaking – to that in the motor system.

In the summer of 2013 at an art exhibition in Sydney, the artist Petra Gemeinboeck told me that she approaches any new project with a clear goal in mind. Because she is an interactive artist, she aims to, in her words, evoke a specific emotion in her audience. Whatever setting or material she works with, she thinks first and foremost about how the viewer will relate to the work. She wants to make them feel wonder, or curiosity, or surprise. This motivation for her art work is a perfectly good example of an ideational RPG. All of Gemeinboeck's steps toward that goal are aimed at satisfying the projected fitness criterion.

Finally, consider the somewhat different case of creativity in which the neural simulator is given very little to work with. A famous instance that comes to mind is the state of physics in the aftermath of the Michelson-Morley experiment, a study in the late nineteenth century that provided conclusive experimental proof that there was no luminiferous ether. The negative result effectively put an end to the Newtonian paradigm, leaving physicists temporarily with no viable alternative. It would appear that there are two ways to move forward in this situation. In the absence of any kind of ideational RPG, an evolutionary algorithm could always ratchet upward blindly and stepwise, as is the case in biological evolution. The other, more exciting possibility is to engage in predictive processing nonetheless. A projection based on little information is of course riskier but might nevertheless simulate a goal representation with some adaptive criteria. This is what Einstein did by, for instance, making the speed of light a universal constant. This decision served as one of Einstein's ideational RPG. Once this ideational missile was up, Einstein could work out how, if at all, the details make sense.

Of course, all this isn't to say that ideational RPGs can't be dead wrong, dooming the Bayesian pathfinder before it starts. Einstein, for instance, could have decided that the moon is made out of green cheese and try his luck thinking through that idea. Anyone who makes a living from creative explorations only knows this too well. But failures, for most creators, are a challenge to spur creativity, not a welcome excuse to give up. So, what successful creators do is simply launch another ideational RPG and try again. The key to this type of creativity, it would seem then, is to come up with the correct, or at least semi correct, ideational RPG.

Cognitive scaffolding

Which brings us to the cognitive scaffolding upgrade, the third of the mind's adaptations. And this mechanism also has its origins in ideational RPGs for the simple reason that a scaffold needs to be attached on both ends to serve its purpose. In biological evolution, each round in the creative process must be instantiated. This is because selection occurs after the fact and, importantly, takes place in the real word. Accordingly, variants are first produced and only then, after they have come into existence, do they get sorted. In brains, selection occurs neither (necessarily) after the fact nor is it (necessarily) located in reality.

In motor control, ordinary decision-making and other cognitive domains, the concept exists that a sequence of emulation steps can evaluate, or reason through, a series of choice points all the while the process is bypassing the realization of each iteration (Hesslow, 2002). The game of chess is a vivid illustration. Good chess players are known to calculate the consequences of several steps in advance before settling on the next move. This also requires a predictive goal representation and bridging scaffolds. But emulation chaining of this type, minor exceptions aside, doesn't count as creativity if we apply the putative definition of creativity as something that is novel, useful, and surprising. The predictive goal representation itself is situated within the boundaries of a recognized and mostly mapped out problem space. The algorithm that needs to be solved is principally known. This is simply a case of clever planning, not creativity.

Cognitive scaffolding bears significantly on two tacit assumptions that many people hold about creativity. First is the notion that the stepwise and analytical way to approach problems is anathema to the glorious inspiration of a creative insight. Ingenious ideas are said to be discontinuous, surprising, and even wild. Consider, for instance, the requirement of the US Patent and Trademark Office that inventions must contain a "non-obvious step." An argument can certainly be made that our phenomenological experience of the sudden appearance of an insightful solution involves some cognitive processes that differ from those underlying systematic, grind-it-out problem solving, perhaps on the basis that the former runs unconsciously while the latter does so consciously. But they are not different in kind. The steps, in either case, are carried out by way of variation-selection algorithms.

I'd imagine that cognitive scaffolding works like this. An ideational RPG, projected into an unknown problem space, can provide a sneak preview of that unexplored topography. The mental projection can set a distant target that is then used, first, to anchor the other side of a scaffold and, second, to orient the search process. With the boundaries of a potential solution space mapped out, Bayesian inference updating can try to make the ends meet. It identifies the appropriate evolutionary algorithms, finds a set of intermediate states, and converges on the creative solution – assuming the ideational RPG has some merit of course. Cognitive scaffolding is perhaps one of the mind's most powerful adaptations because it can temporarily support design elements that are not viable forms in their own right, allowing them to figure into subsequent iterations of the variation-selection algorithm. An arch with a keystone is the canonical example of an interlocking design that must leap over non-adaptive, intermediate forms. Biological evolution cannot do that. The brain's kick-and-rush type of creativity can produce creative designs of an entirely different kind.

Suppose the entire process, goal projection and predictor-controller convergence included, runs unconsciously, as is the case during the incubation phase of problem solving. If we indulge in this speculative possibility for a moment, one can see how such a mechanism might account for two prominent experiences associated with creative ideas. First, given that we have no access to our unconscious brain activity, we might presume that the feeling of discontinuity associated with sudden insights stems from the cognitive scaffolding falling away prior to the conscious representation of the solution. A mental projection into a distant future can readily be independent and disconnected from the present position. A creative insight that is several steps removed from the initial problem configuration can then no longer be *consciously* traced to it in a straight line. Second, and perhaps even a bit more of a stretch, we might also presume that the sense of certainty we often get that a creative idea is obviously just right arises from seamlessly joining the detached initial state with the distant goal state. In Chapter 8, I will explore further the possibility that the discovery of a continuous route between the two might even be the strengthening signal for the unconscious process to generate an aha representation in consciousness in the first place. I don't wish to carry this conjecture too far at this point, but the message we might take from this is that the inability to report the steps leading to the solution doesn't mean that there weren't any steps. Nor does it mean that the steps didn't follow a variation-selection protocol. Accordingly, it is doubtful that the basic cognitive mechanisms underlying the category of systematic problem solving is different in kind from the category of insightful problem solving.

I can also apply a similar line of reasoning to the second tacit assumption people often hold about creativity, the purported difference between "mere" problem solving and creativity. This difference arises in *post-hoc* evaluations of the end product but doesn't lie in the discovery process itself. A solution is deemed creative after a problem has been solved in a manner that violates our expectation. As such, the difference depends on where in the problem space a solution is located, which, of course, we don't know ahead of time. The more it is located in a straight line from our current worldview, the more likely we think of it as a case of mere problem solving. We would say perhaps that such a solution is logical or, to use the US Patent and Trademark Office's phrase, obvious. By contrast, we find a solution creative if it runs counter to our mindset; it is orthogonal to our thinking and thus non-obvious. However, there is no principled reason, let alone evidence, to presuppose that the cognitive processes we engage in to find that solution, irrespective of its position in the problem space, are categorically different. In each case, the discovery process proceeds in the same way, by means of up moves in design space that follow a generate-and-test protocol. Incidentally, it is for this reason that the notions of remote association and lateral inhibition that are often associated with creativity are false categories as far as the discovery process itself is concerned. You will recall Edison's empirical dragnet approach to inventing that yielded 1,093 patents. Clearly, creative products can also arise from close association and lateral facilitation, so to speak.

We see, in conclusion, that heuristics render cultural evolutionary algorithms faster without a proportionate error tradeoff, while scaffolding proliferates design options. Neither is possible without a prediction mechanism.

Foresight and intention

Following tradition, this leaves the mind's best new trick for last. As promised, we will now use the brain's prediction machinery to get to the bottom of the argument from foresight and intention. By universal agreement, the creative process in the biosphere is not teleological or purposeful. It has no ulterior goal and it doesn't deliberately strive toward perfection. It is just as happy to lay waste to what we consider clever engineering as to build it. Human creators, by contrast, act on purpose and create with intent and foresight. This argument, in one form or another, remains the central line of defense for those emphatically opposed to evolutionary approaches in human creativity. To shed light on this confusion, we must go on a little – but fascinating – detour of the way the brain generates the feeling of having intentions and thus our sense of agency and free will. You already know the gist of the conclusion I will reach. What we will find is that these experiences are also phenomenological consequences of the brain's prediction machinery.

Many people believe that free will is a topic for philosophers only. And many aspects of the problem are, perhaps forever, in the realm of metaphysics. But those aspects of our sense of agency that are concerned with the exercise and experience of our intentions to act have been buried under a mountain of neuroscience in recent years (Dietrich, 2007a). So we sidestep, except for a few introductory remarks, any *a priori* arguments for or against the freedom of will offered by earlier thinkers and focus instead on the mechanics and phenomenology of willed action.

The philosopher David Hume made an important observation with respect to free will. He recognized that cause and effect is an inference. Like gravity, we cannot see causality in an object. All we know is a temporal association that A is reliably followed by B. A bowling ball might seem to cause pins to fall but we cannot see a causal force in the ball itself. We must infer cause and effect because causality is an event and not a property of the ball. Accordingly, causal attributions are a habit of the mind. Hume was clear that this also applied to conscious will. In the same way that causation is not a property of an object, it cannot be a property of a person. We cannot see a direct relationship between conscious will and behavior; we can only infer a causal link from the consistent relationship between our intentions to act and the actual behavior. The possibility that a third variable causes both always exists. Our understanding of cause and effect is a theory because it must, by definition, go beyond the evidence.

The question of why we have the experience of agency would seem pointless for someone who believes in free will but it represents somewhat of a paradox for anyone who asserts that free will is an illusion. If we don't have free will why, then, do we privatize our intentions and experience our actions as willed? To answer this, we turn our attention to the brain mechanisms that give rise to the experience of free will and explore their possible evolutionary function. As a first step, we must recognize that conscious will is a feeling. Hume had realized this and defined the will as "the internal impression we feel and are conscious of, when we knowingly give rise to any new motion." The biologist Thomas Huxley stated it even more clearly: "Volition…is an emotion indicative of physical changes, not a cause of such changes." Free will, then, is not so much a mental force but a feeling of causing one's action. We perceive a consistent relationship between motion and its effect and feel that we have caused it. In other words, free will is an ownership-of-action emotion. One consequence of this conceptualization is that the free will-versus-determinism debate is a false dichotomy. Free will is a feeling; determinism is a process.

The psychologist Daniel Wegner (2002) postulates that we infer causality under three conditions: A thought of will must occur prior to behavior (priority), behavior must be consistent with the thought (consistency), and behavior cannot be accompanied by alternative causes (exclusivity). When these conditions are met, we ascribe behavior to conscious will and think that its cause lies within ourselves. It is easy to imagine how the experience of causing action would be undermined if there is no prior thought or the action is inconsistent with the thought. According to Wegner, then, conscious will operates like a magician who fools us into perceiving a causal sequence that doesn't exist. The real cause of our action lies in unconscious brain activity to which we have no access. We only become conscious of the two end-products of this activity, the thought and the motion. We link them and interpret our actions as willed. Imagine looking at a tree and by some miraculous method you would know ahead of time when and how each branch of the tree moves. If the branches do move accordingly it would be quite difficult to avoid the feeling that you caused their motion. As Wegner (2002) put it, "we believe in the magic of our own causal agency."

How, then, does the brain give rise to the sense of agency? The feeling that we own our actions suggests that the sense of agency developed from the brain's self system. Agency and self are not identical, however; we can feel that a particular motion is ours, such as a reflex, but not get the sense of intentionally causing it. To see the agency system as an extension of the self system, recall that the brain represents its body in cortical maps. As we move through our environs, the brain must continuously update these maps with the body's new location and position of all its movable equipment. We accomplish this by monitoring the changes in sensory input that occur as a result of our motion. The experience of our own arm moving is created by kinesthetic feedback from receptors in the muscles and by the visual feedback of seeing the arm moving. On the basis of this, we conclude retrospectively that the executed motion was ours. Because this feedback occurs for involuntary as well as for voluntary motion, it can account for the sense of ownership but it cannot account for the feeling of agency. To experience ourselves as agents we must also have advance notice that our body is about to do something. So, how do brains do that?

And this brings us back to the predictive processing in motor control. It is easy to overlook the fact that motor plans cooked up at the highest level of the motor hierarchy take a sizable chunk of time until they activate muscles. Several cortical and subcortical neural structures are involved in selecting, conceptualizing, programming, and detailing the plan. During these preparatory computations, the motor system engages in a mapping process. It leaks a carbon copy of the plan – the efference copy – to consciousness, effectively providing prior knowledge of the upcoming action (Frith, 1992). Involuntary actions like reflexes are organized by brain regions lower on the motor hierarchy. Such lower-order motor plans are too quickly executed, providing insufficient time for advance knowledge from an internal modeling process.

This model of the agency system is intuitively appealing at the conceptual level but it poses a fundamental problem for neuroscience. How does consciousness interpret motor plans? You will remember that the motor plan, which holds instructions for muscles and joints, must be translated into the only way the brain can understand the upcoming motion, in terms of changes to sensory systems, not motor systems. This is where the efference copy generated by the inverse model of the neural emulator comes back in. Signals from motor regions in the frontal cortex are sent to sensory regions in the posterior cortex that map current motor instructions onto sensory maps representing the body. This mapping process, by way of efference copies, converts the motor plan into a representation that predicts the sensory consequences of the planned action. An important aspect of this mechanism is that the mapping occurs to regions processing sensations so that the nature of the prediction is not what we are about to do but what we are about to experience. The phenomenal result of this representation is what we call an intention. In this view, intention is not prior knowledge of what we are going to do but an expectation of what we are going to find.

These insights into the inner workings of the agency system inform our understanding of the adaptive advantage of the experience of free will. To keep in focus the point we are pursuing with respect to intentional creative behavior, we are not concerned here with the question of whether or not we have free will but how the brain computes the feeling of it, irrespective of its actual existence. Pressures to represent choice consciously may derive from the enhanced ability to differentiate between us as agents and other causes of change in the world. This clarifies the reason why the system that maps motor movements prior to performance is likely an extension of the system that generates the feeling of owning motion. By anticipating sensations that relate to our actions we can label actions as our own, knowledge that we can use to build a self-concept that includes what we like and don't like to do. The ability to predict how our actions will make us feel also allows us to better assess how important they might be to us, which in turn shapes the selection of future behavior. In addition, planned action mapped onto sensory areas might play a crucial role in social interactions. Empathy, for instance, relies on understanding the intentions of others in terms of sensory consequences.

Finally, another advantage of an internal model of the emulated future is that a simulation of the effects of motion provides feedback faster than actual motion; indeed, it provides feedback in the absence of motion. In the context of creativity, the power of such comparator operations lies in the brain's ability to adjust or even stop action prior to execution. The computation of a preview of possible consequences – the feeling of intentions to act, in other words – provides thought trials with the means to equip a selection process with specific merit criteria that can be used to think through specific goals or lines of inquiry before a first step is made.

According to this framework, the sense of agency is created when the prediction of the mapping system is validated by sensory feedback. Thus, our sense of a normal intention-action sequence depends on the adequate mapping of predicted movement and a confirmation report that the expected experience actually occurred. If current motor instructions are not mapped, either because the motor plan is executed too fast by the trigger-happy implicit system or because it is mapped only weakly onto sensory regions, we cannot predict what we are going to see and feel. As a result, our own motion would come as a surprise to us and we get the sense that we didn't produce it intentionally. The reason why human infants and other animals don't seem to experience themselves as agents with intentions and foresight the way we do is likely due to an immature mapping system. For them all action, such as crawling or running, would appear as involuntary. When we engage in volitional acts we do anticipate what we are going to see and feel, which makes the experience less expected and less intense. Incidentally, this is the reason why we cannot tickle ourselves, a conundrum we are going to discuss in more detail in a minute. The sense of agency, in this view, is the misinterpretation of neural activity as conscious intentions when in fact it is a simulation of possible motor plan outcomes. The illusion of free will is completed when ensuing feedback matches the prediction of the simulation.

Ideal agency is based on authentication of motor plans by sensory feedback. The derailment of this process is thought to underlie the abnormal phenomenology of action that characterizes several neurological disorders, in particular schizophrenia (Frith, 1992). Schizophrenia includes both, the overexperience and underexperience of will. The problem is likely a faulty prediction system. In delusions of alien control, or what psychiatrists also call thought insertion, the patient believes that their actions or thoughts are caused by others. Here the brain probably fails to generate a prediction altogether. Without the representation of prior intentions to act, these patients cannot anticipate the consequences of their actions, which creates the impression of being under the direct control of other agents. Imagine how it must feel to never know what to expect from yourself! To the schizophrenic, their own behavior must appear as if guided by magic and it is perhaps not surprising, then, that they tend to misattribute it to some supernatural force. Schizophrenics also suffer from the opposite distortion, experiences of excessive control. They believe they possess Godlike powers and their direct intervention causes, say, the solar motion across the sky. These delusions of grandeur are thought to be created by an overwhelmingly strong prediction system. Fantasies of ruling the world, which we all harbor from time to time, are inadvertently run as simulations on sensory maps. A mere passing thought of the desire to influence world events may thus create the intention to rule the world. When the sun complies, the sense of control is undeniable and irresistible.

We got into the discussion of the brain's prediction imperative in action control because it provides clear leverage to rethink the matter of foresight and intention in creating and designing. The discussion shows that these phenomenological experiences are themselves the computational products of predictive goal representations. This finding certainly deflates the view of a categorical difference between cultural and biological evolutionary algorithms based on the argument from foresight and intention. But it does more. It also demonstrates what kind of propulsive force the brain's prediction machinery is in explicating the mechanisms underlying human creativity in general. Refracted through a prediction prism, intention and foresight are feelings that result from representing the expected future. As such, they merely constitute a change to the blindness parameters of evolutionary algorithms and are thus entirely compatible with an evolutionary explanation of the creative process taking place in brains.

Recommended readings

Bar, M. (2009). The proactive brain: Memory for prediction. *Philosophical Transactions of the Royal Society B, 364,* 1235–1243.

Boden, M. (1996). *The creative mind: Myths and mechanisms.* London: Routledge.

Dietrich, A., & Haider, H. (2015). Human creativity, evolutionary algorithms, and predictive representations: The mechanics of thought trials. *Psychonomic Bulletin & Review, 22,* 1011–1026.

Frith, C. D. (1992). *The cognitive neuropsychology of schizophrenia.* Hove: Lawrence Erlbaum.

Grush, R. (2004). The emulation theory of representation: Motor control, imagery, and perception. *Behavioral and Brain Sciences, 27*, 377–396.

Kawato, M., & Wolpert, D. (1998). Internal models for motor control. *Sensory Guidance of Movement, 218*, 291–307.

Wegner, D. M. (2002). *The illusion of conscious will.* Cambridge, MA: MIT Press.

Wolpert, D. M., Doya, K., & Kawato, M. (2003). A unifying computational framework for motor control and social interaction. *Philosophical Transactions of the Royal Society B, 358*, 593–602.

7
The Brain's Design Studio

We have arrived at a stretch – only a stretch. An examination of the conceptual foundation of current empirical neuroscience work on creativity shows that it cannot find a defensible position within the information-processing theories of neuroscience and psychology. Since it cannot isolate the requirements of its own subject matter – creativity – we can leave the first-round proposals from the 1960s and 1970s behind and consider more capable candidates. It took some vigorous restructuring of the imagination to get this project under way. We first had to free ourselves from the Cartesian shackles and enter the framework of the brain's connectionist architecture that does away with ghosts in machines. Dualist doctrines that wallow in mystery are dead ends – sooner or later – in a quest to find the brain mechanisms of creativity. It is much more exciting, as well as more useful, if we open our eyes.

We also had to disarm one further source of resistance before we could proceed comfortably. The perennial questions of human creativity lie at the heart of anxiety about genetic determinism and often get distorted by a biophobia that is quite distinct from thoughtful skepticism. Some who have sensed the dangers and feel that our creative agency is under threat have seriously misrepresented the generative mechanisms underlying how brains compute new ideas. But from a clear-headed analysis of evolutionary algorithms emerges a thesis that leads the way to a more promising approach that anchors our quest for answers on the brain's upgrades to the blind *ex post facto* drivetrain of the biosphere.

This isn't exactly news to those working on cultural evolution. So why, then, hasn't it percolated through to those working on the neural mechanisms of creativity? Why hasn't it already trumped the current neuroimaging phrenology it must replace? One reason for this is that ultimate (evolutionary) explanations for the mind's highest mental faculties are only too happily disregarded – given the unease they stir – as long as there are no plausible, proximate (neurocognitive) mechanisms for them. Think about it. Where was the foresight supposed to have come from? How could a creator get the special prophetical powers she needed to see the future? It all seemed a bit of a mystery, one might say. To gain some ground on this, I devoted the previous chapter to showing that the brain's prediction machinery can provide a coherent account of how brains implement these superior evolutionary algorithms.

But the journey doesn't end here. We have now equipped ourselves with a bag of thinking tools that can extend our epistemic horizons much further. My task in this chapter will be to apply our newfound knowledge to unpack the mechanisms that might give rise to different kinds of creativity. So far the focus of our journey has been on "how" questions that describe cognitive or computational processes (evolutionary algorithms, Bayes' theorem, etc.) that underlie variation and selection in the brain. Although these processes can inform "where" questions, any proposal on the neuroanatomical localization of creative thinking must be approached with extreme theoretical care. So we better start with a few caveats to keep in mind.

The hardware of thought trials

The position I have been defending from the start is that creativity, as a whole or in the parts we currently understand, is not localizable in the brain, certainly not with low resolution of present-day brain scanning technology. The same goes for processes. Creativity comes in such a variety of shapes and sizes that it cannot, as a whole or in the parts we currently understand, be captured by a false dichotomy pitting one purported creative mental process against another non-creative one.

The tacit assumption that has been driving neuroscience research on creativity, however, is the exact opposite. Creative thinking is obviously special and there must be something, somewhere, that makes it so. Powered by this conviction, psychologists and neuroscientists have made many attempts to make progress on this vexed problem. They first parsed the compound construct of creativity into more manageable chunks. Divergent thinking has been the most influential of these, but we can list plenty of others: defocused attention, low arousal, remote associations, altered states of consciousness, latent inhibition, flow states, unconscious processes, alpha increase, or lateral thinking. The hope was to narrow down the locale from there by assigning these more specific processes to specific brain regions.

The good news is that, in theory, this usually works well. After all, this approach has made cognitive neuroscience so powerful, and there was no reason why it shouldn't work for creativity. The bad news is that the good news cannot be counted on in all instances. It demonstrably doesn't work for creative thinking and a little *reductio ad absurdum* will illustrate why. Recall from Chapter 2 that all these partitions are false category formations. If divergent thinking, or defocused attention, also generates normal ideas and their exact opposites (convergent thinking and focused attention) also gives rise to creative ideas, these *a priori* divisions are incapable of identifying the part that turns information processing into creative information processing. You will also recall the monolithic entity fallacy. The irony is that nearly everyone agrees that concepts like divergent thinking are still compound entities, consisting of various different and quite separate mental processes. No one can say what divergent thinking involves in terms of working memory, attention, spreading activation, or a dozen other cognitive processes. Still, researchers proceed to fall for the same deadly mousetrap and treat those composites as monolithic entities. The basic underlying error in thinking that fueled Franz Joseph Gall's pseudo-science of phrenology over 200 years ago mustn't be forgotten here. As we have seen in Chapter 2, it survives, without modification, in present-day accounts such as the right-brain theory or alpha enhancement. Complex, higher-order psychological phenomena like creativity or divergent thinking – political orientation or religious conviction, if you need other examples – don't have a precise, single location in the brain. Nor are they computed in a single, even if distributed, network! Creativity, or its purported subcomponents, just isn't a cohesive entity at the neural level. Instead, in what I have called the vaudeville conception of creativity, there are multiple processes, implemented over a wide area in many different regions and networks (notice the plural). Divergent thinking remains a hopeful monster that is so broad a construct that it will remain forever intractable by the methods of functional neuroimaging, no matter how high the resolution of future brain-imaging technology.

In a twist that you couldn't make up if you tried, creativity researchers aimed to get around this critique by acknowledging that convergent creativity exists as well. There are now studies that look at "both kinds" of creativity. But all this judo-like move does is to turn the paradigm of divergent thinking from a category error into a question-begging circular argument. Despite the danger of beating a dead horse, the question arises that if both divergent and convergent thinking can lead to both creative and non-creative thinking what is it about either divergent or convergent thinking that is creative or non-creative? No one seems to want to, or is able to, explain this to me.

Unfortunately for us, and for progress, neuroscientists working on creativity have dealt with this issue in the handiest possible way. They ignored it. Even when they mention the problem's existence in their paper's introductory remarks, they then quite predictably continue, as if this acknowledgment somehow turned the water into wine, to use the construct of divergent thinking anyway. It is a disarming reflection of the reluctance, or inability, to come to grips with the fact that creative thinking, in all its forms, is the result of massive global interactions in the brain that are deeply embedded into its many subsystems.

As might be expected from this, the hunt for a mechanistic explanation of creative thinking is adrift from the rest of the psychological sciences. Since the beginning of neuroimaging studies in the mid-1990s, the field has produced a contradictory stew of brain areas and processes that is cloaked in a babble of incommensurate technical jargon and clichés. Depending on whose paper you read, creativity, or some false category of it, has been "discovered" in the prefrontal cortex – one of the few brain areas making multiple appearances – the hippocampus, visual cortex, superior temporal gyrus, density of white matter, anterior cingulate cortex, the temporal-parietal junction, alpha synchronization, default mode network or, the perennial favorite, the right brain (Dietrich & Kanso, 2010). In nearly all cases reported in the literature, the claim is that the identified brain area or process in question is associated with creativity or, to be more exact, with the whole of creativity, because any kind of qualifying remarks are usually absent (Dietrich, 2007b). This, my friends, is phrenology.

Conceptual boomerangs like these, despite their pedigree in the field, are false friends, potent distracters that make us believe that we are hot on the heels of a discovery when in fact we are looking at a mirage. Like the quest for a creativity pill, this path is a fool's errand. We might as well try to locate the brain area where gremlins hide. To be sure, my use of parody to see clearly what the issue is has not been welcomed by everyone, but I think that the theory-induced blindness to the true complexity of the brain's creativity mechanisms is a legitimate target for humorous comment.

So, here's the thing. Until we develop a solid grasp of the cognitive processes involved in creativity – as opposed to non-creative thinking – we should consider the current neuroimaging paradigm as failed. I think that, at the present time, it is possible to commit to only two kinds of partitions of the concept of creativity that avoid the pitfalls of the past. One is to decompose it into the twin processes of variation and selection (Dietrich & Haider, 2015). The other is to distinguish between a top-down or deliberate thinking mode and a bottom-up or spontaneous one (to which I will add the very different experience of flow as a third mode in the next chapter). Since the latter division will occupy us all throughout this chapter, we are keeping it collapsed until we have sorted out the former, the sites of variation and selection processes in the brain.

That's harder to do than you might think. As a matter of judicious theorizing, we begin by acknowledging that no hard data exist that can tie variation and selection to specific brain areas. This is true for the simple reason that there is no psychometric test that can separate these two sub-processes during creative cognition. But the problem with simplistic category formations of creativity is so persistent and the opportunities for blunders so ubiquitous that this wasn't going to stop someone from linking some of the above false divisions to variation and selection. Consider just two such duds. On the face of it, it's certainly tempting to think of the breeding of novelty as occurring in the primitive, unconscious mind, while the clever picking and choosing takes place in the enlightened, conscious mind. As a bonus, this would even go with the idea that the massive parallel computing network of the brain's underworld is perfectly suited for producing a lot of variation while the sophisticated cerebral cortex is best placed for sorting and testing different variants according to some fitness criterion.

There is perhaps no better way to characterize this line of thinking than to use one of the deadpan phrases of H. L. Mencken: "For every complex problem, there is one solution which is simple, neat, and wrong." A few observations will suffice to see that the idea of unconscious variation followed by conscious selection is a mistake. What would we make, for instance, of the common event of an epiphany – complex besides – popping into consciousness in its finished form? Where was the conscious selection process there? And what of all the times when you consciously and meticulously trial-and-erred your way to a new idea? Where was the unconscious variation process in that case? From all we know about the brain, there is no reason, let alone evidence, that prevents us from assuming that variation can also be a conscious process and selection an unconscious one. There are, no doubt, multiple levels of variation and selection in the brain, both in the conscious and in the unconscious mind.

But perhaps nothing competes for the prize for combining false category formations with the monolithic entity fallacy than a recent paper by the neuropsychologist Rex Jung and his colleagues (Jung et al., 2013).

It's difficult to conceive of a more arresting example of what happens when bad theorizing happens to good people. For reasons that may be forever shrouded in mystery, the authors start by resurrecting Donald Campbell's initial blind variation model from the 1960s, which scholars on cultural evolution – and nearly everyone else – have put to rest in favor of partial sightedness some time ago. On the heels of this odd opener, the reader is then asked to accept a real humdinger of a conjecture, namely the claim that one can simply equate variation and selection with – wait for it – divergent and convergent thinking! As for all the well-known problems with the paradigm – compound construct, category error, monolithic entity fallacy, circular argument – the readers are left to wonder about the theoretical grounding of this equivalence claim themselves. It only takes a moment's reflection to see that this cannot be right. Divergent thinking, as measured by divergent thinking tests, obviously contains selection elements, while convergent thinking, as assessed by the Remote Associates Test for instance, still requires variants to be generated before a selection can be made. This case, then, is similar to the unconscious/conscious division. Both divergent and convergent thinking require both variation and selection. Moreover, it misses the point of variation and selection completely, because selection is supposed to work *on* the produced variants! And get this: although the paper is a nonstarter before the introduction section ends, this conjecture was just the warm-up as the authors then proceed to take all the phrenology-tinged neuroimaging data from the divergent/convergent paradigm and treat it as a proxy for the neural correlates of blind variation-selection algorithms taking place in brains. Again, we need a sanity check here. This is nonsense dressed up as neuroscience.

Given the absence of direct evidence for the neural correlates of variation and selection, we have little choice but to search for them by following a trail of theoretical breadcrumbs. While there aren't too many of those lying about, there are just enough to make some headway. In thinking about the variation process first, it is difficult to conceive of anything other than a thoroughgoing anti-localization view, a position I first formulated more than a decade ago (Dietrich, 2004b). The position follows from two basic concepts in neuroscience: modularity and nonlinearity. As we are about to see, they provide the means to keep the bugbear of phrenology at bay. Much like the organs in our bodies, the brain is functionally divided, with different brain structures performing different tasks. The basal ganglia or cerebellum, for instance, are part of the motor system, while the hippocampus deals with the consolidation of explicit memories and the amygdala coordinates the response to threats. This organization into modules suggests that neural circuits that process specific information to yield non-creative combinations of that information – normal thinking, if you like – must also be the neural circuits that generate creative combinations of that information, or creative thinking. This sounds more obscure than it is. All it really says is that the recombination of bits and pieces of content into novel configurations must come from the same neural circuits that normally store those bits and pieces of content. As it happens, this must be conceded simply as part of our understanding of the brain being based on nonlinear dynamics. Indeed, the production of novelty isn't rare in everyday thinking. One only has to consider the combinational potential presented by human language to appreciate the brain's generative capacity. With that much noise in the system, novelty might simply be an inherent feature of such a complex information processor.

A concrete example might help. If we are interested in isolating the elements that turn mental imagery into creative mental imagery, we might want to look at the neural networks that produce mental imagery in general. This wouldn't make any sense at all if we were interested in creative writing, jazz, or mathematics instead, because these abilities engage completely different neural networks. Brain regions that produce novelty in music improvisation cannot be similar to those producing novelty in theoretical physics. This would border on an outright violation of the standard modular conception of brain function. If this is only half right it would be very bad news for the current neuroimaging localizationist camp. The prospect that all brain circuits generate, in principle, variation from the information they normally handle would mean that neuroimaging studies are bound to find activity only in those places the purported creativity test taps into. Use a different test, and the brain would be aglow with quite a different activation pattern.

All this has been a roundabout way of saying that there is no special place for novelty production. Like salt in the ocean, new ideas are everywhere! Although this seems like common sense, it runs counter to the prevailing rationale of neuroimaging studies and their interpretations. Take again the paper by Rex Jung and colleagues who tie variation to the brain's default network, a set of brain areas that we will have to say more about in a minute. Or recall from Chapter 2 John Kounios and Mark Beeman's proposal that creative insights arise in the RH. Once we are clear about the brain's modular organization, such generalized statements about creative thinking, or some subcomponent of it, being located in a specific network are devoid of meaning. These are category errors that betray a commitment to the monolithic entity fallacy.

The thesis that novel information may arise in any network or brain region must be qualified on two accounts, because it overstates the case somewhat. First, the brain isn't an unconstrained generator of new ideas. Not all neural networks possess the same degree of plasticity. At a minimum, we can assume that the more integrative and higher-order the neural network involved in the computation, the more combinational novelty might occur in it. Neuroscience conceptualizes cognition as a functional hierarchy with, roughly, inflexible brainstem circuits at the bottom and the cerebral cortex at the top. Structures such as the prefrontal cortex, then, are simply more likely to contribute to information shuffling but, to drive home the point one more time, the whole brain takes part in the fun. The second restriction concerns working memory, because working memory can upload representations into consciousness that are encoded in long-term memory networks located elsewhere in the brain. This makes it an especially interesting network when the creative thinking is done consciously.

I have a similar anti-localization line of reasoning for the selection component, with one notable exception. I have previously argued that the evaluation of novelty as creative, as opposed to merely new, depends heavily on the engagement of higher-order evaluative networks like the prefrontal cortex (Dietrich, 2004b). But this is not to say that the prefrontal cortex is required for it. Conscious selection perhaps, but not selection in general. Two observations will show that such a crude mapping won't do. One is the sudden representation in consciousness of a complex idea. Evidently, the fact that problem restructuring and solution finding can occur unconsciously, and prior to the solution's representation in working memory, would suggest that selection processes are also at play below the level of the prefrontal cortex. It also seems apparent that spreading activation in a network contains selection criteria for the simple reason that the network nodes are weighted based on previous experiences. This weighting would reflect fitness values. The other observation is the experience of flow, in which conscious processing involving the prefrontal cortex is bypassed altogether. As with variation, then, the indirect evidence supports only the more guarded view that the more integrative a neural structure, the more higher-order selection processes might occur in it. From this modular perspective, selection processes are likely also embedded into the same networks that produce the variation.

Still, the creative process in brains has many different aspects to it, and the prefrontal cortex seems to perform many of the crucial steps that are needed to transform novelty into actual creative behavior. Based on what we know about brains in general, we can think of three tasks for the prefrontal cortex. First, to fully evaluate a novel thought, one has to become conscious of it. Only when posted there, on the black-board of the global workspace for all the mind's demons to appreciate, is the thought conscious, and we can speak of an insight. So, regardless of how, or where, in the brain novelty is generated initially, circuits in the prefrontal cortex are required for further conscious processing. That said, keep in mind that an insight is neither necessary nor sufficient for creativity. Creative products come into existence without the incidence of an anteceding, conscious thought – think flow experience – and creative thoughts have no impact unless converted, often by untold hours of additional creative labor, into an actual product. Second, once consciousness is in the picture, the prefrontal cortex can bring the full arsenal of higher cognitive functions to bear on the problem. We can, for instance, direct our attentional resources to the problem, retrieve relevant memories, and appraise possible future consequences. Information-processing in the explicit system represents a whole new – but not the only – selection level. Many new ideas eventually turn out to be incorrect, incomplete, or trivial upon closer inspection, so judging which ones are worth pursuing and which ones need to be discarded takes prefrontal cortex integration. Finally, prefrontal regions must also implement the expression of the insight. The prefrontal cortex is known to orchestrate action in accordance with internal goals. A finished creative product is often a long way from the initial bright idea and keeping track of all the subtasks while keeping in focus the overall objective depends critically on prefrontal activation. In any domain of creativity, the full expression of a creative insight requires a high level of skill, knowledge, and technique that is dependent upon continuous problem-solving. Great works of art or science are often the result of goal-directed behaviors that took months or years to mature.

So what can we glean from all these complexities about the neuroanatomical location of creativity? One thing seems certain. It is hard to imagine useful neuroimaging data from studies on creativity that blend variation with selection, something all current neuroimaging paradigms do, given that both processes are distributed, occur at conscious and unconscious levels and engage, at each of these levels, different cognitive processes and different brain regions.

Insights into insights

Anecdotal stories abound that portray the creative process as effortless, ephemeral, and unintentional. From Poincaré's realization that Fuchsian functions are identical with those of non-Euclidean geometry to Coleridge's poem Kublai Khan, such sudden flashes of insight are the very cliché of the creative genius. No doubt, there is something in that. But what has been generally overlooked in all this romanticizing about the inspired genius is that the opposite also holds. For all the uplifting stories, the Einsteins riding on beams of light, the Newtons watching falling apples (a myth likely originating from Voltaire), or the Archimedeses displacing bathwater, deep insights about the nature of things can just as easily come into existence by deliberate iterations of trial and error. Think of Thomas Edison's empirical dragnet method that yielded a record number of patents. And what would we make of Watson and Crick's systematic approach to testing the stability of DNA base pairs, Bach's assembly-line tactic to composing hundreds of cantatas, the imaginative ways in which NASA engineers solved the problems of the otherwise doomed Apollo 13 mission, or the countless occasions we converge on creative solutions by orderly, and consciously, eliminating alternatives?

All of this would seem to suggest that the conscious representation of an ideational combination can be achieved in at least two different thinking modes, or types of creativity if you prefer (Dietrich, 2004b). In the deliberate mode, as you would expect from the name, problem-solving is intentional and the retrieval of memory effortful. In the more celebrated spontaneous mode, on the other hand, problem-solving is not intentional and the representation of the solution in working memory is sudden and surprising. These two modes seem to map well on to experience. One involves hard thinking until you feel that steam is about to come out of your ears, while the other flows with intuitive ease and seems to require no mental exertion at all. As always, our task is to find the brain mechanisms that might underpin these differences in phenomenology, and the toolkit of theories and concepts we have now acquired is just what we need to do that. Still, because so many bits of the puzzle remain unknown, I am forced to embellish the facts with some fiction. So what follows is two parts theoretical neuroscience and one part exploratory guesswork.

Paradoxically, I won't drain the drama out of the story if I start by telling you the conclusion. The deliberate mode is powered by activity in the prefrontal cortex. This unleashes the full might of the explicit system with its capacity for conscious representation, cunning prediction machinery, and higher-cognitive functions, all of which feed into its superior evolutionary search algorithms. Enhanced by strongly informed search heuristics, well-aimed ideational RPGs, and the ability to erect scaffolds, the deliberate creativity mode possesses a degree of sightedness that can make short work of a problem space. In the spontaneous creativity mode, the prefrontal grip on the creative process is greatly weakened. How much, no one can say. But what we can say is that access to consciousness is lost and the variation-selection algorithm must ratchet in the brain's unconscious, without the benefit of higher-cognitive functions like working memory or attention. This has consequences, for the search heuristics are less directional, the merit criteria provided by ideational RPGs not as defined, and the degree of sightedness reduced.

But, I must hastily add, we shouldn't confuse the spontaneous processing mode with the flow experience solely because both are unconscious. As we will see in the next chapter, flow is a third type of creativity mode that emanates, unlike the deliberate and spontaneous modes, from the implicit system. The spontaneous creativity mode must be considered as part of the explicit system. It can draw on the omnidirectional knowledge representation of the explicit system, use a scaffold to a goal representation projected into the hypothetical future, and, most importantly, represent its final product in working memory in the form of an insight. The flow mode, which emanates from the simpler, concrete-operational implicit system can do none of that. With no access to the global workspace at all, implicit knowledge cannot become conscious through an internal process. It must go, as it does in flow, through the circuitous route of involving actual behavioral performance. This is a common source of confusion about unconscious creativity, even among neuroscientists and psychologists, and we will sort it out in more detail as we make our way through this chapter.

Economists are forever reminding us that there is no free lunch, and the characterization of the two modes I just sketched out wouldn't be complete without the downside, the tradeoff each creativity mode comes with. For all its computational might and farsightedness, the deliberate mode is only effective if the creative solution is indeed within the boundaries of the predetermined solution space, which of course is a guess – highly educated or not. In the spontaneous mode, the opposite constraint arises. Without the explicit system firing on all pistons, the spontaneous mode isn't as efficient a search algorithm, but it therefore has the potential to chance upon a creative solution that happens to be located out in left field. There is nothing contradictory about this. Attention, for instance, has an analogous tradeoff. We can focus on a specific object but this prevents us from seeing the big picture. If, on the other hand, we zoom out and take in the grand view the details become hazy. We can't do both at the same time.

With this in mind, we can now attempt to explain the boosting of *some kinds* of creative thoughts in *certain kinds* of states of consciousness (note the italics), most notably mindwandering, dreaming, meditation, flow, and LSD (long slow distance) running. The decomposition of creativity into variation and selection aside, this deliberate/spontaneous division of creative thinking is, as said, the only one that seems to have sufficient empirical and theoretical support.

Suppose you face a task requiring your creative thinking. As you consciously think about it and try to find possible solutions, you can draw on all the higher mental faculties of the explicit system. As you will be aware, this is generally a good thing. First, you can furnish the equations that make for powerful search heuristics. You see, the prefrontal cortex has a kind of search engine that googles the brain's intranet and deliberately pulls into working memory knowledge that might be relevant to a solution. In that way, the evolutionary algorithm is informed by a vast database of folk wisdom and everything else you've learned in life. Once that knowledge is online – fully conscious – it can also be flexibly combined to narrow down a promising search area further. Second, you can launch a clever ideational RPG into the tapered search space to gain some sightedness on its topography. You will recall that this predictive goal representation is the step that internalizes the selection process, because its specs serve as the merit criteria for a hypothetical fitness function. Finally, once a predictive goal state is in place, you can attach a scaffold between it and the initial problem configuration and let the two converge using Bayesian inference techniques. Should the ideational RPG turn out to be a dud and the two components of the neural emulators (forward and inverse model) fail to connect, you simply repeat the trick with another ideational RPG, which you can now launch into an even smaller search space, given knowledge of the preceding failure. If the solution is indeed inside the borders of the preset solution space, it won't hold out long until the deliberate mode finds it.

We have all reasons to assume that this powerful computational machinery is inherently biased toward up moves that are linear in kind rather than radical breaks from the past. Being at the top of the neural pyramid, the prefrontal cortex also houses a person's cultural values and belief system. This gives the deliberate mode – initiated and supervised by the prefrontal cortex as it is – a number of critical built-in predispositions as it generates new ideas. Prior experiences, expectations, preferences, common schemas, or accepted wisdom are all factors informing the search engine, formulating ideational RPGs, and

The Brain's Design Studio 151

structuring emulation processes. Which brings us back to the tradeoff that lurks in the deliberate mode. By placing all eggs in only a few baskets, the deliberate mode is, for all its sightedness, pretty useless when the solution violates something we think is true about the world. In the deliberate mode, we are liable, for the sake of efficiency, to exclude such possibilities from the start. To quip, while the deliberate mode has the advantage of superior algorithms, it has the disadvantage of superior algorithms! It isn't unlike looking for the keys under the lamp post.

In connectionist lingo, the prefrontal dominance of the deliberate mode alters the configuration of the task set, the parameters that determine how we see and approach the creative task. The top-down input containing a person's expertise and worldview recalibrate the network's frequency of occurrence values and the strength of their connections to more polarized settings. Lowering the values of some nodes while increasing those of others is, in effect, how search heuristics, fitness functions, and predictive processes are implemented at the level of the knowledge structure. Mind you, a (fading) task set is also in place in the spontaneous mode. But by amplifying the task-set values further, the deliberate mode creates even greater information-processing speed differentials for good as opposed to bad solutions. In evolutionary biology, this would be considered a case of strong selection pressure. Programming a high number of bottlenecks into the network's pathways strongly directs the spreading activation toward adaptive ideas. Those ideational combinations that have a higher speed of processing on that particular network configuration will generate the feeling that we are on the right track. The eventually correct solution would breeze through the network with much greater ease still. If the heuristic algorithm and the ideational RPG are generally accurate, the deliberate mode is a good bet you wouldn't want to do without. But, again, a highly weighted task-set configuration also renders the knowledge structure less flexible for the simple reason that strong weight values, in either the plus or minus direction, provide less opportunity for spreading activation to go off on remote tangents.

This is a good place to forestall the ever-present temptation to relapse into a false category and align the spontaneous mode with divergent thinking or defocused attention and argue, on that basis, that creative products generated in the deliberate mode don't count as real creativity. It is a mistake to discount creative achievements generated in the deliberate mode simply because they buttress the currently accepted paradigm. To use examples from the arts this time, think of all the masterpieces of the Renaissance, Romantic Period, or Impressionism that embody the ideals and techniques of their time. Often truly great pieces of art are not those that break new ground but those that emerge at the height of a prevailing paradigm. This is as true for Picasso's Guernica as it is for Goethe's Faust. It would be difficult to argue for remote associations or divergent thinking here, given Picasso's and Goethe's earlier styles of creation. These great works of art might be remote associations to us, but the creative process in these cases happened in their brains, not ours.

A visit to the creative underworld

The brain is a wonderful thing. It starts working the instant you're born and never stops until you must write something on deadline. Like all forms of functional fixedness, writer's block is an utterly frustrating and draining experience. Suppose you have the milder version of it, not the full-blown type in which the mere thought of writing causes immense anxiety. Imagine yourself sitting in front of the computer screen trying to put a paragraph together but all that comes out is clichéd and dull. You're stuck. What do you do? If you are like most people – nine out of ten by some estimates – you try to break the impasse by removing the problem from consciousness. Some people go for a stroll in the woods to jump-start their creativity. Others cook or do Tai Chi. And then, out of the blue, it happens. While you mind is goofing off in la-la land, a sudden stroke of inspiration hits you. You run to your computer and write the whole article, start-to-finish, in a few hours. Like that.

How can we not stand in wonder of the mysterious ways the mind works? The sudden appearance of knowledge without intentional reasoning seems so inexplicable to us, so discombobulating, that it isn't at all surprising that such Eureka moments are often described by being hit by a ton of bricks. The job of psychologists and neuroscientists is to find mechanisms for precisely these kinds of experiences, solid explanations that fit without a miraculous addition, to use Darwin's famous phrase again, into the canon of science. But a mechanistic view of the human mind doesn't diminish the wonder. Far from it. In the contrary, the brain becomes ever more fascinating the more we understand its inner workings.

Suppose a creative task requires a solution that is located in a region of design space ruled out by the strong directional guess of the deliberate mode. As an example, you can pick any of the major revolution in science. They all start by someone not simply taking another step but by someone looking in a completely new direction. No amount of logical maneuvering would have persuaded an ancient seafaring Phoenician of the theory of relativity, genetic engineering, or cell phones. The fact that groundbreaking discoveries in science are the result of the mind idling in neutral should give us pause the next time we want to credit creative thinking solely to the higher cognitive functions of the cerebral cortex. It's more complicated than that.

Since we don't know ahead of time which project necessitates revolutionary thinking, we typically tackle a new challenge by consciously exploring the well-trotted paths of our intellectual comfort zone. In many – perhaps most – cases, the deliberate creativity mode manages just fine and will yield a creative solution in short order. Should the solution be located beyond this zone, this approach won't work. It only leads to frequent gridlock and much frustration. But creative people are nothing if not tenacious. They don't stop trying until all the logical knobs have been turned and all plausible options exhausted. Only when that moment comes – and for these kinds of problems it will come – do they give up and turn their attention to other matters. But thanks to task-set inertia, the problem doesn't just disappear. The brain merely shifts it from a deliberate mode of processing to a spontaneous one. The incubation phase has begun and with it a whole stack of adjustments occur in the brain's networks that changes profoundly the way we process the task.

Based on what we know, which isn't much but probably more than you expected when you started reading this book, we can now string together a tentative narrative of how, during the incubation phase, creative insights come into existence. We start by tracking the tuning changes that ripple through the brain's networks when we shift to the spontaneous creativity mode. From the moment you turn your attention away from the creative task and stop thinking about it consciously, a massive redistribution of the brain's resources is under way. This is simply a matter of mental economy. To begin with, the prefrontal, top-down control is gone, which is another way of saying that the spontaneous mode benefits much less from the higher cognitive function and clever forecasting ability of the explicit system. Most importantly, a new neuronal coalition has ascended to consciousness and is now the reigning task set in the global workspace. This relegates our task set – its goal representation, especially – to the fringes of working memory, where it doesn't possess the same complexity and influence it had on center stage. But even without the halo of consciousness, this downgraded goal representation retains some strength to help organize activity in the now deposed task set.

Much the same can be said about the nodes in the knowledge structure. As soon as the task set is demoted into the unconscious, the activation in this network changes in strength and quality. Right away, this triggers a drop off in overall network intensity, probably dramatically so. Whether this happens fast or slow, we find inertia in the network, a kind of residual activation that continues to process information related to the task. Due to the loss of top-down input from the prefrontal cortex, this general decline in liveliness is accompanied by the resetting of all relevant knowledge nodes to more moderate values. The task-set representation for our creative task is now both, weaker and more neutral. The disengagement of higher-order thought also puts an end to the highly selective retrieval of knowledge from long-term memory, which has helped bias the combinatorial shuffling of information toward linear and logical new ideas. At all events, the network now effectively runs generate-and-test algorithms below the threshold of consciousness, but with much less vigor, precision and direction.

What is still missing in all this are the prediction processes that occur in the spontaneous mode. What can we say about them? As it is, given the broad slowdown in activity, and the more level playing field in the knowledge structure, evolutionary algorithms in the spontaneous mode cannot have the degree of sightedness that lifts their cousins in the deliberate mode to such lofty creative heights. Search algorithms in the spontaneous mode must contend with larger solution spaces for the simple reason that they cannot enlist higher-cognitive functions to restrict them further. They must also roam these larger spaces with less sightedness, for the same reason. Which brings us to perhaps the most decisive factor. Unconscious processes don't have the computational sophistication to launch clever new ideational RPGs. At best, they probably operate on the old one which has, on top of that, lost the crisp representational format it once had in the deliberate mode. This toppled RPG probably contains little more than the vague information that there is still a problem out there in need of a solution. That still works as a fitness function for the spreading activation – along with the remaining value settings in the knowledge structure – but we are now looking at a case of weak selection, because requirements for speedier processing are less stringent. Are we to assume then that the spontaneous mode runs second-grade algorithms that are more haphazard and aimless? Well, in a word: Yes. And this rather neatly takes us back to the tradeoff. Let's not forget that the ideational RPG, with its prefrontal-imposed traditionalism, is what got the deliberate mode into trouble in the first place.

It doesn't take much for incubation to start. It happens, for instance, every time a new event captures our attention. Cerebral resources are immediately redirected toward the new task set holding sway in consciousness and all that is left for the task set grappling with our creativity problem is the spontaneous processing mode. You may just recall from an earlier chapter that we called this the Russian-Revolution scenario, a strong neuronal coalition outcompetes all others for access to consciousness and takes control of the conscious mind. Recall also the Fall-of-Rome scenario in this context. As anyone who tried to sit through a boring lecture can attest to, it is difficult to concentrate on one thing for a long period of time. The longer attention is engaged the more difficult it is to maintain. So during the inevitable times when the brain's attentional system is downregulated, daydreaming takes over and no powerful new task set manages to install itself in working memory. Instead different task sets take brief turns at the top, and the sequence of thoughts in the stream of consciousness becomes erratic and mercurial, an unsystematic drifting from one imaginary dreamscapes to another. Either scenario – Russian Revolution or Fall of Rome – leads to incubation. But only the latter, for reasons we are about to see, seems to help with creative thinking.

Before we get too excited about unconscious creativity, let us pause for a moment and consider the spontaneous creativity mode in the larger set of altered states of consciousness, of which daydreaming is only a very mild sort. Other putative altered states include the contemplative karma of meditation, hypnosis, the chemical never-never lands of mind-altering drugs, the euphoria of the runner's high, and the nightly slideshow of the bizarre otherwise known as dreaming. Many people view some of these outer frontiers of the mind with suspicion – some sort of abstruse psychopathology at the lunatic fringe frequented mostly by potheads and meditating yogis. This bias is further exacerbated by the excessive use of esoteric language used to describe them, which does little to disabuse others of the aura of lawlessness and unscientific hogwash that surrounds altered states. But not all cultures understand altered states as neurological junk or signs of temporary insanity. In other cultural traditions, they are valued highly as sources of insight and truth. Often people attach great spiritual significance to them and interpret the brain's computations as visions that allow them a glimpse into other realms, worlds inhabited by their ancestors and gods. Whatever view you hold – sacred meaning or random glutamate fire – all altered states of consciousness seem to have creative potential.

The orthodox view is that consciousness is composed of various mental faculties, such as self-reflection, attention, memory, perception, or arousal, which are ordered in a functional hierarchy with the prefrontal cortex necessary for the top attributes. Although this implies a holistic view in which the entire brain contributes to consciousness, it is evident that not all brain regions contribute equally to consciousness. This layering concept localizes the most sophisticated levels of consciousness in the zenithal higher-order structure: the prefrontal cortex. From this perspective, I have formulated a few years ago the transient hypofrontality theory, or THT for short (Dietrich, 2003). The central idea behind the THT is that the brain mechanism common to all altered states involves a transient downregulation of prefrontal activity. Because the prefrontal cortex is the neural substrate of the topmost layer, any alteration to consciousness should, first and foremost, affect this brain area followed by a progressive shutdown of regions that compute more basic mental processes. In other words, the top layers of consciousness are most vulnerable when the brain's operations are altered. It follows from this onion-peeling principle that mental functions, such as working memory, sustained attention, costly inhibition processes, and temporal integration, are compromised first as consciousness is distorted. Anecdotal evidence supports this. All altered states share the gradual disappearance of mental content that depends on the prefrontal cortex, such as the ability to mental time travel (only the here and now counts), adherence to social norms, or focused attention.

Consider, by way of example, one of the most common experiences, especially in profound altered states: the loss of ego boundaries. People routinely report merging with one's surroundings; they may unite with the forces of nature, dissolve into the Universal Ocean, or attain mystical oneness with the Void. Of course, the experience may also be less sacrosanct and people become one with the astray or melt into the wallpaper. Whatever meaning you attach to such experiences, they can all be understood in terms of prefrontal downscaling, as it is there that we form a sense of the self and delineate it from other selves.

As the altered state deepens, induced by the progressive disengagement of prefrontal areas, more phenomenological subtractions occur and the experience becomes one of ever greater departure from normal consciousness. In altered states that are marked by severe prefrontal hypofunction, such as dreaming or the various psychopharmacological heavens and hells, this modification results in an extraordinarily bizarre phenomenology. In altered states that are marked by less prefrontal deactivation, such as endurance exercise, the change to experience is milder. In any event, the individual simply functions on the highest layer of phenomenological consciousness that remains fully functional (Dietrich, 2003).

It is probably not too much to say that the transient hypofrontality theory hasn't won me many friends among psychonauts, to put it in the most salutary terms possible. This is largely because one logical consequence of the theory argues against a widely held belief about altered states. The concept of hierarchically structured mental functions entails that full-fledged consciousness is the result of a fully operational brain. But what this also means is that default consciousness is the highest possible manifestation of consciousness, and all altered states are, by virtue of being an alteration to a fully functional brain, a reduction in consciousness. This is also true for altered states that are seen – presumptuously, in my view – as higher forms of consciousness, such as transcendental meditation or "mind-expanding" drugs. It is difficult to imagine what truly higher consciousness might look like in terms of brain activity or phenomenology, but shouldn't it entail an enhancement of mental abilities ascribed to the prefrontal cortex rather than their subtraction? But we better stop here. The pros and cons of that discussion are another book.

I mention all this to underscore the point that the brain mechanisms of the spontaneous creativity mode also bear on, with perhaps a few modifications, other mind states associated with incubation. But to return to daydreaming, the downshifting of the prefrontal cortex into safe mode produces a mental state in which no dominant, global task-set rules in working memory – the Fall of Rome scenario. Rather, there are several task set representations weakly activated, all of which are locked into an internal power struggle. Whenever one ascends to consciousness, its reign there is likely to be short-lived for the simple reason that in a state of hypofrontality it wouldn't have the resources to uphold the costly inhibition processes necessary to suppress other contenders and remain in power. Another way of saying this is that the hypofrontality process deludes the task set and relaxes self-imposed constraints, leaving more room for diversity among the brain's many independent units. The upshot is a state mindwandering, a journey full of kaleidoscopic and phantasmagoric images that hop from one dreamy thought to another.

Suppose now that an unexpected event occurs to you, say, a jump into the bathtub displaces a lot of water. We have already touched in an earlier chapter on the fact that incoming stimuli make contact with a set of knowledge nodes greater than those in the focus of attention. Archimedes' famous Eureka moment (the word is derived from the same root as heuristic) shows that serendipitous incidents can prime a fading task set that still busies itself with a search for answers. As the task-set inertia interacts with perceptual networks that decode displaced bathwater, or falling apples to take another example, the spreading activation pathways are changed. Of course, this kind of interference takes place in both, the deliberate and spontaneous mode. The crucial difference is that the deliberate mode has a single, overriding task set in force. It is unlikely that interference ripples get very far under the oppressive thumb of a dictator. A powerful task set actively inhibits exactly these sorts of ripple effects for the obvious reason that they pose a threat to its rule. In point of fact, the inhibition of extraneous stimuli is one of the main duties of a task set. Moreover, the ruling task set filters the new sensory information – displaced bathwater, falling apples, etc. – and files them away under the category of irrelevant. Its singular focus makes it unable to recognize the meaning of the unexpected event. Incidentally, this is also the reason why incubation works better when problem solving in the deliberate creativity mode is followed by daydreaming rather than a task switch.

Now contrast this with daydreaming, a mindset in which several neuronal coalitions are weakly activated. The plurality alone probably increases the odds that one of them can assign meaning to the extraneous input. What is likely to be a more important factor, however, is the weak activation of the task sets, not their number. The interference ripples a new event can possibly make in a more fragile and less polarized network are simply greater. This, in turn, improves the chances that a novel combination of information is forged that will pass through the network with high speeds. Recall that the speed of processing, by virture of being a fitness criterion, might be the mechanism that can recognize meaning. After all, we cannot leave this decision to some Cartesian Designer. If the processing speed of the thought trial exceeds a threshold, possibly set by the merit criteria embodied in an ideational RPG, a creative insight might emerge into consciousness.

The brain's global highways

Before we take up the neural mechanisms of the famed flow experience in the next chapter, we must bring another aspect of the brain's anatomy up to date by considering the large-scale networks that crisscross the brain. Getting clear about these global highways provides extra inoculation against our natural inclination to think about the relationship between complex psychological phenomena and their neural underpinnings in terms of phrenology. We know that more basic functions are indeed located in discrete brain structures. The amygdala, for instance, does coordinate the fear response to clear and present dangers. But complex cognitive functions like creativity are distributed. By way of comparison, it is easy to point out England on a map, but you cannot find all people in the world who speak English that way.

The brain computes multifaceted traits and talents by linking local circuits and units – each contributing one part to the bigger picture – into large-scale networks that span the length and width of the brain. There are at least three prominent ones, and for our purposes we can restrict them further to two, the central-executive network and the default mode network. These two core brain networks come into the story because they control cognitive functions that map rather well to the deliberate and spontaneous mode we have covered in this chapter. This connection gives us a way to better understand the neuroanatomy of creativity while remaining ever vigilant about the booby traps of localization.

Starting with the latter, the default mode network is a set of neural regions that is most active during stimulus independent thought – daydreaming, to the rest of us – as well as a number of specific mental tasks, such as remembering the past and imagining the future (Raichle et al., 2001). If you can handle the heavy dose of brainspeak, here is a shortlist of brain structures involved in it: Several areas of the medial temporal lobe, especially the hippocampus and the parahippocampal cortex, the medial parietal and lateral temporal cortices, especially the precuneus and the temporal-parietal junction, as well as the medial prefrontal cortex, cerebellum, and thalamus.

The default network derives its name from the fact that it is spontaneously active during passive control tasks in neuroimaging studies. Consider a study in which experimenters ask people to ponder a moral dilemma while their brains are being scanned. As always, a good experiment needs a control condition. To draw valid conclusions, experimenters must compare the brain activity during moral reasoning to some sort of standard brain activity. But what is standard? To get around this problem, they ask participants to give their brains a rest and not think about anything at all. The assumption was – a rather peculiar one, in retrospect – that this would give them the baseline activation they needed for proper comparisons. What they saw instead, time again and irrespective of the study's main purpose, was a collection of interconnected brain regions that showed increased activity during these periods of intended rest. From this humble beginning as a mere control condition for other research questions, it took a while before the default network was noticed and became of interest in its own right. But eventually neuroscientists realized that this network of brain areas was doing something. At a minimum, it supported a state of mindwandering or moments of introspective self-talk and thought.

The discovery of a default network was not only serendipitous, it was also unexpected (Buckner, 2012). Look at it this way. Brain activity is costly. Roughly 20 percent of all metabolic resources are consumed by an organ making up only 2 percent of body weight. So why is there default activity at all? What good accrues to us by doing this? Why not just rest? Additional research aimed specifically at studying this default network brought more surprises. In particular, it revealed that several other associative cognitive processes, such as episodic recall and thinking about the future, also activated this common set of distributed brain areas. This led to the conclusion that remembering the past and imagining, or simulating, the future are subserved by the same neural substrate.

The meaning of default network activity – the point of mindwandering, in other words – has been the subject of a thought-provoking debate. The question guiding deliberations is the possibility that the various functions that have been ascribed to it actually minister for a more universal, overarching purpose. Proposals on that front have ranged from a construction system that is involved in the fabrication of imaginary scenarios over mediating contextual associations in general to self-projection, the capacity to envision the world from alternative perspectives. Examined from a step back, what these initial proposals all pivot on is the idea of prediction, the ability to simulate worlds that differ mentally, temporally, and physically from the present. We have already seen this conclusion emerge in the previous chapter as an important piece of a broader framework that sees the brain as a prediction machine. Memory is essentially an epistemic device for simulation and its reconstructive and associative nature renders it a process identical to imagination. Incidentally, this also explains why the brain can't just rest. The point of a proactive system is to constantly anticipate, so there must be a continuous search process taking place to reduce uncertainty even when, just to be prepared, no task is at hand.

The default network has an opposing twin, the grandly named central-executive network (Bressler & Menon, 2010). In point of fact, they behave like two components of a flip-flop circuit, as their activation strength is inversely related one another. While one is at full tilt, the other is subdued. The central-executive network is anchored in the dorsolateral prefrontal cortex and several areas of the posterior parietal cortex, among much else. In accordance with its name, it controls executive functions like working memory and inhibition processes and is called into action whenever we have to focus our attention on a specific task. Another way of contrasting these two systems is to say that the default network is associated with endogenous activity, while the central-executive network is driven by exogenous input. Finally, just to complete the brain's communication infrastructure, there is a third large-scale network that goes by the name of salience network. From its hubs in the anterior insula and the anterior cingulate cortex, the salience network facilitates the yin-yang between the other two. All the bells and whistles of these grids and their global interactions would take us too far afield. We remain focused here on the possibility that the central-executive network is the crank behind the deliberate creativity mode, whereas the default network powers the spontaneous creativity mode.

As with most things in life, fashion comes into it too. It is a curious fact that a number of powerful ideas – evolutionary algorithms or task-set inertia, for instance – have been completely overlooked in neuroscience explanations of creativity, while the discovery of the default network has been seized upon swiftly by people in the field. The default network now makes sudden and surprising appearances in many scientific papers where it has no real business. I have the foreboding sense that a brain network for mental doodling appeals to many for the unfortunate reason that it readily fuels long-standing but, again, misbegotten category formations of creativity, namely divergent thinking and defocused attention. Proceeding with more enthusiasm than sense, many researchers now seem be to climbing over one another to claim that people with more default mode network activity are more creative. Well, that explains it then, doesn't it! And why not just stick, while we are at it, to the right brain theory? It is hard to say which is more remarkable, the persistence of this kind of phrenology or the number of different incarnations it can assume. Evidently, people seem unwilling, or unable, to just snap, crackle, pop out of it.

Let's assume, for the sake of argument, that current psychometric tests of creativity actually test real creativity and that their validity is based on a sound theoretical and conceptual foundation. Even then, two points need to be kept in mind. First, lab-based tests of creativity, by their very nature, require the full commitment of executive functions and attentional control from the central-executive network. Participants must consciously attend to the test questions and work on them in an effortful and intentional manner. How data from such a paradigm can be recruited to argue for the default network in creativity escapes basic logic. Indeed, by all evidence, lab tests of creative ability must be counted as an instance of deliberate problem solving. In the same vein, you will recall that it is demonstrably false to associate daydreaming, flow, or any other of altered states with enhanced creativity tout court, irrespective of a neural basis for these mind states. There is no reason or evidence to suppose that default mode activity cannot also be uncreative and the activity in the central-executive network creative. Liking the default mode to creativity is yet another false category formation. What type of creative thought is facilitated or inhibited by what kind of cognitive process, and in what circumstances, is a pressing issue for future research. But either/or doesn't come into it at the resolution of large-scale networks.

We turn next to a third type of creativity that I have postponed. It is the flow experience and it marks the last stop in our tour through the working parts of the creative mind. This chapter has focused on creativity mechanisms in the explicit system, and we have come a long way to distinguish deliberate and spontaneous modes of creative thinking in terms of anatomy and predictive computations. We have now reached a place where we can appreciate the utterly different neural drivetrain that powers the flow state. For it is in flow that the implicit system shows its capacity for creative behavior.

Recommended readings

Bressler, S. L., & Menon, V. (2010). Large-scale brain networks in cognition: Emerging methods and principles. *Trends in Cognitive Science, 14*, 277–290.

Buckner, R. L. (2012). The serendipitous discovery of the brain's default network. *Neuroimage, 62*, 1137–1145.

Dietrich, A. (2003). Functional neuroanatomy of altered states of consciousness: The transient hypofrontality hypothesis. *Consciousness and Cognition, 12*, 231–256.

Dietrich, A. (2004a). The cognitive neuroscience of creativity. *Psychonomic Bulletin & Review, 11*, 1011–1026.

Dietrich, A. (2007a). *Introduction to consciousness.* London: Palgrave Macmillan.

Jung, R. E., Mead, B. S., Carrasco, J., & Flores, R. A. (2013). The structure of creative cognition in the human brain. *Frontiers in Human Neuroscience, 7*, 330.

8
Flow Experiences: From Mystery to Mechanism

The lead guitarist of R.E.M, Peter Buck, once made the following observation about the band's most famous song:

> When I think about *Losing My Religion*, I think about the process of writing and recording it, and how dream-like and effortless it was. The music was written in five minutes; the first time the band played it, it fell into place perfectly. Michael had lyrics within the hour, and while playing the song for the third or fourth time, I found myself incredibly moved to hear the vocals in conjunction with the music. To me, *Losing My Religion* feels like some kind of archetype that was floating around in space that we managed to lasso. If only all song writing was this easy.

Ask any athlete or artist about flow experiences, and you will be treated to sound bites about time flying by, ecstatic experiences, being lost in the moment, and spontaneous joy, never mind the best job they have ever done. Flow is a common experience and the concept is intuitively appealing. For those who haven't come under its spell, here is a short description. Flow is a highly attentive state of consciousness characterized by effortless, fluid, and graceful action. A flow experience ensues when one becomes so deeply focused on a task and pursues it with such passion that all else disappears, including the passage of time, worry of failure, or the sense of authorship. The person enters a tunnel, an almost euphoric state of bliss, in which the task at hand is performed, without strain or effort, to the best of the person's ability (Dietrich, 2007a). According to the psychologist Mihaly Csikszentmihalyi (1996), the high priest of the flow state, any activity can produce flow as long as it is a challenging task that demands intense concentration and commitment, contains clear goals, provides immediate feedback, and is perfectly matched to the person's skill level.

The topic of optimal human functioning has a long history in humanistic and health psychology. In the 1940s, the psychologist Abraham Maslow called such memorable moments of self-actualization peak experiences and described them as being filled with happiness, fulfillment, and achievement that create a feeling of realizing one's human potential. Some say that flow – if not an altered state – is at the very least a special state of consciousness. To be sure, a shortlist of key phenomenological features includes the usual suspects. People invariably report the typical one-pointedness of mind, the mental singularity that occurs when the muscle of attention is flexed and a single event becomes the exclusive content of consciousness. Activities in flow are done for their own sake, the ego takes a leave of absence, and distractions are eliminated from awareness, especially complex, meta-analytical processes such as self-reflection, worry of failure, or fantasies of success. Time loses its meaning, and one becomes so immersed in the task that the here and now is the only realm of existence. The flow experience, you understand, is not limited to musicians, painters, or freestyle skiers. It can also occur, and regularly does, in unsung activities like house cleaning, garbage collecting, or on-the-fly lying about your whereabouts. Total immersion by itself alone isn't enough. Being absorbed in watching a movie or reading a gripping novel doesn't count. The essence of flow is the merging of perception and action, the smooth, rapid-fire integration of sensory input and motor output that cleanly bypasses the centers of higher thought and consciousness. That's why meditation, for instance, isn't a flow state. It doesn't include a skilled movement sequence.

Now the question that has occurred to most of us at some point is this. What could possibly be happening in the brain to bring about such wonderful and exceptional human performance? We might be forgiven for thinking that such all-you-can-be moments must be associated with the brain operating at full capacity, with all your neurons gushing dopamine and singing hallelujah. So it did come as a bit of a surprise when I upended this assumption a few years ago and proposed that the exact opposite makes more neuroscientific sense (Dietrich, 2004a). To fully understand what is going on, we start by saying a bit more about the tradeoff between implicit and explicit processing that we introduced in Chapter 3, in particular the computational fact that behavioral efficiency precludes cognitive flexibility and vice versa. We then add the theory of transient hypofrontality to it, and the neural basis of the flow experience comes readily into clear view.

Once this is in the bag, we finally have all the pieces of the puzzle to appreciate a bird's-eye perspective of the creativity mechanisms in the brain. All that's left to do is to bring back into the frame the two creativity modes of the explicit system and go out on a couple more theoretical limbs to settle remaining issues. The reward is a grand view of the current state of play.

The efficiency-flexibility tradeoff

We saw in Chapter 3 that we have two independent systems for knowledge representation. There is the very sophisticated explicit system supported by the super-charged prefrontal cortex. This system creates higher-order and abstract mental representations, a format that enables conscious processing. The counterpart is the more basic implicit system that simply embeds its information directly into the knowledge structure itself. For reasons that will now become clearer, this renders the information unavailable for conscious processing and verbal expression.

The first question to ask, and answer, is this. Why go through the trouble of evolving two separate systems? What good does this do? A little illustration will show why. Suppose a frog has two inflexible and stereotypical behaviors to react to visual input. It responds to small, prey-like objects by snapping, and to large, looming objects by jumping. These instinctive behaviors are controlled by rigid and reflexive but fast and efficient neural circuits. But what would the frog do if a medium-sized object comes into view? Snap for food or jump to safety? As the number of such fixed, hardwired circuits must grow to handle ever more intermediate situations, such an organization becomes patently uneconomical. A more advantageous solution is to evolve a single system that is capable of temporarily activating multiple representations, so that the organism can examine them and make more flexible decisions (Crick & Koch, 1998). This is particularly useful when two or more of the brain's circuits generate conflicting plans of action.

Explicit knowledge dramatically increases cognitive flexibility because it can weigh and integrate conflicting hypotheses. The complex format includes meta-information – additional information about the information – the fact, for instance, that the system contains the knowledge it contains, which makes it possible to retrieve it in a context different from the one it was acquired. Both, the omnidirectional access and the indexing function, permit the information to be broadcast to a global workspace, so that it is known to, and hence useable for, all other parts of the system. This, incidentally, is also the reason why this kind of knowledge is verbalizable.

Contrast this with the setup of the more primitive implicit system that neither stores its knowledge independent of context nor represents meta-information about it. Instead, it embeds all its information, without indexing it, straight into the procedure itself. This simpler storage format makes the information unavailable for representation in the conscious mind. By fully implanting it into the specific context or application, the implicit system cannot retrieve it for use in other situations. It is because of this encapsulation that the implicit system cannot tell the explicit system that it knows what it knows, and why you find it so difficult to verbalize how to tie shoelaces, to use a previous example.

We have now a way of bringing in the efficiency-flexibility tradeoff without being stomped. The key insight is that both information-processing systems have fundamentally different, mutually exclusive purposes. The explicit system has evolved to enhance cognitive flexibility because it can represent knowledge at an abstract level. In the Darwinian calculus of evolution, however, there is always a cost. It's exactly this complex representational format that limits its use in a specific instance for the simple reason that a representation that is general in type would have to be first converted to a specific one before it can be used, a translation that takes time and is prone to errors. Nowhere is this more apparent than in situations that require fluid, rapid, and efficient motion (Dietrich & Audiffren, 2011). As we all know, textbook knowledge of a motor skill is of little help when performing the skill. The forte of the explicit system, then, is the type of complex problem that can only be solved offline and outside real time. The canonical example is scientific discovery. Recall the earlier point about science being unkind to common sense. The implicit system would have never learned that the Earth is round, has a molten core, or lies at the outer arm of an insignificant galaxy, to say nothing of eleven-dimensional string theory. The explicit system owes its flexibility to its capacity for abstraction, but the tradeoff in speed and efficiency that comes with cognitive flexibility makes it a liability when time is of the essence.

The inverse is true for the implicit system. Implicit knowledge is limited in its generalizability and flexibility but therefore faster and more efficient in real-time execution. Being embedded into the application itself, the implicit system cannot represent its knowledge as a hypothetical, abstract possibility, which makes it specific and idiosyncratic (Dienes & Perner, 1999). But the advantage of not being burdened by higher-order complexity is speed. Implicit knowledge is contained in the application of the procedure and need not be extracted from general rules that are represented at a higher-order level and then applied to a concrete example.

It's worth digging a bit further into the efficiency-flexibility tradeoff to render vivid and robust a few insights that would seem otherwise contradictory. Recall also from Chapter 3 that language acquisition in childhood is implicit. Without specific schooling, we cannot state the rules that govern sentence construction in our mother tongue; yet, we make very few mistakes during free speech. The reason is the implicit nature of language representation. The rules are contained in the application of the procedure itself and cannot be extracted from an instance-dependent format. This simplicity is the key to the high processing speed and fluidity of native speakers. The computational flipside of this form of encapsulated representation is also the reason why we are unable to extract the rules and verbalize them. Exactly the opposite is true for a second language acquired later in life, and for the same reasons. In this case, the explicit system acquires the skill through books and deliberate exercise and represents the rules in the general format it learned them. While this gives us conscious knowledge of the underlying regularities, and thus verbalizability, it also takes time when we need to apply them to construct a specific sentence. The resulting clumsiness is the source of much pain for those trying to speak a second language. In short, the abstract, metacognitive format of explicit knowledge permits conscious processing and verbalization but makes real-time usage a protracted agony. Procedural knowledge, by contrast, delivers the speed when you need it, but it cannot be taken out of its embedded form and used for some other application.

The differences in design and function between the two cognitive systems lead to a remarkable fact that has bedeviled our understanding of expertise for a long time. Suppose you learned a motor skill in early childhood – a tennis serve, for instance – and only possess, for the sake of argument, an implicit representation of it. If you wish to teach others how to hit such a nice serve, your explicit system is called upon to explain something for which it wouldn't have a mental representation. A private, internal chat between the two systems is not possible. Due to its encapsulation, implicit knowledge cannot cause explicit knowledge directly. What you must do is execute the movement so that the explicit system can observe what the implicit system knows. Only through the circuitous route involving actual behavior can the explicit system extract the critical components of an implicitly learned skill. To give another example, how would you recall a phone number that you have dialed many times before but that has momentarily slipped your mind?

You would probably try to dial it on an imaginary phone dial. This works because the execution of implicit knowledge triggers explicit representation. The fact that we don't have direct conscious access to our implicit knowledge leaves us often with little choice but to explain that our behavior was guided by intuition. Sometimes the unfortunate misnomer muscle memory is used to describe this phenomenon. My body knows how to do it; I just go along! This is a particularly common experience when trying to explicate a skilled movement.

The efficiency-flexibility tradeoff is perhaps most vividly exposed when we think of the deleterious effects of transferring the neural control of a complex movement from implicit to explicit. When a task is represented in both systems it can be executed by the explicit system and/or the implicit system. But an explicit-predominant movement proceeds from a mental representation that is different in kind from one that is implicit-predominant. Since a highly-practiced, implicit skill is still performed by a conscious person, it is possible for the explicit system to partake in its moment-to-moment execution. To stay with tennis, this occurs when a player consciously represents information extraneous to the motor sequence – thinking about stroke technique or reflecting on the game's importance – in a higher-order representation and allows such analysis to guide the movements. Due to the explicit system's complexity, it should be clear that any amount of transfer of the skill from implicit to explicit affects the speed and accuracy of the movement negatively. John McEnroe apparently knew this intuitively. The story is told that when he played an opponent who was in the zone and could do no wrong with his, say, backhand, McEnroe would call it to his rival's attention during the switching of sides. "Hey, excellent backhand you have there! How do you do it?"

We can sum this up by saying that a fully automated motor skill deeply inserted into implicit networks is best left alone. The motto would be: To be fast, keep it simple. Explicit interference in the execution of a well-learned skill only decreases the skill's speed and accuracy, or to state it the other way around, the degree of implicitness of motor competence is positively related to the speed and quality of the performance (Dietrich, 2004a).

We must rigorously apply this efficiency-flexibility tradeoff that exists between the implicit and explicit systems if we want to understand the effortlessness of the flow experience. Indeed, this position needs to go as far as it can go; it has considerably more explanatory utility than has been generally recognized. The inherent efficiency of implicit knowledge is paramount to flow because the flow experience is a type of creativity mode that occurs online and in real time. The fast and fluid sensorimotor tasks that characterize flow cannot be micro-managed by the explicit system. Its representational format is simply too complex and hence too slow.

Flow and the effortlessness of being

It took some hard work to get to this point but once we are clear about the computational yin-yang involved, we can lean on it to make inferences about the underlying brain activity. You will remember that the explicit system is powered mostly by the prefrontal cortex. It follows from this that a brain state with less neural activity in the prefrontal cortex would weaken the explicit system and minimize the chances that explicit processes compromise the smooth, implicit execution of an automated motor skill. In fact, from an evolutionary perspective, such a transient state of hypofrontality must occur in a pressure situation involving physical motion; it simply isn't adaptive to engage higher-order executive processes, at least not to the extent humans can, when you need to be quick (Dietrich & Audiffren, 2011). Not only will thinking *about* the movement be of little use, it will mess up the movement itself. Perhaps no one ever articulated this more succinctly than the Austrian skiing great Franz Klammer, who famously said after winning a giant slalom event: "You can't win a thing by thinking."

The problem of explicit interference, we can presuppose, only arises in humans because other animals simply don't have enough explicit processing capacity that possibly could wreck the sleekness and ease of implicit motor performance. The downregulation of the prefrontal cortex, then, has evolved in humans to offset the influence of metacognitive processes in the one situation this is most definitely not useful, when the devil takes the hindmost. Powering up your explicit system and pondering the meaning of life when you are being chased by a grizzly bear isn't something that would help you contribute further to the gene pool. Optimal performance of a real-time sensorimotor integration task is associated with maximal implicitness of its execution.

Notice that a hypofrontality account is also consistent with the way the flow state feels. While the movement itself is performed with ease, the psychological experience is marked by phenomenological subtractions of exactly those higher-cognitive functions that are encoded in the prefrontal cortex. With the notable exception of focused attention, flow lacks a sense of self, intention and agency, abstract thinking, mental time travel, or the ability to consider the possible consequences of

the ongoing action. Should any of these sophisticated mental faculties return, flow is gone; as anyone who has felt the flow experience
come and go can tell you (Dietrich, 2004a). Daniel Dennett (2004) once
quoted the painter Philip Guston as saying:

> When I first come into the studio to work, there is this noisy crowd
> which follows me there; it includes all of the important painters in
> history, all of my contemporaries, all the art critics, etc. As I become
> involved in the work, one by one, they all leave. If I'm lucky, every
> one of them will disappear. If I'm really lucky, I will too.

There is nothing analytical about flow. Otherwise flow wouldn't flow.

So, ok, fine. The online and real-time requirements of speedy
stimulus-driven responding make it impossible for the flow experience
to be coordinated by the higher-cognitive functions of the explicit system. But this can't be right, I hear you say. What about painting or
free jazz improv? This is high culture, very sophisticated art. And all
the things you have to know to write beautiful poetry? Isn't that highly
cerebral? It simply doesn't make sense that all those creative activities
and positive feelings one experiences in flow are enabled by a process
that tends to deactivate the pinnacle of human evolution, the prefrontal
cortex.

What is going on here? This apparent paradox arises, it seems, from
the often presupposed but seldom examined idea that more (brain
activation) must be better (mental health, creativity, happiness, etc.),
which climbs right into bed with our hallowed regard of the creative
genius, to make a potent combination that has led many astray in their
theorizing about the flow experience. You may recognize this line of reasoning as a close relative of the idea that altered states must be states of
higher consciousness, perhaps accompanied by a spectacular symphony
of excitatory postsynaptic potentials. We can see the mistake clearly in
a parallel argument. A team sport like basketball surely requires a whole
array of prefrontal-dependent, executive processes. Players must, among
much else, do strategic planning, deliberately retrieve memories, focus
attention, time events, keep in mind the score, and so forth. How can
this be reconciled with the hypofrontality process, which, according to
the transient hypofrontality theory, takes place in the player's brains at
the time of the game?

To see why a supposedly strategic, coordinated activity such as basketball is unlikely to require activation of the explicit system during
the game, and thus substantial prefrontal involvement, compare the

five-member basketball team of, say, North Carolina State University, to a five-member bona fide wolf pack hunting for dinner. In both cases, there is a broad strategy, an overall goal, a number of intermediate goals toward the main goal, retrieval of relevant memories, temporal integration, as well as sustained and directed attention. What's more, success depends on keeping in mind, at any one time, the preferences and capabilities of your teammates and opponents (or prey), their positions, the layout of the land, and countless other factors. These cognitive processes are all, without a doubt, executive processes, are they not? Yet, the tiny prefrontal cortex of a wolf is entirely adequate for the hunt (Dietrich & Audiffren, 2011). Laying it on this thick helps, I hope, to see where the problem lies. Theorists tend to overestimate the extent a specific task really requires explicit processes.

Consider next flow experiences reported by stand-up comedians, simultaneous interpreters at the UN, or lawyers making closing arguments. To see such impromptu, off-the-cuff speech in the same light, we have to know that language production, spoken or written, is not a multidimensional tasks but a serial one. It is generated by stringing together existing and automated units but components of these units are not integrated along one or more dimensions (phonology, semantics, or grammar) before an output decision occurs. Language is produced from a small set of conjunctive rules that are applied sequentially as speech moves forward (e.g., subject-verb agreement), which eliminates a nearly infinite number of mistakes that are possible if all components were to be combined freely in all dimensions. A task – however complex initially – in which the requirements can be chunked or sequenced is amenable to automation and thus can become controlled, over time and with much practice, by the implicit system. It is worth remembering that a person's native language is represented in the implicit system. Without training, we cannot name the grammatical rules that govern, say, conditional clauses in English, but we hardly make a mistake when we talk. This is the epitome of implicit knowledge. To be sure, the explicit system can steer language production toward a topic, or direct the implicit system to stick to a strategic plan in tennis – avoid opponent's backhand! – but moment-to-moment execution must always rely on reflexive loops that, as a result of thousands of hours of practice, have the application directly embedded in the procedure itself.

Much the same can be said about free-jazz improvisation. It's a conjunctive task in which the musician arranges well-learned melodic units – "licks," as they are known in musical jargon – into a flowing string. Because the string advances by each unit triggering the next, the application becomes part of the procedure. The end product can be creative; indeed, if the string is long enough it must be creative due to the complexity of the musical system. The string as a whole can even be multidimensional but each individual step is not. Free-jazz performance is the classic example of flow and it surely won't surprise you by now to learn that well-controlled neuroimaging studies of musicians have shown prefrontal deactivation (Limb & Braun, 2008).

To pull all we have learned together into a crisp summation, the flow experience relies on two mechanisms. The first is the automation of the task so that the implicit system can be fully entrusted with running the program. Simultaneous interpreters at the UN, for instance, have memorized the translation of countless phrases of standard political jargon – The American people deserve ... (fill-in-the-blank: better, less taxes, answers, more education, etc.) – for which they have ready-to-go equivalent counterparts in their language. No thinking required (although it's still one of the most stressful jobs because of the remaining uncertainty). The second is the powering down of the explicit system so that the implicit system can do its thing without having its efficiency nullified by pointless meddling from the smarty-pants explicit system.

The essence of flow is the fusing of perception and action into a graceful behavioral sequence. Flow, therefore, is a creativity mode that does not – cannot – involve engagement of the explicit system; to be flowy, the behavior must be run implicitly. This brings into sharp focus the primary difference between flow and the two creativity modes I detailed in the previous chapter. Flow emanates from the implicit system, the deliberate and spontaneous modes emanate from the explicit system. This fundamental difference in their neural basis explains why the creativity of flow is online, inside real time, and outside conscious awareness, while the creativity of both explicit modes is offline, anytime, and proceeds via a conscious insight. This leaves us with one more fudge factor before we can make it to home base. All three creativity modes also differ in their prediction capabilities, a parameter that changes the sightedness of the evolutionary algorithms they can run. To this we are going to turn our attention to next.

Why does flow flow?

In Chapter 6, I proposed the explicit system's predictive machinery as the neural mechanism behind the mind's four upgrades that make cultural evolution so much more powerful than biological evolution. The proposal explains (1) where the coupling of variation to selection and the resulting partial sightedness come from, (2) how the establishment of merit criteria for a notional fitness function is accomplished, (3) what makes the scaffolding effect possible, and (4) why the experiences of intention and foresight cannot serve as a category boundary to set human creativity apart from the creativity in biology and artificial intelligence. In Chapter 7, I added to this by arguing that only the deliberate creativity mode possesses the fully upgraded package. The spontaneous mode operates unconsciously and must make do with much less prediction competence. But let's not forget, the spontaneous mode still arises from the explicit system. So, it retains some degree of sightedness, uses ideational RPGs (Representations of Predicted Goals) to scaffold and enjoys access to consciousness, as evidenced by the capacity to represent its final products in working memory in the form of a conscious insight.

None of this occurs in flow. The implicit system doesn't have the computational cleverness to generate ideational RPGs for problem spaces that are abstract or unknown, or both. Let me elaborate on this. Recall that the implicit motor system does have a prediction mechanism. The system relies heavily on emulators and inverse models, which are, of course, representations of the future. But the motor prediction machinery only works for actions that have been learned previously. In other words, the goal state must be known beforehand so that a predictor-controller pair can be established and allowed to converge using Bayesian inferences.

At the risk of stating the obvious, creativity is an adventure into parts unknown. How does the motor system render a prediction in that case? Well, it doesn't. It can't. When the situation is unknown, the motor system must first learn what the goal state is and it can only accomplish that by doing. The implicit system must acquire knowledge of goal states on the basis of a learning process that is stochastic, stepwise, and blind. It simply tries out, by trial and error, solutions to environmental contingencies (Perruchet & Vinter, 2002). This slowly and gradually shifts the weights in the knowledge structure, which introduces a bias for subsequent information processing (Cleeremans, 2008). By embedding the new information into the network itself, the implicit system forms expectations that can then be used to make predictions the next time the situation arises. Suppose you want to perform a movement that is totally new to you, some activity you have never done before – a new dance, say. This is a true challenge for the motor system. It has no way of making a prediction in this case. It doesn't know what the movement's endpoints are, because it wouldn't have learned inverse models for them. And without such action memories, the motor system wouldn't even know the algorithm that it needs to solve (Wolpert et al., 2003). Of course, the fancy explicit system would handle such a challenge by launching an ideational RPG into the dark. But the implicit system cannot do that. Its concrete-operational setup lacks the computational means to generate a controller that is imaginary. The fact that the implicit system cannot model the entire sensorimotor loop internally is the reason why a first-time movement feels so weird to us. We simply cannot anticipate what we are going to see or feel.

This boils down to the following. The implicit system possesses partial sightedness in its search algorithms alright, but that is true for known fitness landscapes only, a situation that doesn't normally qualify as creativity (except, as we will see just below, for the flow experience). For explorations in terra incognita, implicit forward models are reduced to blindness because the selection process occurs *ex post facto* by natural selection, or more precisely, feedback from the environment. This doesn't mean that the implicit system cannot be creative in uncharted territory. It only means that the implicit system cannot be creative there above and beyond the zero-coupling exhibited by biological evolution (Dietrich & Haider, 2015). Of course the explicit system can always try to generate an ideational RPG and *imagine* how it must feel to perform the new dance, but, as we are also about to see, this would have to be a simulation rather than an emulation.

All this changes for the explicit system, especially in the deliberate creativity mode. The source of this is, once again, the working memory buffer in the prefrontal cortex and the omnidirectional access of explicit knowledge. They give the explicit system a prediction mechanism that provides degrees of sightedness not only for known problem spaces but also for unknown ones. The ability to project an ideational RPG into virgin territory internalizes the selection process and allows for a scaffolding process. The knowledge we have about the adaptive landscape is also the difference between creativity and planning, both of which are simulation chains extending into the unknown future. In planning, however, the design space neighborhood is principally mapped out and the outcome of a series of hypothetical thought trials in that landscape will neither be novel nor surprising.

From this analysis, we can also derive the answer to this section's heading: why does flow flow? The evolutionary algorithm of the implicit system operates without goal representations and so cannot anticipate more than one step at a time. Note that this is true both for known and for unknown solution spaces. Each element of the perception-action sequence depends entirely on the directly preceding one and links up to the immediate next. There's no scaffolding, no leaping over unfit intermediates, and thus no discontinuity. To see this clearly, picture the lightning-fast escape maneuvers of a squirrel. Lacking an overall strategy or plan, the squirrel gets to safety entirely by relying on moment-to-moment adjustments. Such smooth, feedback-driven motor strings can produce extremely complex and elegant movement patterns that can serve a higher goal (safety), yet requires no more than the reaction to immediately preceding input. This is not unlike a baseball outfielder trying to catch a flyball. Starting with only a vague idea as to the ball's ultimate location, the player progressively approximates that location by constantly adjusting his movements based on updates of the ball's trajectory and speed as it approaches. The creative process in flow is grounded in the same constraint. Flow feels continuous because all units of the chain must follow from a previous one. If the chain is broken, flow is kaput.

Emulation versus simulation

There is one more layer of complexity in the prediction machinery that we have been keeping clamped all this time. We can no longer continue to ride roughshod over the fact that two different types of predictive processes exist, mental emulation and mental simulation. I have been using these terms interchangeably so far but this distinction might turn out to matter a great deal for creative thinking.

In the most general terms, simulation is the use of one process to acquire knowledge about another. All simulations, mental imagery and imagination included, essentially make predictions. By answering "what if" questions, they generate knowledge that makes explicitly accessible the possible consequences of being in an alternate time and place. But this modeling can be done by two types of processes, and they don't deliver the same kind of predictive information (Moulton & Kosslyn, 2009).

The basic difference is quickly explained. One type is a first-order simulation, which only mimics models in an abstract way. What these first-order simulations don't do is to model also the intermediate processing steps that convert one scenario into the next. A computer model of a hurricane is an example. Although the sequence of the modeling process is functional – each step critically constraining the next – and not epiphenomenal, the algorithms transforming successive states differ categorically between the simulator and the real system.

Simulation of this type occurs when we imagine the changing scenery on a drive through the countryside without also modeling the corresponding steps causing the change in scenery – turning the steering wheel, for instance. Mental emulation, by contrast, is second-order simulation. It's a special type of simulation that imitates not only the content but also the processes transforming the content. This is to say, both simulation and emulation operate by sequential analogy, but one is theory-driven (simulation), the other is process-driven (emulation).

Why does this matter for creativity? To anticipate the key point, I'd like to pitch here the speculative idea that emulation might be a critical factor for an unconscious thought trial to nudge across the threshold of consciousness and become an insight. Could the additional how-to information of emulation indeed make the difference in strengthening a neuronal coalition to reach global ignition? If so, first-order simulations, which don't contain this detail, might simply lack the oomph to compete for access to consciousness. Anecdotal evidence would seem to corroborate this. We often get it only when we know how to do it.

Let's approach this prospect with a little intuition pump. Take the deceptively simple question of why we cannot tickle ourselves. Although the stimulus applied to the belly is roughly the same, being tickled by someone else evokes hysterical laughs while tickling oneself causes boredom. The standard response to the conundrum is that much of our behavior is guided by our expectations of specific consequences. If we tickle ourselves we know what is coming and that makes just about everything less funny. The problem with that explanation is that if we were told exactly how we will be tickled, it would still feel ticklish, despite the fact that we know precisely what is coming. The real reason is that a mere first-order simulation, imagining how it would feel, doesn't provide sufficiently detailed information about the predicted sensory consequences. Self-tickle, on the other hand, involves emulation. In this case, our motor system generates a motor command which holds instructions for all the state-to-state transitions. The efference copy, containing the same detailed information, is used to match the predicted outcome to the sensory feedback. So, unlike a first-order simulation, an internal model of the entire sensorimotor loop also models the transformational steps. Subtracting the emulation from the actual sensory feedback lessens – anticipates – the experience properly (Blakemore & Decety, 2001).

If I decide to tickle myself, I also generate an efference copy that tells me whodunit. If someone else tickles me, I don't initiate this emulation process and I can only simulate – *imagine* – the sensory consequences. Incidentally, this also explains the reason why some schizophrenics can tickle themselves. Due to their brain damage in the prefrontal cortex, they probably fail to generate an efference copy that can be mapped onto the sensory cortex. Without it, they are unable to distinguish between self-touching and other-touching solely from the perceptual feedback they are getting.

It would appear that implicit predictions are necessarily emulations, not simulations. To see why, remember that the implicit system cannot compute hypotheticals. It must therefore proceed on a step-by-step basis, and by using the exact same operator as the real system. This disqualifies simulations. To avoid getting confused here, keep also in mind that this only applies to familiar terrain. In unknown solution spaces, the implicit system has, anyway, no prediction capabilities. It can neither emulate nor simulate, making its evolutionary algorithm blind. So what can this tell us about creativity in the flow experience? This is harder to answer than you might think. In creating a painting, for instance, the artist's actual hand movements are nothing new to the motor system, and each stroke of the brush would be emulated. In fact, flow cannot occur in a situation in which the motor system would have to learn a new movement. For flow to flow, the movements must be automated. It turns out, then, that the creativity in flow is a more interesting case than expected. Since flow could arise only in solution spaces that are known in principle to the implicit system, the creative act cannot be in the steps themselves but must emerge from the overall pattern produced by the entire action-perception sequence. This also holds for jazz improvisation or poetry. A series of individual, uncreative steps produces an overall, creative final configuration because the sequence is strung together in a state of optimal sensorimotor integration. For flow in sports, on the other hand, creativity isn't so much the issue, as no surprising and novel pattern is generated. Rather the optimal performance can win gold medals.

It hardly needs saying that the explicit system can also run simulations. Thanks to its higher-order representations, it can readily compute operators that are different from the real system. This, in turn, exponentially increases the realms we can envision with our imagination. We can conceive – predict the effects – of events that we cannot even reproduce with our bodies, such as ocean waves or, to use the chemist August Kekulé's famous discovery, whirling snakes forming a (benzene) ring. The explicit system, then, makes use of both prediction processes, emulation and simulation.

Having disentangled this tricky issue, we can now continue to pursue the idea of emulation as the critical process in insight formation. To start, there is no need to make the very strong claim that all creative ideas depend on a reference to an efference copy and hence emulation. To leave open the possibility that some forms of creativity get by with simulation, or analogue reasoning, is simply a matter of cautious theorizing. We mustn't forget that there is no hard data on the subject. However, emulation done offline by the explicit system seems a much more powerful candidate for generating aha moments. This hypothesis is supported by at least three reasons. The first is self-evident, if you think about it; emulation contains additional information. When neural emulators can be pressed into service, we get, over and above the creative idea, a roadmap on how to get there from here. The second reason is likely a consequence of the first. Modeling the transformational steps should make a solution more compelling because it leaves no gaps in the path from A to B. Insight events are accompanied by the strong feeling that the answer just *is* right. Although this intuition can be wrong, a concrete, unbroken thread joining the problem constellation with the far-flung ideational RPG could very well be the source of this feeling of certainty. If so, the successful Bayesian convergence of the forward and inverse models would be the decisive trigger to strengthen an unconscious combinatorial process and generate a conscious representation.

The third reason to favor emulation over simulation is based on the paradigm of embodied cognition and demands a bit more elaboration (Barsalou, 2009). Embodied cognition is the idea that thoughts, emotions, and actions are grounded in bodily interaction with the environment. This concept is now an integral part of many disciplines, including robotics, linguistics, and cognitive psychology. A few findings will illustrate the basic idea. In one study, for instance, the researchers asked participants to compare two poses of a human model in an unusual body configuration. The pictures were presented in two versions. Either the visual angle had changed but the body position remained identical, or the body position had changed as well. The task was simply to determine whether or not the body position of the model had changed. While viewing the pictures, participants also engaged in a secondary movement task. They made unconstrained, nonrepetitive movements of either the arms or the legs. If a body schema exists, it should be used in both, the primary, visual task to encode the model's body position and the secondary, movement task to ensure that they are nonrepetitive. The results showed that arm movements reduced error rates when the model's arm position changed and leg movements helped recognition when the model's leg position changed. This suggests that representations of one's own bodies contribute to the performance in a visual task (Reed & Farah, 1995).

Or consider the "snarc" effect (spatial numerical associations of response codes), which refers to the finding that a left-hand reaction to small numbers is faster than a right-hand one and a right-hand reaction to large numbers is faster than a left-hand one (Dehaene et al., 1993). Word meanings also seem to be grounded in sensorimotor representations. Reading a word activates those sensorimotor brain areas that are also active when we actually hear the sounds produced by that object. In yet another study, experimenters asked participants to judge sentences were sensible while making either a forward or a backward movement. The meaning of the sentence was either compatible with the movement or not. Again, the movement mattered. Responses were faster when movement and sentence meaning were congruent. This action-sentence compatibility effect occurred even for sentences referring to abstract actions (Glenberg & Kaschak, 2002). Finally, and most interestingly perhaps, is that higher-order cognitive processes are also affected by movements. In one experiment, participants were instructed to solve a classical insight task. Before doing so, they were first asked to move their arms either back and forth or sideways. Problem solving was significantly higher in the back and forth condition (Thomas & Lleras, 2009).

In sum, there is overwhelming evidence that actions and movements play an important role in trying to understand the world. Actions can change our perception and, more importantly, our thoughts. Similarly, thinking about an object activates associated embodied states. Cognition, then, is not merely a process of abstract symbol manipulation but relies heavily on the brain's modality-specific systems as well as on current bodily states. The type of body human beings possess and the manner in which this type of body interacts with the environment determines how we think about the world. If we had other bodies, our thinking would also be different.

Let's take a concrete example. Imagine you need to cut a sheet of paper but don't have a pair of scissors at hand. Scanning the environment for suitable alternatives you are unlikely to simply consider objects on the basis of their characteristics. Rather, you try for each object you see to emulate the motion of cutting, and it is this emulation process that helps you decide if an object is suitable for the task. Such an assessment cannot be done solely by analyzing an object's features. Emulation helps to detect if an object can be used for the intended goal. What's more, the intention to cut actually guides the perception of the object so that you might not even notice the object's original function.

Linking this to the generation of creative ideas, the fact that our cognition is embodied implies that movements, or the emulation of movements, are important in finding new ways to solve problems. Think about it. Why else did Einstein need to ride the beam of light himself? The answer might lie in the additional how-to information that comes with emulation. Too see if his ideational RPG – making the speed of light a constant – fits with the known facts, a first-order simulation of the consequences wasn't enough. To fully understand all the implications, Einstein needed to emulate his way through this part of design space. Creativity, at least this type of creativity, can thus be said to involve finding the evolutionary algorithm that binds an adaptive RPG to the initial problem state by way of a series of motor plans (Table 8.1).

Table 8.1   Prediction interaction

	Known Problem Space	Unknown Problem Space
Mother Nature	Blindness	Blindness
Implicit System	Emulation	Blindness
Explicit System	Emulation Simulation	Emulation Simulation

The search algorithm of organic evolution is always blind. Since it doesn't produce a model of the world at all, there is no prediction mechanism that can provide some sightedness. It can accumulate design but that must evolve through inheritance from one (blind) iteration to the next. The implicit system can at least generate a model in known regions of design space. On the basis of previous experiences, it can compute a paired controller and emulate possible consequences. This ability is nicely exploited in the flow experience to generate overall patterns that are creative. In unknown landscapes, the implicit system is as blind as biological evolution, because its procedural platform lacks the capacity to compute a goal state that is hypothetical. And without such a paired controller, it cannot model a situation it has never encountered before. It doesn't follow from this that the implicit system cannot be creative in unknown solution spaces; it only follows that the creative process is blind in that case, that is, cannot be driven via predictive processes. For the explicit system, this changes for the simple reason that it can compute ideational RPGs even for unfamiliar landscapes. There are two ways of doing that: mental simulation and mental emulation. Simulations are abstract models of expected future environments that don't represent the transformational steps. The implicit system cannot use this process at all, not even in known solution spaces, because it relies on a concrete-operational format. Emulations are modelling processes that also contain all transformational steps. The implicit system does use emulation but can only do so for familiar situations. The explicit system can use both, simulation and emulation, to model the future but emulation could prove to be the more powerful process in generating conscious insights.

A trinity of creativity modes

We can now zoom out and enjoy an integrative view of all the brain's creativity mechanisms. Table 8.2 summarizes what we have distilled in the previous chapters about the three creativity modes and the parameters hidden in their evolutionary drivetrains. Following tradition, let us start at the top. The deliberate mode has the good fortune to count on the explicit system running at full throttle. Its evolutionary algorithm is powerfully upgraded from the blind, variation-selection algorithm of biological evolution. It makes use of predictive computations to build informed heuristics; launch ideational RPGs that furnish the fitness criteria for selection processes that must operate in the unknown reaches of design space; erect scaffolds to create more complex, interlocking designs; and generate a conscious preview of the sensory consequences in the form of a sense of agency and feelings of intentions. Moreover, thought trials in the deliberate mode are not limited to emulation processes. Thanks to the capacity for abstraction, the explicit system can also substitute the operator of the system it models and run first-order simulations. The only drawback of all this computational wizardry is conventionality. The deliberate creativity mode crashes easily if the solution is quirky.

So far so good. What remains most in need of sorting out is this. The spontaneous creativity mode and the experience of flow are similar in that they both operate in the mind's unconscious hinterland. But this is also where the similarities end. We shouldn't forget that neuroscientists still know little of the goings-on in there, but several considerations should give us much confidence to presuppose that the spontaneous mode stems from the explicit system. Much of the power of the deliberate mode is certainly taken out, but one thing

Table 8.2 Summary table

	Cognitive System	Prediction Process	Degree of Sightedness	Feeling of Intentions
Deliberate Mode	Explicit System	Simulation Emulation	Substantial	Yes
Spontaneous Mode	Explicit System	Simulation? Emulation	Modest	No
Flow Experience	Implicit System	Emulation	Blind	No

An oversimplified summary of the brain's three creativity modes and their association to the two cognitive systems, different prediction processes, sightedness and the sense of agency.

we know for certain is that scaffolding takes place during incubation. The scaffold itself doesn't make it to consciousness; it falls away, like a Wittgensteinian ladder, before the aha moment occurs. But the feeling of discontinuity, the fact that the solution is several steps removed from the problem constellation, leaves no doubt of a scaffolding process. We also know that goal pursuit continues in the spontaneous mode, which suggests the existence of ideational RPGs, internal selection processes, and predictive fitness functions. The single most telling indicator, however, is that the unconscious generate-and-test computations have access to the global workspace at all. That the solution can be represented in consciousness means that – by definitional fiat – the spontaneous creativity mode cannot, despite being unconscious, be part of the encapsulated implicit system. We can say then that the evidence points to a few modest degrees of sightedness in the evolutionary algorithm of the spontaneous mode, but there is not enough prefrontal activity to run a mapping process to compute conscious intentions.

What is much less clear is the question of whether the spontaneous mode, surviving as it might on task-set inertia and fringe working memory, can run first-order simulations. To do so, it would have to be able to model a sequence of events without using the same operator that causes change in the real system. This, however, represents an additional level of abstraction and the spontaneous mode might not have the computational means. Also, I argued in the preceding pages that emulation is a more powerful modelling process because accurate knowledge of what causes transformations in the real system increases precision. I even speculated that it could be the decisive factor that triggers conscious representation. But we can also turn this question around and ask if the spontaneous mode possesses sufficient abstraction power at all. If it doesn't, emulation wouldn't merely be a propulsive trigger but rather a necessary precondition. This matter must await empirical testing. It cannot be settled based on the little we currently know.

In contrast to the spontaneous mode, the flow experience emerges from the implicit system. The implicit evolutionary algorithm has no access to consciousness, no ideational RPGs, no scaffold, no foresight, and no feeling of authorship. Its prediction mechanism is limited to emulation processes in known solution spaces. There, neural emulators system map a predictor – the forward model – onto sensory cortices to anticipate possible consequences of the planned action, but can only do so for already acquired controllers. Switch to an unknown solution space and the selection process can no longer be internalized because the implicit system lacks the necessary processing power to deal with hypotheticals. So, in unknown solution spaces, the implicit system can only take creative strolls in the landscape of all possible designs in the blind, *ex-post-facto* way biological evolution does, based on selection processes that exist in the environment. Flow is an interesting exception. It's a creativity mode in which the process itself occurs in a known solution space, which normally doesn't qualify as creativity. But here the sensorimotor efficiency of the implicit system is exploited to create an overall pattern that can be novel, useful, and surprising.

Recommended readings

Barsalou, L. W. (2009). Simulation, situated conceptualization, and prediction. *Philosophical Transactions of the Royal Society B, 364*, 1281–1289.

Blakemore, S.-J., Wolpert, D., & Frith, C. (2000). Why can't you tickle yourself? *NeuroReport, 11*, 11–16.

Crick, F. H. C., & Koch, C. (1998). Consciousness and neuroscience. *Cerebral Cortex, 8*, 97–107.

Csikszentmihalyi, M. (1996). *Creativity*. New York: Harper Perennial.

Dienes, Z., & Perner, J. (1999). A theory of implicit and explicit knowledge. *Behavioral and Brain Sciences, 5*, 735–808.

Dietrich, A. (2004). Neurocognitive mechanisms underlying the experience of flow. *Consciousness and Cognition, 13*, 746–761.

Dietrich, A., & Audiffren, M. (2011). The reticular-activating hypofrontality (RAH) model of acute exercise. *Neuroscience & Biobehavioral Reviews, 35*, 1305–1325.

Dietrich, A., & Haider, H. (2015). Human creativity, evolutionary algorithms, and predictive representations: The mechanics of thought trials. *Psychonomic Bulletin & Review, 22*, 1011–1026.

Downing, K. L. (2009). Predictive models in the brain. *Connection Science, 21*, 39–74.

Limb, C., & Braun, A. (2008). Neural substrates of spontaneous musical performance: An fMRI study of jazz improvisation. *PLoS ONE, 3*, e1679.

Moulton, S. T., & Kosslyn, S. M. (2009). Imagining predictions: Mental imagery as mental emulation. *Philosophical Transactions of the Royal Society B, 364*, 1273–1280.

9
In Search of the Artificer

A hundred – or a thousand – years from now, future historians might mark the day of January 25, 2005, as a watershed moment in Earth's history. That's the day machines crossed the Rubicon and became creative agents in their own right. Huh? Machines are creative? Well, consider the criterion. On that day in early 2005, the US Patent and Trademark Office (USPTO) awarded the first ever patent to a non-human designer – a software program, to be more precise. Recall that the USPTO defines an innovation as something that is a novel, useful, and non-obvious extension of an existing idea. The non-obvious part of the definition means that the machine didn't just solve a logical problem by making a forced move. It was, by established convention, demonstrably creative. Clerks at the USPTO didn't know that they were looking at the invention of a thing by a thing so you could say that artificial intelligence passed a sly version of a Turing test – a game computer scientists play to see if a computer can hold up one end of a conversation with a human without being spotted as a machine.

If you still don't feel this in the marrow of your bones, look at it this way. This machine holds intellectual property rights – not its human designer, John Koza, but the pile of metal itself! But wait, back up!, I can hear you say, John Koza made the thing that made the thing? Ah, that explains it. It is he then who is the real inventor! But, as you will see in this chapter, pushing back the credit like this is problematic. First, this line of reasoning is hard to maintain, a slippery slope that isn't really different to saying that Koza also owns the creative deeds of his flesh-and-bones children – who Koza also supplied the initial programming for, if that's the right phrase to use here. Second, it doesn't answer the question of how the invention came into existence. We can't stop our search for mechanisms once the creative act is off-loaded onto a member of *Homo sapiens*. For neuroscience, this is the point where it all starts, not where it ends. It cannot be said too often: we can't let the Designer back into the design process, certainly not now after pages and pages of stalwart naturalistic demystification.

I often conduct informal surveys in my courses, a quick show of hands to see who thinks that computers will ever be creative. That the day will come when they compose moving symphonies, design sexy women's shoes, or write funny jokes. I take care to emphasize that I am after the principle. Will they ever? Not today, not tomorrow, but ever? To be sure, there are the odd students here or there – two or three in a hundred perhaps – who raise their hand. But by and large, it is fair to say that the results of the opinion poll are, to a first approximation, unanimous. No one thinks so. In point of fact, it isn't uncommon to see students laugh out loud and look at me as if I just ask them if one day two and two could be five. Fuhgeddaboutit! The trouble starts only once I asked them to tell me why.

If the creative mind is nothing but an exquisite network of neural circuitry computing partially sighted evolutionary algorithms – no ineffable extra ingredient anywhere in sight, no immaterial muse to set off sparks in the occipital cortex – why couldn't there be one made of semiconductors? The matter of machine creativity has never been a topic that lends itself naturally to sober, intellectual discourse. There are people – nearly everybody, it seems – who think that this is a pipe dream. But there are also people like Marvin Minsky (1986), a trailblazer in the field of AI, who famously predicted that the next generation of silicon intelligentsia would be so clever that we would "be lucky if they [would be] willing to keep us around as household pets." In this tug-of-war, positions are hardened and there is much paranoia about erosion. You can't give them an inch, not even in principle, or they'll take a mile. This polarization is probably inevitable, given what's at stake is nothing less than the nature of our souls. But in their zeal to protect the human mind from the steady march of science, naysayers often erect barriers too early, thinking it is better to defend too much than risk losing the precious mind to materialism. The result is that they end up defending an indefensible position, because it forces them to invoke, beyond said barrier, a miraculous force of some kind.

As always, there is much to be gained from abandoning the absolutist dichotomy of us versus them, of soulless machines with no creative potential whatsoever and inspired brains that have it all. As soon as we do this and place creativity on a continuum, it is easier to give both extreme positions a bit of a squeeze. At the human end, I have been on about deflating our grandiose view of the Designer ever since we started on our journey. So our task in this chapter will be to boost the computer end of things and get a better sense of what they might be capable of in the future. In the end, the difference between us versus them might evaporate altogether, like the Aristotelian categories of the heavens and earth. Or we might find that machines are indeed different when it comes to creativity. But at all events, let's not forget that we are dealing with mechanisms on either sides, since a retreat into mysterian fogginess is a throwaway not worth entertaining in a scientific arena.

Rise of the machines

It is worth taking a bit of time to understand how we got here. The basic idea of machines mimicking human thinking goes all the way back to antiquity, but it wasn't until the seventeenth century that Blaise Pascal built the first calculating machine. It was a mechanical contraption that operated on rotating cylinders and did some basic transformations – addition, subtraction, multiplication, and the like. Gottfried von Leibniz later improved the device to make it more practical but these first attempts didn't go very far because the design had a fatal flaw: its functions were fixed.

In the mid-1800s, the mathematician Charles Babbage kicked off the modern era when he conceived of the first multipurpose device. The innards of his Analytical Engine, as he called it, consisted of a series of interlocking cogs and wheels – the hardware – which formed a (central) processing unit. The centerpiece of Babbage's invention was the interchangeable punch card – the software – that controlled the operation of the unit. Each card had a pattern of holes which coded a particular mathematical function that then specified how the unit worked. By swapping the punched cards, the device could execute any logical function. Put another way, the machine was programmable and flexible, the first version, in principle, of the digital computer. Babbage got the idea of punch cards from the textile industry, where a series of innovations in loom design prior to the 1830s culminated in the Jacquard loom. It automated the weaving of intricate patterns into fabrics with the use of these interchangeable punched cards. Babbage's creation didn't take the world by storm. Even he never had the chance to see his brainchild labor away. It is acknowledged that the schematics would have worked, but the machine was simply too complex to be built at the time. The first functional general-purpose computing machines didn't see the light of day until World War II – over a hundred years after Babbage – to decipher encrypted code. And even then, the engineering feat involved was prohibitive. The computing power that now comfortably fits onto a modern microchip occupied basements filled with diodes, vacuum tubes, switches, and cables.

While there was little progress on the hardware side, mathematicians and logicians made progress on the software side. AI can only simulate systems that are formalized, which is to say that all the statements and permissible transformation rules manipulating them must be fully specified and given a definite shape. This is known as a formal system, the representation of a system in abstract, symbolic language. What was needed to precisely explicate a system in that manner was a solid understanding of formal logic (i.e., the properties of propositions, the logic of numbers and classes, etc.) and the foundation of mathematics in logic, namely the underlying logical structure of geometry, algebra, and arithmetic. All this doesn't make for a terribly exciting narrative but is vital for understanding the capabilities of AI. At any case, this was an ongoing project in the nineteenth century and between 1910 and 1913 the mathematicians Bertrand Russell and Alfred Whitehead startled the world – or at least the little bit that was paying attention – with their publication *Principia Mathematica*, which runs to three volumes and revolutionized formal logic.

The mathematician George Boole, a contemporary of Babbage, took the next step by expressing logical problems in terms of algebraic equations. Boolean algebra laid the theoretical groundwork for formal automata theory and computing, developed in the 1930s and 1940s by the mathematicians John von Neumann, Alan Turing, and others, because it restated logical relationships in a way that made them solvable mathematically. At the same time, the engineer and father of information theory, Claude Shannon, applied Boolean algebra to electrical circuits. Just as the symbols and rules of algebra can be stated in a binary code using 1s and 0s, the switches and relays in electronics operate in a binary fashion, "on" and "off." By using Boolean algebra to describe the behavior of switches and relays, logical problems could be translated into formal systems and then manipulated systematically. Shannon called one unit of information a "bit," which is short for "binary digit." Finally, in the 1940s, von Neumann built on these ideas and designed the basic computing architecture that now bears his name.

All these developments paved the way for any system, human cognitive processes included, to be embodied in a machine. By the 1950s, engineers also built computers powerful enough to handle more complex formal systems. This put into play all the bits and pieces needed for AI to lift off. And lift off, it did. In 1956, Marvin Minsky, of keeping-humans-as-pets fame, and John McCarthy organized the famous Dartmouth conference – famous to AI people anyway – and coined the term AI. This event, attended by all those clued in at the time, is considered to be the birth of AI. At that time, people also started working on software that could simulate mental processes in computers. The first such programs in the 1950s were the Logic Theorist followed by the General Problem Solver, both of which were designed to solve problems of logic (Newell & Simon, 1972). They even played chess.

Since then, the co-evolution of ever more powerful computers that could accommodate increasingly sophisticated software programs has proved to be among the most impressive scientific and technological achievements of our time. Now, as then, the business of making artificial minds continues to advance nonstop on these two parallel fronts. One salvo comes from engineers relentlessly increasing brute computing power, an effort that is flanked by cognitive scientists doing their best to formalize human mental processes. The formalization of human cognition has always been the bottleneck in this research endeavor, and still is. Any system that is formalized can be embodied in a program. The problem is that we just don't know well the mechanisms brains use to compute consciousness, creativity, or morality, which makes it difficult to reproduce them in a silicon program.

It was the mathematician Alan Turing who first developed the notion that a machine capable of doing a series of automated steps could solve algorithms (Turing, 1950). A Turing machine could be put to work on any problem that is described by a well-defined computational procedure. The concept of a Universal Turing Machine goes further in that it assumes that any procedure can be realized by a device of any composition – silicon, neurons, cogs and wheels, or beer cans strung together with wires and powered by windmills, to use John Searle's memorable phrase – as long as it executes the same function. The digital computer, for instance, is one type of Universal Turing Machine. This abstraction of function from structure fueled the first comparisons between mind and computer (Putnam, 1960). If the structural constitution performing the mental operations is irrelevant, as this theory of mind maintained, then the brain can be thought of as a computer, a peculiar instance of a Universal Turing Machine, and the mind as a program that runs on it. Brains just happen to be one of many possible kinds of hardware configurations that can implement minds. This has been the guiding assumption behind the goal of AI to design programs that exhibit genuine intelligence.

The realization that this is possible in principle led to the belief in the 1950s and 1960s that it is surely only a matter of time until the highest mental faculties become subject to replication in a machine. If thinking is, as everyone in AI assumed it is, a product of computational complexity, the puzzle should be solved in a few decades. In the 1970s, during the heady days of this computational functionalism, we appeared to hurdle toward inevitable computer domination, a scenario not lost on Hollywood. The rapid progress indeed left everyone breathless. Today, computers can do many wonderful things and you should be impressed. They calculate theorems, build your car, beat Russians in chess, look for life on Mars, monitor the local weather, and optimize your stock portfolio. But as time has shown, it isn't nearly so simple. All but the hardiest members of the AI community now realize that the road is thornier than initially thought. While some problems were solved with ease, others turned out to be next to impossible to translate into computer code. Only brains can laugh out loud, throw a fit, be a proud citizen, sulk for days, hope for the best, fake an orgasm, look for itself, or dance salsa.

This is now, but what of tomorrow? Clearly, AI is not putting on the brakes any time soon. Its seemingly unstoppable motor of progress forces us, nearly every year, to redraw the boundary line, albeit ever so slightly, of what mental faculties – if any – will forever remain off limits for AI. For creativity, the issue can be cast like this. Suppose in a future time, cognitive neuroscientists will have formalized all mental processes related to creative thinking in the super-duper program Virtual Mind 6.2. As the dust of the achievement settles, will these silicon minds be creative? Will they write poetry, choreograph a ballet, or come up with weird new theories about the origins of the universe?

Alan Turing, whom we last encountered as the man behind the Universal Turing Machine, also devised the famous Turing test, a would-be experimental test of machine intelligence. In his 1950 seminal paper, he proposed a criterion that would serve as a benchmark to decide whether a machine truly thinks. Turing hazarded no metaphysical guesses as to what thinking is, nor did he discover some magical way of shining a light down into the engine room of machines to check for signs of inner musing. Instead, he proposed a functional test based on what machines can do. A machine is said to pass the test, and thus be granted the status of thinking creature, if it can fool people into thinking it is human. In other words, it holds machines to the same standard we hold ourselves. Actually, the setup of the Turing test is like this. People submit questions in typing and independent judges determine whether the typed replies originate from a human or another computer. The task for both, human and computer, is to convince the judges that they are the human. Naturally, the trick is to ask questions that would reveal the computer's true identity. It may interest you to learn that the Turing test is a fiendishly difficult one for AI. Asking the computer to compare the meaning of metaphors typically suffices to do it in (while asking a mathematical question usually does the human in). That no computer has come even close to passing the Turing test is testimony to the moving fact that wet brains are truly sophisticated machines. Critics of the Turing test argue that a mere conversation criterion dismisses the phenomenal content of consciousness. A machine's capacity to fool people into thinking it is human merely shows its dazzling capacity to simulate thought; it isn't sufficient, however, for real thoughts, real creativity, and real consciousness. Anticipating this objection, Turing argued that if a machine plays the imitation game and wins, there is no reason to consider it different to the human player – even in terms of phenomenology. Whatever the machine is doing inside, it evidently thinks, otherwise it couldn't pass the test.

The first 30 years of AI are known as Good Old-Fashioned AI, or GOFAI, as they say in computer science (Haugeland, 1985). It was a time marked by the development of ever more complex systems. But the architecture of GOFAI systems – regardless how complex – had a fundamental limitation. Its internal hardware connections were fixed, which meant that it couldn't adjust its performance based on feedback; it always did things in the same exact way. It could only execute operations that were precisely specified beforehand. In short, if it wasn't programmed in, GOFAI systems couldn't do it. This changed, in the mid-1980s, with ANNs which is shorthand for artificial neural nets. This new generation of systems is built on a connectionist architecture in which units are connected like real neural networks. They are, in a literal sense, computer models of the brain. In these circuits, it isn't necessary to specify every operation *a priori* because they can be trained. This works because the platform is dynamic, changing its configuration as it processes information.

To give you a quick taste of machine learning, each node in the network has a particular weight that is adjusted – strengthened or weakened – as the system learns a task. Take the ability to recognize complex patterns, such as those of faces, a tricky problem for AI because faces, like speech or emotions, exhibit statistical, nonlinear irregularities that make formal specification very difficult. But with ANN computer scientists can circumvent the problem of programming something that they don't fully understand themselves. They just let the system learn for itself. This is not a trick with mirrors. It works like this. The network is fed examples of faces to which it produces answers, say, whether the face is male or female. Depending on the feedback – right or wrong – the ANN gradually varies the weights of its connections until it arrives consistently at the correct answer. It does this by way of a back-propagation algorithm in which the feedback is rippled backward through the network and those connections that contribute to a successful match are strengthened while those that don't are weakened. As training continues the error rate drops until the system categorizes even novel faces with high accuracy. What really happens inside the system is that all nodes are adjusted so that each contributes, statistically speaking, in the right proportion to the determination of sex. The network's final architecture reflects structurally, just as it does in the brain, the system's past experience. An interesting consequence of this process is that it is impossible to tell, even for the machine's maker, how, in the end, the machine manages to correctly categorize faces.

A second major breakthrough since the GOFAI days is robotics. From the start, AI has been plagued by what is commonly known as the grounding problem. All software programs do is abstract computation; they know nothing about the meaning of what they are computing. Creating cybernetic art or tallying spreadsheets; it's all the same number-crunching – just ones and zeros. The computations are not grounded in the real world. AI people think this is due to the fact that programs are disembodied. Locked up in plastic cases, they don't interact with the real world and so cannot understand anything about it. The obvious solution to this problem is to give programs bodies. For AI, this means robotics. Embodiment is thought to be the solution, because interaction with the environment is the way we acquire meaning ourselves (Harnad, 1990). By housing programs in robots, AI can create entities with moveable equipment (arms, hands, legs) and sensory systems (eyes, ears, pain sensors) that can make contact with the world they are supposed to represent. It wasn't long before AI started to merge this behavior-based robotics approach with the knack of ANNs to learn from experience. Could an artificial brain equipped with a body be one day an autonomous creative agent?

The final innovation in our quick flyover of AI is genetic programming. The basic idea to apply the variation-selection ratchet of biological evolution to computer science was pioneered by the engineer John Holland in the mid-1970s (Holland, 1975). Consider a routine engineering problem, say, how to improve the occupancy-to-capacity ratio of an

airline company. A software program based on evolutionary computation would start by randomly varying single specs of the system – flight
routes, plane types, holiday schedules, etc. – and retain any mutation
that improved the system's performance – however tiny the advantage
in question. Sometimes this takes less than a few generations of breeding. For more complex problems, it can take hundreds. But the program
keeps with the generate-and-test procedure until the specs are satisfied.
They are excellent optimizers and come up with solutions that human
designers wouldn't. Granted, this tinkering to optimize pre-specified
goal parameters isn't the sort of creativity that quicken the pulse of any
but a software engineer, but we also have one more step to go.

In the early 1990s, John Koza (1992) turned the process on itself.
By using genetic programming to make programs alter their own code,
the process became open-ended. It can all begin to seem terribly complicated, and in some ways it is terribly complicated, but from there, it's
basically Evolution 101. The trick is to mate bits of computer code with
each other and generate, from that parent code, a second generation
that is then field-tested. Any offspring code that improves the program's
performance becomes the parent code for the following generation.
Code with lower fitness values is expelled so as not to contaminate the
pool of adaptive code. This process is then repeated over and over again.
In genetic programming, the program is procreating and so evolves, in a
series of almost imperceptible steps, new and unexpected code. In other
words, it's a method for computer programs to make better computer
programs, virtually without human guidance. It won't have escaped
your attention that it was this process that led to the USPTO patent with
which we began the chapter. The important point for us to remember is
that John Koza, after setting the process in motion, no longer controls
it. He doesn't know where the program is going or understand how,
eventually, it does what it does. He admits as much, and we are left
wondering who (or what) should receive credit for the patent.

The line between mind and machine is blurred further by the fact that
this isn't a one-off case. Genetic programming is a runaway success, if
you pardon the expression. It's very efficient in evolving programs that
can find creative solutions to complex engineering problems. To this
date, there are more than 20 cases of genetic programming duplicat-
ing or infringing on an existing patent. In addition, there are at least
two instances in which the method created a patentable new invention. Of course, if you have a dye-in-the-wool silicon bias, none of
this is likely to impress you beyond perhaps the obvious engineering
feat. Remarkable, yes; reconsidering my view on machine creativity,

no! Fair enough. But you have to admit that this starts to look scary. Where does this go next? We shouldn't forget that the human mind has passed through the ultimate screening program: over three and a half billion years of biological evolution. AI, on the other hand, is only a few decades in. How about a few centuries of this kind of progress? The core question we are pursuing after all is whether machines can be creative in principle and, arguably, a good case can be made that this era is already upon us.

And they will never be creative

A few years ago, I had an eye-opening conversation with a computer scientist about genetic programming, and the USPTO patent it had received. He was convinced that machines can't be inventive. They can aid humans in the creative process, he told me, but they cannot do it alone. Knowing that the generative (variational) nature of genetic programming can't be denied, he had no choice but to have a go at the selection component of creativity. So he argued that Koza's program pumps out umpteen strings of code and that it was in fact Koza who selected the most promising ones and submitted them to the USPTO. Machines, he concluded, have no intrinsic creativity; a human is always required.

When thinking through knotty issues containing lots of unexamined background assumptions, a few acts are as salutary as adopting a version of the children's habit to ask a never-ending stream of why questions ("Sweetheart, you need to eat breakfast." "Why?" "Because it is good for you." "Why?" "Because it makes you healthy." Why?"). Just as a toddler isn't going to be satisfied with "Because I said so", we shouldn't be satisfied with an explanation until that explanation contains real mechanisms. So I ask the computer scientist what difference it would have made had Koza submitted all the waste, too. Of course it wouldn't have made any, and he realized this immediately. Notice that my question would push the "act of creation" to the clerk working in the USPTO office. Even if, for the sake of argument, we accept this, we would then have to come at it with yet another follow-up question. How does the clerk's brain do it? ("Daddy, why do I have to go to school?" "Why can't I stay home and play?"). Suppose the brain mechanism of selection is, as I argued in previous chapters, the speed of processing, why couldn't machines simulate a fitness function based on that variable? The irony of the story was, of course, that my computer scientist friend regularly uses genetic programming to generate art, but it had apparently never occurred to him to apply the same line of reasoning to the human brain. His thinking betrayed a commitment to the tacit assumption that our creativity isn't mechanistic, a charge he'd surely deny holding instantly as soon as it is stated explicitly.

People seem to think that computers are not, by themselves, creative. What's more, people also seem to think that this isn't going to change – not tomorrow, not next year, not ever! When the suggestion that robots might someday be creative artists or ingenious scientists is put to lay people they would, no doubt, sniff at it, declaring that we members of *Homo sapiens* will forever have the monopoly on *true* creativity. It's just common sense to them. But what makes them so sure? What, if pressed, are the actual arguments they'd use to justify their certainty that AI – however advanced – will never write sketches of Pythonesque quality or compose piano concertos as moving as those by Rachmaninov? Let's round up the top naysaying claims against robotic creativity and hose them down to see if any of them can be made to stick.

Objection #1 is by far the most common of the bunch. It's also the first one my students try – in a knee-jerk fashion almost. Computers can only do what they are told. Without a human being around, they can't do a thing, they wouldn't even exist, for that matter. Even the current alpha male among supercomputers, the Cray Jaguar with a serene 1 quadrillion calculations per second, is just programmed, by us, and so possesses in its clunky algorithmic programs no independent creativity, originality, or self-initiative.

Keeping in mind the principles behind ANNs and genetic programming, we can readily see that this line of attack quickly ends in a belly flop. It's nothing more than a psychological talisman. Even the unwieldy silicon beasts of the GOFAI era did creative work by any barbed definition one cares to uphold. Recall the Logic Theorist, a program built in the 1950s to handle logical problems. It proved 38 of the 52 theorems in Russell and Whitehead's *Principia Mathematica*, but – and that's the key point – came up with a new and more elegant proof for one of them, Theorem 2.85. Had a mathematician done it, no one would have questioned the creative nature of the deed. And that's just GOFAI systems. These days, with the upgrades to ANNs, robotics, and genetic algorithms, AI makes this argument look simply uninformed. Computers routinely do things that are not programmed in. The fact that we can't even trace back the computer's output speaks to this loud and clear. Given this, one way to save objection #1 is to claim that the initial programming is still done by a human. While that's true, this retreat also makes it impossible to retain the ownership of the part of the process that is creative. Finally, we mustn't forget to direct the same line of inquiry toward us. What's good for the goose is good for the gander, as they say. So we must dare to quibble with the question of how much of our own creativity is the result of programming, hardwired or culturally acquired. How independent are we of that?

Objection #1 is actually a special case of objection #2: Computers will never do X. No sooner did the possibility if thinking machines come into sight, did people feel compelled to hoist the mind above them. This has often taken the form of a human-only list containing mental faculties that people just couldn't imagine being performed by a lifeless, mechanical apparatus. As is often the case in predicting future developments, such failure to imagine is just that, a failure to imagine. Descartes, for instance, nominated language and reasoning (Wouldn't he just?). He'd surely be surprised to learn that the real troublemakers aren't the higher faculties that set us apart from beasts but rather lower-order processes like emotions, perception, and motion. In any case, this list keeps on shriveling, as AI picks off one ability after another. This perpetual retreat alone ought to make one cautious about never, ever statements. Computers are long past being glorified adding machines and people prophesying AI's ultimate destiny must do so at their own peril. Perhaps the day isn't far off when computers make lists of things humans will never ever be able to do, such as imagining the fifth dimension, eliminating prejudice and poverty, solving the Riemann hypothesis, or understanding the mechanisms of creativity.

Where does this leave the aspiring would-be skeptic? Recall that AI can simulate anything as long as it is formalized. But what if brains work in a way that eludes characterization in a formal system? If this is the direction in which you want to proceed, you may be inclined to go for a close relative of objection #2, objection #3: Non-computability. This position is motivated by the claim that brains don't use formal logic but instead do their thinking in an unspecifiable, non-algorithmic manner. Some – most prominently the mathematician Roger Penrose – press a version of objection #3 by leaning hard on quantum theories of the mind (Penrose, 1989). This class of theories envisions complex mental events – creative ideas, mystical experiences, consciousness, etc. – as emergent properties that defy computational proof. From that vantage point, a creative insight is, in a word, noncomputable. As an example, Penrose cites mathematical knowledge, which he considers of such complexity that neurons and networks cannot realize them by any algorithm in any finite amount of time. Forget variation-selection heuristics, search functions, or Bayesian inferences, Penrose reckons that: "Mathematical ideas have an existence of their own, and inhabit an ideal Platonic world, which is accessible via the intellect only. When one 'sees' a mathematical truth, one's consciousness breaks through into this world of ideas, and makes contact with it."

Penrose is no dualist; he just thinks that creativity goes beyond mere algorithmic computation. He underscores this doubt by invoking Gödel's famous incompleteness theorem. The mathematician Kurt Gödel proved that in any finite, formal system there are statements that cannot be proved or disproved from within that system. This is typically interpreted to mean that brains contain truths that may never be knowable to brains themselves. It follows that we have a built-in epistemic horizon and, as a result, can never fully know our own mind. What is required for creativity, then, is a different kind of method, one that is capable of seeing complex truths at once, without computation. This, Penrose thinks, is quantum gravity.

So what, you are bound to ask, can quantum theories tell us about the mind and, by extension, creative insights? Some say nothing. For others quantum physics and consciousness are weird in similar ways – similar enough to take the analogy seriously. The debate over quantum minds comes down to whether or not quantum effects manifest themselves in brains. Quantum events happen at the level of subatomic particles of course, but cancel out at higher levels, even long before we get to the scale of molecules. To have them act upon larger-scale systems like brains, they need to stretch further in space-time. A quantum field across a neural network isn't an inconceivable occurrence. There are a few quantum events in which an astronomical number of particles join up in the same energy state and collectively make a splashy appearance in the human-scale world. In the parlance of physics, these are known as Bose-Einstein condensations, with superconductors and lasers being the best known examples. Having said that, I must quickly throw in that, at present, quantum phenomena in brains are not supported by so much as a shred of empirical evidence. The quantum mind is an entirely fictional entity.

To better appreciate the lure of non-computability based on quantum weirdness, let's carry the analogy a bit further. Quantum systems have emerging properties that aren't present in their individual parts or their relations. In that sense, all quantum phenomena are emerging. Spin, velocity, momentum, or even particles don't exist in the system until they get measured. Prior to observation, they are mere potentialities. Indeed, which of the potentialities moves to actuality is itself an emerging property, one in relation to the measuring method. Because a quantum foundation lurks underneath all matter, everything in this world is, strictly speaking, an emerging property. What's more, when quantum systems meet, their potentialities are superimposed creating a newly intertwined system that brings out emerging properties that don't exist prior to the entanglement. In physics, this effect is appropriately called quantum holism. In applying this kind of talk about quantum emergence to creative insights, things move swiftly into the direction of obscurity. Ultimate mindfulness without the hassle of computations? One thing going for quantum theories of the mind is the irresistible resemblance of quantum holism to the sudden and seemingly out-of-nowhere occurrence of a creative insight – enlightenment through entanglement, we might say.

To most neuroscientists, such analogies to quantum mechanics sound kooky, the sort of ideas people have who spent too many hours in a hot tub. Not surprisingly, they have been given a thorough shakedown (Grush & Churchland, 1995). It isn't just the fact that brains don't condense Bose-Einstein style or that all the evidence we have points to computations in neural networks. Logicians also disagree with Penrose's conclusion regarding the relevance of Gödel's theorem to human information-processing, and philosophers lament that quantum theory doesn't address any of the puzzles facing the study of consciousness. How, exactly, is quantum holism related to creative insights? The lack of explanatory power and the absence of a research program that could change this are a colossal fiasco for the non-computability camp. As the philosopher Patricia Churchland (2002) puts it: "Pixie dust in synapses is about as explanatorily powerful as quantum coherence." At this point, quantum theories of the mind are wonderful brain-teasers, but until we find some hard evidence, we must be content with their – admittedly considerable – entertainment value.

I mention all this to show that non-computability isn't the get-out-of-jail card people wish it to be. For one thing, it is clear that we get nowhere near a sound explanation of creativity by pulling quantum rabbits out of metaphysical thin air. But for our purposes, objection #3 fails on even more important grounds. Here's why. Suppose an interdisciplinary team of scientists finds, against all odds, quantum happenings inside brain cells. Are we now finally in a position to conclude that machines can't be creative? Well, Naw. The reason is the arrival of quantum computing. Although still in its infancy, quantum computers perform operations on data by using the principles of quantum mechanics. The main difference to digital computers that are based on binary, on-off transistors is that quantum computers use qubits (quantum bits) which computes information in a sequence of qubit states that are on *and* off. Needless to say, the details of that realm must be taken up elsewhere. If quantum effects can also occur in a computer, objection #3 goes bust as far as machine creativity is concerned. It would still be possible to see a difference – if one squints hard enough – between humans and machine creativity, but this is about as far as you can take it. It doesn't follow from non-computability based on quantum emergence that computers cannot be creative. From the looks of it, I have brought you a long way only to end up back at that irritating place called square one.

And on that sobering note, it's time to proceed to objection #4. This one comes from different quarters and asserts that creativity requires life. Machines are inanimate things, twisted threads of heavy metals and metalloids, that cannot possibly become inspired or stirred to passion. Technically called the carbon argument, it is reminiscent of the nineteenth-century position of vitalism, which conjured up a life-giving force – élan vital – to explain why organic tissue has life, while objects made from metal, stone, rubber, or glass don't. Like the objections that have come before it, objection #4 has initially a triumphant air about it, as if the bull has finally been taken by its horns and AI, with its preposterous research program, is in deep trouble.

Objection #4 forces us to look closer at the stuff of life to see if creativity might require it. Most college students, if they were reasonably attentive in Chemistry 101, can tell you that life is composed of four elements of the periodic table: carbon, hydrogen, nitrogen, and oxygen. Actually, the order is a little different. Of every 1,000 atoms in your body, 630 are hydrogen, 255 are oxygen, and just 95 are carbon, with the remaining 20 coming from nitrogen (15 atoms) and all the other elements (5 atoms). Mind you, this is not counting the immortal clumps of soulstuff that are above the fray! This focuses objection #4 more sharply: What is so special about carbon? Does it have any intrinsic property that qualifies it as the sole agent of creativity? Carbon's most distinguishing feature seems to be its sociability. In Bill Bryson words: "[Carbon] is the party animal of the atomic world, latching on to many other atoms (including itself) and holding tight, forming molecular conga lines of hearty robustness..." (Bryson, 2003). While this indeed is different to the reactivity of silicon, it is far from clear how that property translates into beautiful paintings and astonishing architecture. Wet brains and silicon computers are both information processors; the difference, in terms of constitution, is that they are decision-making devices made from a different elements of the periodic table, one with an atomic number of

6 (carbon), the other with one of 14 (silicon). If you are committed to a materialist view and believe that mind and matter are one, you must concede that the carbon argument falls right here. There is no principled reason why a carbon-based information processor ought to be unique with respect to creativity.

The next thing in tow is objection #5: Humans have evolved while computers are designed. Notice that this argument is nested within objections #1 (only programmed) and a variation on objection #4 (requires life). Notice too that ideas such as top-down, intention, purpose, planning, and foresight all hit essentially this very same spot but from a slightly different angle. Since we have been on this theme throughout the book, a single-sentence reminder should suffice to break the back of objection #5. To be sure, a top-down mechanism can make for a different kind of proximate explanation, as it may involve processes not found in bottom-up mechanisms, but it cannot be enlisted as an ultimate explanation of complexity because ultimate explanations – to be true explanations – must always come bottom-up. No skyhooks allowed. If quantum physics can't come to the rescue, we are safe in considering objection #5 as failed.

Finally, a last argument against artificial creativity is objection #6: Computers lack phenomenal content; they have no inner experience, subjectivity, or sense of what it's like to be someone (or something). They are zombie systems, all dark inside, with no-one home. As you might imagine, this objection has a long and checkered history, and its most famous rendering is the so-called Chinese room thought experiment by the philosopher John Searle (1980). Since objection #6 is driven by a clear commitment to the intuition that consciousness is something extra, something riding on top of the neural machinery, the standard arguments against dualism apply. So, before we enter the basic playground fight of the field of consciousness – you've left something out, no we haven't! – we dismiss objection #6 on the simple grounds that we are searching here for mechanisms, and dualism – regardless of how it's packaged – always ends up inventing a special difference that is somehow essential but nevertheless unknowable and invisible. Dualism demands that you sooner or later to take a leap of faith, a maneuver not too terribly popular among scientists.

I would wager good money that you didn't think it would be so hard to find a defensible position for something so obvious. For a dualist who believes in immaterial soul-particles with halos hovering above them, the entire exercise of thinking through the issue of machine creativity would seem pointless. But for a materialist who maintains, in one and the same breath, that consciousness fits neatly into the natural order of things, a naysaying position is clearly somewhat of a problem.

In conclusion, of the six objections considered, none constitutes, in spite of their intuitive appeal, an *a priori*, knockdown refutation of machine creativity. Most are based simply on a lack of understanding of what is involved in the process whose replication by silicon is being doubted. Moreover, the non-computability objection only allows one to hold on the trivial position that machines might have a different kind of creativity, not that creativity is impossible. Finally, the argument from phenomenology is based on intuition, which is not a plausible starting point in the search for the truth within the logical framework of science.

The robot artist

Now what? A calm examination of the perennially attractive conclusion everybody is aching to make – machines just don't have it – leaves us in an uncomfortable position. Having considered the standard counterarguments, we cannot find a secure hiding place from the relentless advance of AI. It isn't my goal here to convince you of the opposite claim, the inevitable coming of the creative machine. I am rather out to plant the seed of doubt in what looks like a premature call. For the purpose of edification and entertainment, I now want to turn the tables in the few pages that remain to us and give robots a chance to make their case, to show us how far they have already come. A USPTO patent for an engineering solution is one thing, but can machines also create art, compose music, or be curious about the world they inhabit?

There is, turns out, a subfield of AI that tasks itself with exactly that goal. A few years ago, I was invited to give the keynote address at its annual meeting. Computational creativity, as the field is known, is a small but fascinating area of AI. It defines itself as "the art, science, philosophy and engineering of computational systems which . . . exhibit behaviors that unbiased observers would deem to be creative." You will have notice the word "unbiased," which alludes to its ambition to pass the Turing test. A typical conference draws a few hundred people and has a decidedly underground feel to it. Most AI people calling this field their intellectual home write software programs that are intended to help creative people be more creative. These programs might aid designers in making sketches or produce new ringtones for cell phones, but there are also researchers who have more ambitious plans. Some develop autonomous robots, for instance, while others work on programs that paint or write poetry. To give you a sense of their exploits, we consider two remarkable projects. You might think that they fall comically short of true and genuine creativity but keep in mind that all we are after at this stage is a proof of concept.

The first of these is an art installation called Accomplice, created by the AI scientists and artists Rob Saunders and Petra Gemeinboeck (2013). Accomplice features a pair of curious robots and the curious thing about these robots is that they themselves are curious about the world they inhabit. Their problem is, at least initially, that they find themselves on the backside of a wall, clearly not the best place to be if you are curious. But Saunders and Gemeinboeck have equipped the robots with a hammer – a motorized punch, essentially – an array of sensors, such as eyes that can detect changes in color, motion, and shape as well as a microphone, which they can use to communicate with each other. The robots can also move along a sliding carriage so they can cover the length and width of the wall. The centerpiece of Accomplice, however, is the robots' personality, an AI program that is really interested in only one thing: novelty.

A novelty-seeking robot makes for an agent that is both curious and autonomous. The program is based on a computational model of creativity that combines unsupervised learning and reinforcement for novelty. The more the robots see, the more they memorize and compare any new image to their ever-growing datasets. The overall goal of the learning algorithm is to maximize an internally generated reward for capturing interesting images. The program also allows the robot to discover strategies for moving about the wall, how to use the hammer, and position the camera. Equipped like this, the robots' exploratory behavior isn't predetermined but emerges from interactions with the environment.

In the beginning of the installation, the robots face the backside of a cardboard wall. But even the smoothest of walls isn't entirely uniform. There may be dirt on it or small surface irregularities. Or the manufacturer's label is still printed on it someplace. Since the robots seek novelty, anything that looks different from the surrounding, they will find these spots on the wall and start hammering away at them. Soon cracks and holes appear in the wall, which create more novel patterns that the robots find even more interesting. So they move on to those. It isn't long until they punch through the wall, at which point a whole new world opens up to them, because the installation is located in an art gallery and the front side of the wall is full of visitors who are just as curious about the jarring banging noises coming from behind the wall as the robots are about them.

As the pair of robots proceeds to demolish the wall, they can peer through ever larger holes at the constantly changing settings that are the art gallery's visitors who have come to see them. But from the robots' point of view, the audience is the object of interest because they perceive people as changes to their environment, complex patterns that offer a great deal of novelty. Faces are especially fascinating to them. So, being curious, they study them. They even track them. This draws the visitors in, also because the robots' eyes – a camera framed with LED lights – resemble human eyes. But for people to keep the robots focused on them, they would have to constantly provide some kind of new experiences to them. People realize this rather quickly. Just being there isn't enough. The robots simply get bored, lose interest, and move on. I visited the exhibition with a female friend of mine who objected to my use of the adjective "bored" to describe the behavior – or state of mind – of a robot. She was adamant that this is just wrong. So I stopped saying it for reason can be safely left to the imagination.

People's reaction to the robots is varied. Some are disconcerted; others amused. Saunders told me that people often respond to them like visitors in a zoo. It is interesting, he says, how keen people are to be seen by the robots. They will go through a lot of trouble to keep their gaze on them. Some even provoke the robots by making faces or noises. Others start to perform for them. Still others openly speculate about the intent of the machines. In doing all this, the audience becomes part of the artwork. What interests Saunders and Gemeinboeck isn't just the system's creative drive, or the spectacle of the machines, but the encounter between robots and humans. Their work transforms the traditional relationship between visitors and robots such that the visitors become performers for the robots (see Figure 9.1).

Saunders and Gemeinboeck's projects demonstrate the concepts of autonomy and curiosity, two central elements of creativity. For our second example, we take things further and consider what is surely the most remarkable foray in computational creativity, David Cope's Emmy (Cope, 1996). Emmy, which stands for Experiments in Musical Intelligence, is a software program that composes classical music. Starting in the early 1980s, Cope programmed Emmy with the elements and themes of Bach's chorales (four-part vocal hymns). Emmy would then reassemble these bits and pieces and compose new chorales, in the style of Bach. As you'd expect from such a simple shuffling, the music was klutzy and predictable, easily spotted as artificial by connoisseurs of Baroque music. Cope realized that the genius of Bach's music lies in breaking the musical rules of the time and pushing the boundaries of

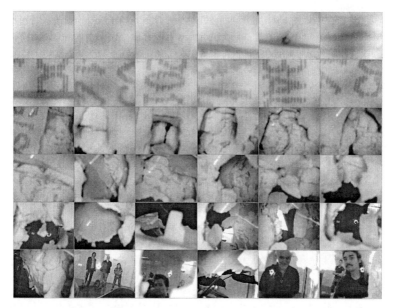

Figure 9.1 Curious robots
The world from the robot's point of view. Accomplice is a fascinating example of combining computational creativity and robotic art. Autonomous robots embedded into the walls of a gallery transform their environment through the enactment of curiosity, and the onlookers become accomplices in the art.

what was then permissible. To accommodate this insight, Cope built some randomness into the program, to spice up the predictability. The results were surprising. According to Cope, Emmy developed a personality, its very own personal style of composing Bach-style music. It also created thousands of original Bach-style sonatas in just minutes, what would have taken Bach, no slouch himself in the production department, several lifetimes to do. After many unsuccessful attempts to get musicians to play Emmy's compositions, Cope finally succeeded and released Emmy's first album, *Bach by Design* in 1993. *Virtual Mozart* and other albums followed, all original scores in the spirit of classical heavyweights.

For AI, Emmy is a small triumph. Though musicians and composers have often expressed skepticism, Emmy has also attracted praise from all quarters, including musicians. But the most common reaction from first-time listeners, says Cope, is stunned silence, followed, after a little reflection, by anger. People often react as if the human spirit has just been desecrated and that they have been treated to an abomination of music. Such is the pitch of some critics that it can only be described as spiteful. The composition are awful, they claim, lacking soul, pace, and vibrancy, or some quintessence that only human composers can supply. Mind you, these comments are all with 20-20 hindsight. Cope once Turing-tested an audience, playing Bach and Emmy-written Bach without telling which is which. Not only were people unable to tell the difference, some described Emmy's music as superb. For die-hard enemies of Emmy, such blind tests won't do. It's just obvious to them that Cope's enterprise is doomed. It won't surprise you to learn that Cope has a complex relationship with his critics, to put it mildly. On occasion, he has called them racists and accused them of being prejudiced against all computer. This exchange of fire continues. Most authors who write about Emmy articulate either pure admiration or, more commonly, pure hate, with both sides shouting past each other in arrant hyperbole. Consider for instance this anonymous blogger:

> A machine is able to rehash music with rules written for a composer, what's so incredible about that? They will never be able to fabricate music with lyrics (which is half of music). They will never be able to build a song that is happy or sad or some other emotion without someone telling them that is happy or sad or whatever. We will always be able to program computers to extend ourselves, the machines will never have intelligence or soul.

Emmy's success is rooted in Cope's deep understanding of music. Cope is not only a computer programmer but also a musician and composer. He has never opened Emmy's black box and showed the guts of his program to the world. But the process works, conceptually at least, something like this. To get Emmy to emulate style, it wasn't enough to formalize the musical system. Cope also had to develop his own categories of musical drama – things like tension and release, urgency, or harmony – and tie them to the preferences of famous composers, since each had his own tendencies to use a series of notes, combination of chords, melody, or the tonal range of a particular instrument to express these categories. When Emmy is fed a composition by, say, Mozart, it would deconstruct it, identify elements based on Cope's classifications, and create a new score by reassembling and re-sequence the bits back together, plus a bit of randomness. Before we are tempted to question whether this constitutes *true* creativity, we should, again, ask ourselves how Bach's brain might have done it. What, exactly, does it mean to have a particular style? Bach or Mozart also absorbed the music that came before them, recombined the elements in new ways, and then, in an act of inspired plagiarism merged them once more. In doing all that, they didn't, as far as we know, use a brain mechanism that violates Turing computability.

If Emmy doesn't rattle your nerves, this should: Emmy is a rule-based GOFAI system! In Cope's own assessment, it reached the level of C student in a sophomore musical composition class, demonstrating the basic ingredients that go into composing music. After 11,000 original scores, Emmy is now unplugged and replaced by its daughter, Emily Howell (the human-sounding name is intended). Emily Howell is a much more sophisticated connectionist platform and its first album *From Darkness, Light* was released in 2010. A second called *Breathless* followed in 2013. Cope is in constant conversation with Emily Howell. He feeds it bits and pieces from its parent, Emmy, so Emily Howell's compositions are now at least twice-removed from Cope. It is perhaps not too surprising that Cope has been approached by pop bands to churn out hits, and it is hard to believe that it isn't just a matter of time until a computer program claims the No. 1 spot in the Billboard charts. One thing seems certain, Emily Howell is a growing headache for all those who think that only humans can write music that moves us to tears. But why not make your own judgment? There are samples on the Internet you can check out.

Agents of creativity

It will not have gone unnoticed that the advent of creative machines would add a third agent of creativity to planet Earth. There is Mother Nature, of course, the creator of all artifacts in the biosphere. Based on the hardy DNA molecule, this was the first instantiation of the quality crank of evolution. After billions of years of steady up moves in the lower regions of design space, this most basic version of an evolutionary algorithm had evolved a computational machine that is the second agent of creativity, the human brain. The mind can run upgraded evolutionary algorithms because it is capable of representing the world, a design improvement that betters the wasteful business of blind variation-selection by adding a wee bit of sightedness. This shouldn't really surprise us. A process that creates things would, sooner or later, create a thing that improves the very process of creating things. The result is human culture, an evolutionary system that brings into existence artifacts of an entirely different kind.

This second instantiation of the bootstrapping process of evolution took a mere 50,000 years to make a third, a fraction of the time it had needed to go from first to second. In the same way that one particular artifact of biological creativity – the brain – has become a creative agent in its own right, one particular artifact of the brain – the computer – has become a creative agent in its own right. Again, this shouldn't surprise us. A bold creativity machine like the brain wouldn't just use its superior evolutionary algorithm to create fancier things. It would also search for ways to improve the algorithm itself. This took the form of a new kind of material for inheritance – silicon – and the intellectual framework – AI – to program variation-selection iterations to run on it. If human culture is an upgraded Darwinian system, then AI is the grandchild of biological evolution, a kind of Darwinism three-point-0. It's a sobering thought that we humans might just be a passing stage in the open-ended process of creativity.

These three agents of creativity all now make their own tracks in the vastness of design space. There is overlap, of course, but the differences in their drivetrains also guarantee that each is unique. Apart from the physical substrate each is based on – DNA, neurons, silicon – the main differences seem to lie in just two parameters of the algorithmic function: the turnover speed of iterations, which is a quantitative factor, and the degree of sightedness, which is a qualitative factor because it increases the algorithm's overall hit-to-miss ratio. Since brains are an improvement over Mother Nature on both, cultural evolution has opened up regions of design space that biological evolution alone cannot reach. Computers (will) have higher speeds and superior sightedness still, making them capable of entering regions that are off-limits to both biological and cultural evolution. But brains also have, due to their evolutionary past, quirks in their evolutionary algorithm – emotions, for instance – that are likely to be skipped by computer evolution. This might be a good thing. It provides some diversity in exploring the single design space that unites all possible designs, be they biological artifacts, human artifacts, or for a lack of a better phrase, artificial artifacts.

Recommended readings

Brooks, R. A. (2002). *Flesh and machines*. New York: Pantheon.
David Cope: Samples of Emmy: http://artsites.ucsc.edu/faculty/cope/mp3page .htm.
Dennett, D. C. (1995). *Darwin's' dangerous idea*. New York: Simon & Schuster.
Grush, R., & Churchland, P. S. (1995). Gaps in Penrose's toilings. *Journal of Consciousness Studies, 2,* 10–29.

Hofstadter, D. R. (1979). *Gödel, Escher, Bach.* London: Penguin.

Penrose, R. (1989). *The emperor's new mind.* London: Vintage.

Saunders, R., & Gemeinboeck, P. (2013). Creative machine performance: Computational creativity and robotic art. In M. L. Maher, T. Veale, R. Saunders, & O. Bown (Eds.), *Proceedings of the Fourth International Conference on Computational Creativity* (pp. 205–209).

References

Abbott, R. J., James, J. K., Milne, R. I., & Gillies, A. C. M. (2003). Plant introductions, hybridization and gene flow. *Philosophical Transactions of the Royal Society of London B, 358*, 1123–1132.

Allport, A., Styles, E. A., & Hsieh, S. (1994). Shifting intentional set: Exploring the dynamic control of tasks. In C. Umiltà & M. Moscovitch (Eds.), *Attention and performance 15: Conscious and nonconscious information processing. Attention and performance series* (pp. 421–452). Cambridge: MIT Press.

Anderson, J. R. (1996). ACT: A simple theory of complex cognition. *American Psychologist, 51*, 355–365.

Arden, R., Chavez, R. S., Grazioplene, R., & Jung, R. E. (2010). Neuroimaging creativity: A psychometric view. *Behavioural Brain Research, 214*, 143–156.

Ayers, M. (1968). *The refutation of determinism: An essay on philosophical logic.* London: Methuen.

Baars, B. J. (1988). *A cognitive theory of consciousness.* Cambridge: Cambridge University Press.

Bar, M. (2007). The proactive brain: Using analogies and associations to generate predictions. *Trends in Cognitive Science, 11*, 280–289.

Bar, M. (2009). The proactive brain: Memory for prediction. *Philosophical Transactions of the Royal Society B, 364*, 1235–1243.

Barsalou, L. W. (2009). Simulation, situated conceptualization, and prediction. *Philosophical Transactions of the Royal Society B: Biological Sciences, 364*, 1281–1289.

Blackmore, J. S. (1999). *The meme machine.* Oxford: Oxford University Press.

Blakemore, S.-J., & Decety, J. (2001). From the perception of action to the understanding of intention. *Nature Reviews: Neuroscience, 2*, 561–567.

Blakemore, S.-J., Wolpert, D., & Frith, C. (2000). Why can't you tickle yourself? *NeuroReport, 11*, 11–16.

Boden, M. (1996). *The creative mind: Myths and mechanisms.* London: Routledge.

Borges, J. L. (1956). La biblioteca de Babel. In *Ficciones.* Buenos Aires: Emece Editors.

Bressler, S. L., & Menon, V. (2010). Large-scale brain networks in cognition: Emerging methods and principles. *Trends in Cognitive Science, 14*, 277–290.

Brooks, R. A. (2002). *Flesh and machines.* New York: Pantheon.

Bryson, B. (2003). *A short history of nearly everything.* New York: Broadway Books.

Boyd, R., & Richerson, P. J. (1985). *Culture and the evolutionary process.* Chicago: University of Chicago Press.

Buckner, R. L. (2012). The serendipitous discovery of the brain's default network. *Neuroimage, 62*, 1137–1145.

Burke, J. (1995). *Connections.* New York: Little Brown & Co.

Calvin, W. H. (1996). *The cerebral code.* Boston: MIT Press.

Campbell, D. T. (1960). Blind variation and selective retention in creative thought as in other knowledge processes. *Psychological Review, 67*, 380–400.

Campbell, D. T. (1974). Unjustified variation and selective retention in scientific discovery. In F. Ayala & T. Dobszhansky (Eds.), *Studies in the philosophy of biology: Reduction and related problems* (pp. 139–161). London: Macmillan.

Churchland, P. S. (2002). *Brain-wise: Studies in neurophilosophy*. Cambridge: MIT Press.

Clark, A. (2013). Whatever next? Predictive brains, situated agents, and the future of cognitive science. *Behavioral and Brain Sciences, 36*, 181–204.

Cleeremans, A. (2008). The radical plasticity thesis. *Progress in Brain Research, 168*, 19–33.

Collard, M., Shennan, S., & Tehrani, J. J. (2006). Branching, blending, and the evolution of cultural similarities and differences among human populations. *Evolution and Human Behavior, 27*, 169–184.

Cope, D. (1996). *Experiments in musical intelligence*. Madison, WI: A-R Editions.

Cope, D. (1996). Samples of Emmy. http://artsites.ucsc.edu/faculty/cope/mp3page.htm.

Cowan, N. (2005). *Working memory capacity*. Hove: Psychological Press.

Crick, F. H. C., & Koch, C. (1998). Consciousness and neuroscience. *Cerebral Cortex, 8*, 97–107.

Crick, F., & Koch, C. (2003). A framework for consciousness. *Nature Neuroscience, 6*, 119–126.

Csikszentmihalyi, M. (1996). *Creativity*. New York: Harper Perennial.

Dehaene, S., Bossini, S., & Giraux, P. (1993). The mental representation of parity and number magnitude. *Journal of Experimental Psychology: General, 122*, 371–396.

Dehaene, S., & Changeux, J.-P. (2011). Experimental and theoretical approaches to conscious processing. *Neuron, 70*, 200–227.

Dehaene, S., & Naccache, L. (2001). Towards a cognitive science of consciousness: Basic evidence and a workspace framework. *Cognition, 79*, 1–37.

Darwin, C. (1859/1968). *The origin of species*. London: Penguin.

Dasgupta, S. (2004). Is creativity a Darwinian process? *Creativity Research Journal, 16*, 403–413.

Dawkins, R. (1976). *The selfish gene*. Oxford: Oxford University Press.

Dawkins, R. (1986). *The blind watchmaker*. New York: W.W. Norton.

Dawkins, R. (1999). Foreword. In S. Blackmore (Ed.), *The meme machine* (pp. vii–xvii). Oxford: Oxford University Press.

Dennett, D. C. (1991). *Consciousness explained*. Boston: Little, Brown & Co.

Dennett, D. C. (1995). *Darwin's' dangerous idea*. New York: Simon & Schuster.

Dennett, D. C. (2004). Could there be a Darwinian account of human creativity? In A. Moya & E. Font (Eds.), *Evolution, from molecules to ecosystems*. Oxford: Oxford University Press.

Dienes, Z., & Perner, J. (1999). A theory of implicit and explicit knowledge. *Behavioral and Brain Sciences, 5*, 735–808.

Dienes, Z., & Perner, J. (2002). A theory of the implicit nature of implicit learning. In R. M. French & A. Cleeremans (Eds.), *Implicit learning and consciousness* (pp. 68–92). New York: Psychology Press.

Dietrich, A. (2003). Functional neuroanatomy of altered states of consciousness: The transient hypofrontality hypothesis. *Consciousness and Cognition, 12*, 231–256.

Dietrich, A. (2004a). Neurocognitive mechanisms underlying the experience of flow. *Consciousness and Cognition, 13*, 746–761.

Dietrich, A. (2004b). The cognitive neuroscience of creativity. *Psychonomic Bulletin & Review, 11*, 1011–1026.

Dietrich, A. (2007a). *Introduction to consciousness*. London: Palgrave Macmillan.

Dietrich, A. (2007b). Who is afraid of a cognitive neuroscience of creativity? *Methods, 42*, 22–27.

Dietrich, A., & Audiffren, M. (2011). The reticular-activating hypofrontality (RAH) model of acute exercise. *Neuroscience & Biobehavioral Reviews, 35*, 1305–1325.

Dietrich, A., & Haider, H. (2015). Human creativity, evolutionary algorithms, and predictive representations: The mechanics of thought trials. *Psychonomic Bulletin & Review, 22*, 1011–1026.

Dietrich, A., & Kanso, R. (2010). A review of EEG, ERP and neuroimaging studies of creativity and insight. *Psychological Bulletin, 136*, 822–848.

Downing, K. L. (2009). Predictive models in the brain. *Connection Science, 21*, 39–74.

Dreisbach, G., & Haider, H. (2009). How task representations guide attention: Further evidence for the shielding function of task sets. *Journal of Experimental Psychology: Learning, Memory, and Cognition, 35*, 477–486.

Fink, A., & Benedek, M. (2014). EEG alpha power and creative ideation. *Neuroscience and Biobehavioral Reviews, 44*, 111–123.

Fisher, R. A. (1930). *The genetical theory of natural selection*. Oxford: Oxford University Press.

Fisher, J. C. (2006). Does simulation theory really involve simulation? *Philosophical Psychology, 19*, 417–432.

Foster, P. L. (2004). Adaptive mutation in *Escherichia coli*. *Journal of Bacteriology, 186*, 4846–4852.

Frith, C. D. (1992). *The cognitive neuropsychology of schizophrenia*. Hove: Lawrence Erlbaum.

Gazzaniga, M. S. (1992). *Nature's mind*. New York: Basic Books.

Gazzaniga, M. S. (2000). *The mind's past*. Berkeley: California University Press.

Gigerenzer, G., & Gaissmaier, W. (2011). Heuristic decision making. *Annual Review of Psychology, 62*, 451–482.

Guilford, J. P. (1950). Creativity. *American Psychologist, 5*, 444–454.

Glenberg, A., & Kaschak, M. (2002). Grounding language in action. *Psychonomic Bulletin & Review, 9*, 558–565.

Gould, S. J. (1979). Shades of Lamarck. *Natural History, 88*, 22–28.

Grush, R. (2004). The emulation theory of representation: Motor control, imagery, and perception. *Behavioral and Brain Sciences, 27*, 377–396.

Grush, R., & Churchland, P. S. (1995). Gaps in Penrose's toilings. *Journal of Consciousness Studies, 2*, 10–29.

Haider, H., & Rose, M. (2007). How to investigate insight: A proposal. *Methods, 42*, 49–57.

Haider, H., & Frensch, P. A. (2005). Empirical research on the generation and functional role of consciousness. *Psychological Research, 69*, 313–315.

Harnad, S. (1990). The symbol grounding problem. *Physica, D42*, 335–3346.

Haugeland, J. (1985). *Artificial intelligence: The very idea*. Cambridge: MIT Press.

Helie, S., & Sun, R. (2010). Incubation, insight, and creative problem solving: A unified theory and a connectionist model. *Psychological Review, 117*, 994–1024.

Hesslow, G. (2002). Conscious thought as simulation of behavior and perception. *Trends in Cognitive Sciences, 6*, 242–247.

Hofstadter, D. R. (1979). *Gödel, Escher, Bach*. London: Penguin.

Holland, J. H. (1975). *Adaptation in natural and artificial systems*. Ann Arbor: University of Michigan Press.

Hommel, B. (2004). Event files: Feature binding in and across perception and action. *Trends in Cognitive Sciences, 8*, 494–500.

Hoyle, F. (1984). *Evolution from space: A theory of cosmic creationism*. New York: Touchstone.

Hull, D. L. (2001). *Science and selection: Essays on biological evolution and the philosophy of science*. Cambridge: Cambridge University Press.

Huxley, J. (1942). *Evolution: The modern synthesis*. London: Allen & Unwin.

Ingold, T. (2007). The trouble with "evolutionary biology." *Anthropology Today, 23*, 3–7.

Jablonka, E., & Lamb, M. J. (2005). *Evolution in four dimensions: Genetic, epigenetic, behavioral, and symbolic variation in the history of life*. Boston: MIT Press.

James, W. (1880). Great men and their environment. *Atlantic Monthly, 46*, 441–459.

Jung, R. E., Mead, B. S., Carrasco, J., & Flores, R. A. (2013). The structure of creative cognition in the human brain. *Frontiers in Human Neuroscience, 7*, 330.

Kahneman, D. (2011). *Thinking fast and slow*. London: Penguin Books.

Kounios, J., & Beeman, M. (2014). The cognitive neuroscience of insight. *Annual Review of Psychology, 65*, 71–93.

Koza, J. R. (1992). *Genetic programming: On the programming of computers by means of natural selection*. Cambridge: MIT Press.

Kronfeldner, M. E. (2007). Is cultural evolution Lamarckian? *Biology and Philosophy, 22*, 493–512.

Kronfeldner, M. E. (2010). Darwinian "blind" hypothesis formation revisited. *Synthese, 175*, 193–218.

Laland, K. N., & Sterelny, K. (2006). Seven reasons (not) to neglect niche construction. *Evolution, 60*, 1751–1762.

Lamarck, J.-B. (1809). *Philosophie zoologique*. Bruxelles: Culture et Civilisation.

Lehrer, J. (2008). The eureka hunt. *The New Yorker*, July 28.

Lewontin, R. C. (1970). The units of selection. *Annual Review of Ecology and Systematics, 1*, 1–18.

Lewontin, R. C. (1991). *Biology as ideology*. New York: Harper.

Limb, C., & Braun, A. (2008). Neural substrates of spontaneous musical performance: An fMRI study of jazz improvisation. *PLoS ONE, 3*, e1679.

Llinás, R. R. (2001). *I of the vortex: From neurons to self*. Boston: MIT Press.

Martindale, C. (1990). *The clockwork muse: The predictability of artistic styles*. New York: Basic Books.

Martindale, C. (1999). Darwinian, Lamarckian, and rational creativity. *Psychological Inquiry, 10*, 340–341.

Mayr, U., & Kliegl, R. (2000). Task-set switching and long-term memory retrieval. *Journal of Experimental Psychology: Learning, Memory, and Cognition, 26*, 1124–1140.

Mednick, S. (1962). The associative basis of the creative process. *Psychological Review, 69*, 220–232.

Mesoudi, A. (2008). Foresight in cultural evolution. *Biological Philosophy, 23*, 243–255.

Mesoudi, A., Whiten, A., & Laland, K. N. (2006). Towards a unified science of cultural evolution. *Behavioral and Brain Sciences, 29*, 329–347.

Minsky, M. (1986). *Society of mind*. New York: Simon & Schuster.

Monsell, S. (2003). Task switching. *Trends in Cognitive Science, 7*, 134–140.

Moulton, S. T., & Kosslyn, S. M. (2009). Imagining predictions: Mental imagery as mental emulation. *Philosophical Transactions of the Royal Society B: Biological Sciences, 364*, 1273–1280.

Newell, A., & Simon, H. A. (1972). *Human problem solving*. Englewood Cliffs: Prentice Hall.

Öllinger, M., Jones, G., Danek, A. H., & Knoblich, G. (2013). Cognitive mechanisms of insight: The role of heuristics and representational change in solving the eight-coin problem. *Journal of Experimental Psychology: Learning, Memory, and Cognition, 39*, 931–939.

Penrose, R. (1989). *The emperor's new mind*. London: Vintage.

Perruchet, P., & Vinter, A. (2002). The self-organizing consciousness. *Behavioral and Brain Sciences, 25*, 297–388.

Pinker, S. (2002). *The blank slate: The modern denial of human nature*. New York: Penguin.

Popper, K. R. (1974). Campbell on the evolutionary theory of knowledge. In P. A. Schilpp (Ed.), *The philosophy of Karl Popper* (pp. 1059–1065). LaSalle: Open Court.

Putnam, H. (1960). Mind and machines. In S. Hook (Ed.), *Dimensions of the mind* (pp. 138–164). New York: Collier.

Raichle, M. E., MacLeod, A. M., Snyder, A. Z., Powers, W. J., Gusnard, D. A., & Shulman, G. L. (2001). A default mode of brain function. *Proceedings of the National Academy of Sciences, 98*, 676–682.

Reber, A. S. (1993). *Implicit learning and tacit knowledge*. Oxford: Oxford University Press.

Reed, C. L., & Farah, M. J. (1995). The psychological reality of the body schema: A test with normal participants. *Journal of Experimental Psychology: Human Perception & Performance, 21*, 334–343.

Richerson, P. J., & Boyd, R. (2005). *Not by genes alone: How culture transformed human evolution*. Chicago: University of Chicago Press.

Runco, M. A. (Ed.). (1991). *Divergent thinking*. Norwood: Ablex Publishing Corporation.

Runco, M. A., Millar, G., Acar, S., & Cramond, B. (2011). Torrance tests of creative thinking as predictors of personal and public achievement: A fifty year follow up. *Creativity Research Journal, 22*, 361–368.

Russ, S. W. (1999). An evolutionary model for creativity: Does it fit? *Psychological Inquiry, 10*, 359–361.

Saunders, R., & Gemeinboeck, P. (2013). Creative machine performance: Computational creativity and robotic art. In M. L. Maher, T. Veale, R. Saunders, & O. Bown (Eds.), *Proceedings of the Fourth International Conference on Computational Creativity* (pp. 205–209), University of Sydney, Australia.

Sawyer, K. (2011). The cognitive neuroscience of creativity: A critical review. *Creativity Research Journal, 23*, 137–154.

Schacter, D. L., & Buckner, R. L. (1998). On the relationship among priming, conscious recollection, and intentional retrieval: Evidence from neuroimaging research. *Neurobiology of Learning and Memory, 70*, 284–303.

Schooler, W. J., & Dougal, S. (1999). Why creativity is not like the proverbial typing monkey. *Psychological Inquiry, 10*, 351–356.

Searle, J. (1980). Minds, brains, and programs. *Behavioral and Brain Sciences, 3*, 417–457.

Selfridge, O. (1959). Pandemonium: A paradigm for learning. In *Proceedings of the Symposium on the mechanization of thought processes held at the National Physics Laboratory, November 1958.* London: HM Stationary Office.

Shin, Y. K., Proctor, R. W., & Capaldi, E. J. (2010). A review of contemporary ideomotor theory. *Psychological Bulletin, 136*, 943–974.

Simonton, D. K. (1997). Creative productivity: A predictive and explanatory model of career trajectories and landmarks. *Psychological Review, 104*, 66–89.

Simonton, D. K. (1999). Creativity as blind variation and selective retention: Is the creative process Darwinian? *Psychological Inquiry, 10*, 309–328.

Simonton, D. K. (2003). Scientific creativity as constrained stochastic behavior: The integration of process and person perspectives. *Psychological Bulletin, 129*, 475–494.

Simonton, D. K. (2007). The creative process in Picasso's Guernica sketches: Monotonic improvements or nonmonotonic variation. *Creativity Research Journal, 19*, 329–344.

Simonton, D. K. (2011). Creativity and discovery as blind variation: Campbell's (1960) BVSR model after the half-century mark. *Review of General Psychology, 15*, 158–174.

Simonton, D. K. (2013). Creative thought as blind variation and selective retention: Why creativity is inversely related to sightedness. *Journal of Theoretical and Philosophical Psychology, 33*, 253–266.

Sternberg, R. J. (1998). Cognitive mechanisms in human creativity: Is variation blind or sighted? *Journal of Creative Behavior, 32*, 159–176.

Sternberg, R. J. (1999). Darwinian creativity as a conventional religious faith. *Psychological Inquiry, 10*, 357–359.

Thomas, L. E., & Lleras, A. (2009). Swinging into thought: Directed movement guides insight in problem solving. *Psychonomic Bulletin & Review, 16*, 719–723.

Tooby, J., & Cosmides, L. (1992). The psychological foundations of culture. In J. Barkow, L. Cosmides, & J. Tooby (Eds.), *The adapted mind: Evolutionary psychology and the generation of culture.* New York: Oxford University Press.

Torrance, E. P. (1974). *Torrance test of creative thinking.* Lexington: Personal Press.

Turing, A. (1950). Computing machinery and intelligence. *Mind, 59*, 433–460.

Uttall, W. R. (2001). *The new phrenology.* Cambridge: MIT Press.

Wegner, D. M. (2002). *The illusion of conscious will.* Cambridge: MIT Press.

Weisberg, R. W. (2004). On structure in the creative process: A quantitative case-study of the creation of Picasso's Guernica. *Empirical Studies of the Arts, 22*, 23–54.

Weisberg, R. W. (2013). On the demystification of insight: A critique of neuroimaging studies of insight. *Creativity Research Journal, 25*, 1–14.

Whittlesea, B. A. (2004). The perception of integrality: Remembering through the validation of expectation. *Journal of Experimental Psychology: Learning, Memory, and Cognition, 30*, 891–908.

Wolpert, D. M., Ghahramani, Z., & Jordan, M. I. (1995). An internal model for sensorimotor integration. *Science, 269*, 1880–1882.

Wolpert, D. M., Doya, K., & Kawato M. (2003). A unifying computational framework for motor control and social interaction. *Philosophical Transactions of the Royal Society Series B: Biological Sciences, 358*, 593–602.

Yoruk, S., & Runco, M. A. (2014). The neuroscience of divergent thinking. *Activitas Nervosa Superior, 56*, 1–16.

Index

218   *Index*

CPSIA information can be obtained
at www.ICGtesting.com
Printed in the USA
LVOW10*2056301117
558172LV00012B/344/P